The Panasonic Lumix DMC-G2

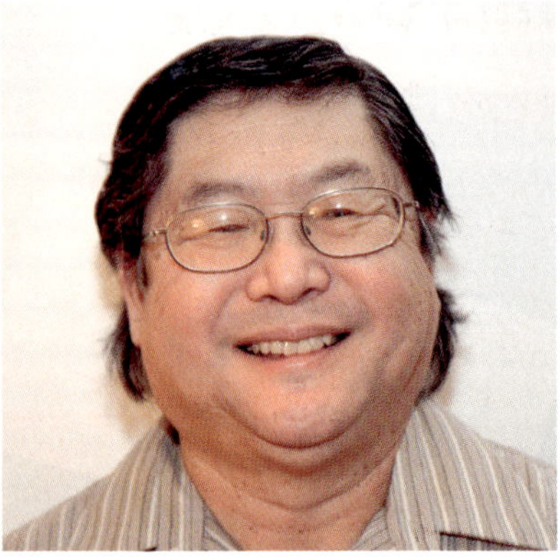

Dr. Brian Matsumoto is a retired research scientist who has worked for 30 years recording his experiments with a wide range of film and digital cameras. Now he spends his time photographing with a variety of equipment ranging from microscopes to telescopes.

He carries a camera on all his hikes and enjoys photographing nature. In addition to the two books he has written for Rocky Nook, Dr. Matsumoto has published several articles and has had his photographs published in a number of periodicals. He is experienced in the technical aspects of photography and has taught courses on recording scientific experiments with digital cameras.

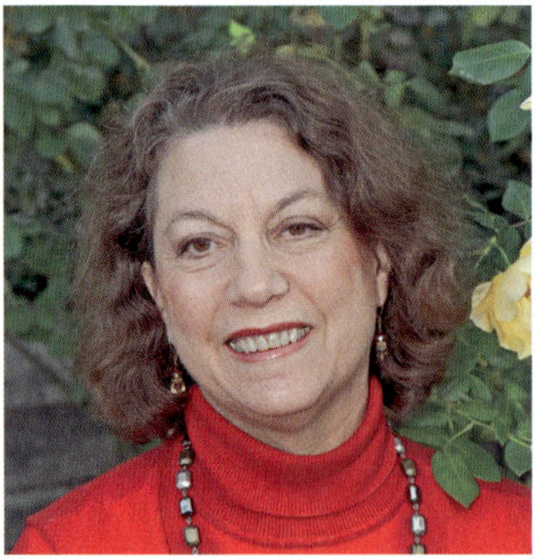

Carol F. Roullard has been an avid photographer since high school, where she first experimented with black and white artistic composition. She has continued photographing (mainly nature and architecture) throughout the years. Carol has used a variety of cameras covering a wide range of makes and models, from simple point-and-shoot cameras to complex professional cameras. She has been using the latest Panasonic G series models for the past several years.

Carol is a Project Management Quality and Compliance engineer by trade and has spent a number of years developing procedural and quality control methodology for IT projects. In addition, she has developed and conducted training sessions that cover best practices for procedural and quality control, breaking down complex subjects into easy-to-use approaches to learning.

The Panasonic Lumix DMC-G2

The Unofficial Quintessential Guide

Brian Matsumoto
Carol F. Roullard

rockynook

Brian Matsumoto
Carol F. Roullard

Editor: Gerhard Rossbach
Copyeditor: Judy Flynn
Layout and Type: Darrell Young
Cover Design: Helmut Kraus, www.exclam.de
Printer: Sheridan Books, Inc.
Printed in USA

1st Edition 2011 (2nd reprint, March 2013)

Rocky Nook Inc.
802 E. Cota Street, 3rd Floor
Santa Barbara, CA 93103

www.rockynook.com

Library of Congress Cataloging-in-Publication Data

Matsumoto, Brian.
The Panasonic Lumix DMC-G2 : the unofficial quintessential guide / Brian Matsumoto, Carol F. Roullard. -- 1st ed.
p. cm.
ISBN 978-1-933952-77-2 (soft cover : alk. paper)
1. Lumix digital camera. 2. Photography--Digital techniques. I. Roullard, Carol F. II. Title.

TR263.P36M38 2011
771.3'3--dc22

2010048768

Distributed by O'Reilly Media
1005 Gravenstein Highway North
Sebastopol, CA 95472

I dedicate this book to my mother and father who inspired me and gave me the confidence to believe that I could reach my dreams and the foundation to make my dreams a reality.

A special thanks to my beloved husband and two children who continuously encouraged and supported me throughout this endeavor.

Carol

Table of Contents

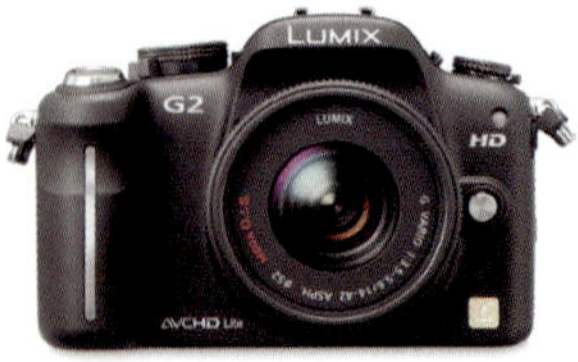

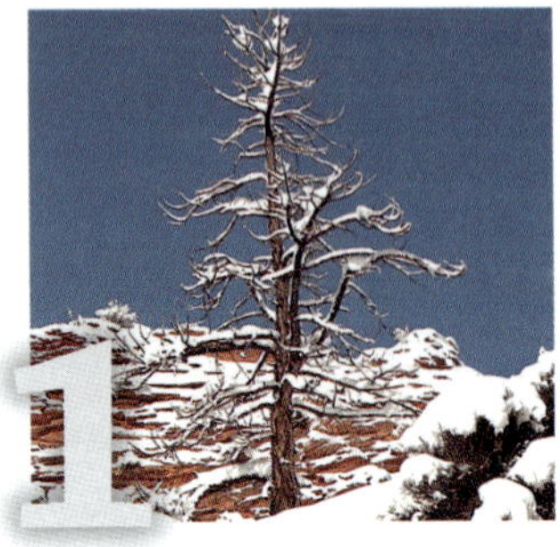

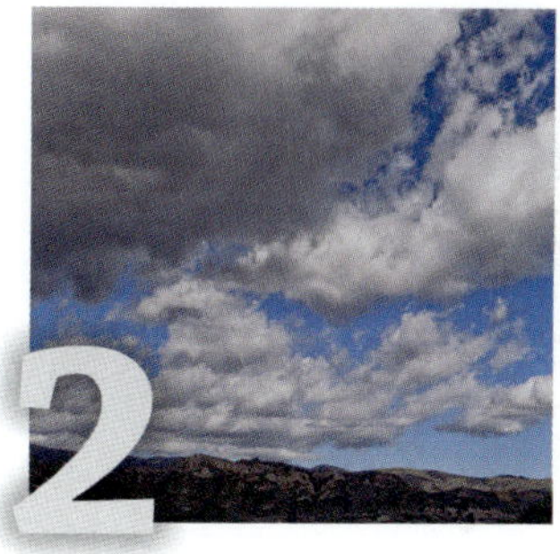

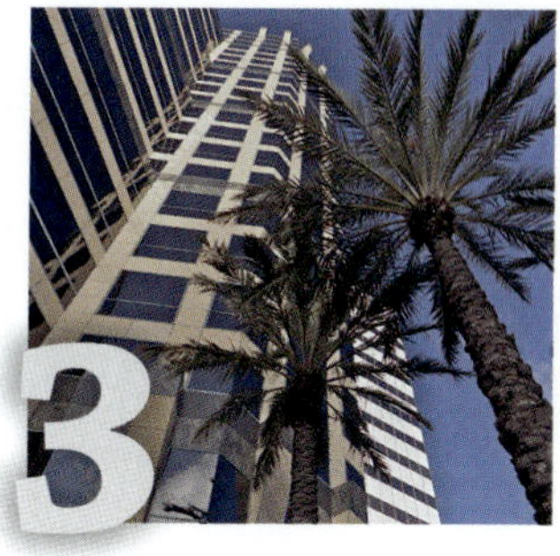

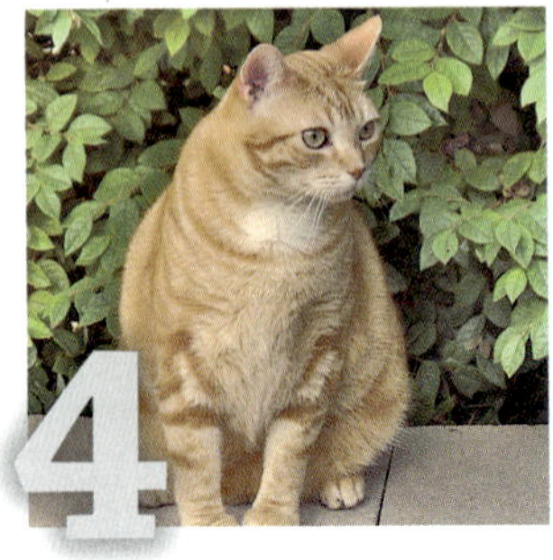
4

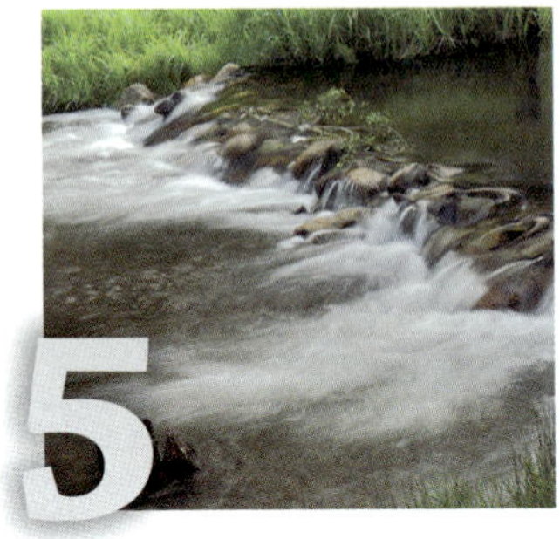
5

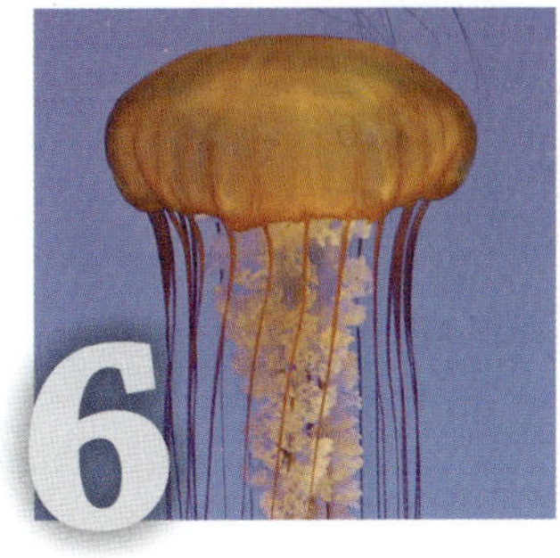

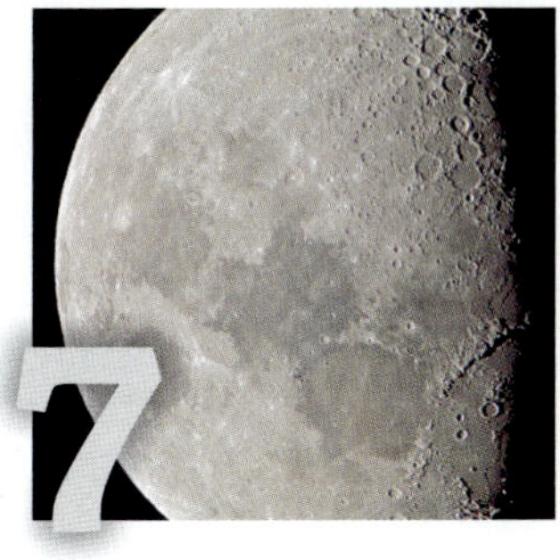

8

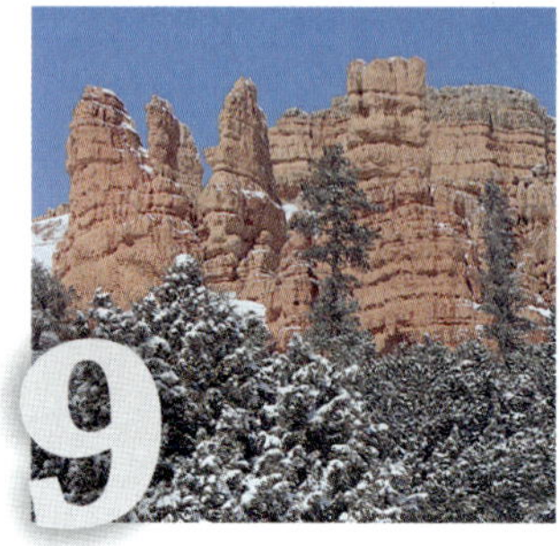

9

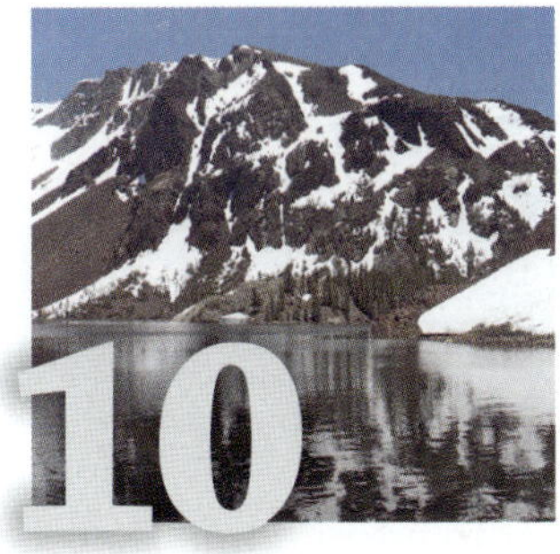

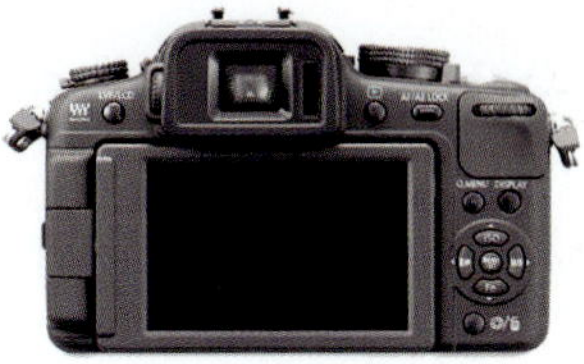

Downloadable Resources Webpage

There is a downloadable resources webpage for this book. It contains additional Appendix sections that provide added information on camera operation. The webpage is located at the following website address:

http://rockynook.com/PanasonicG2

All references in this book to Appendices B–D refer to information that is available from the downloadable resources webpage.

Preface

The Panasonic G2 camera is a remarkable photographic tool. Its innovative design makes it one of the most versatile cameras available to the consumer. The electronic viewfinder provides a bright, easy to focus, highly magnified image of the subject when composing a photograph. The resulting pictures and videos are of excellent quality. Its selection of interchangeable lenses gives you the flexibility to work with fisheye wide angles, extreme telephotos, and everything in between. To increase the camera's versatility, a simple adapter will allow you to mount and use manual focus lenses from older film cameras.

As an added bonus you can explore a variety of different subjects by mounting the Panasonic G2 camera body to a microscope or a telescope. You must focus the camera manually when used on these instruments, and many of the qualities found in a Panasonic electronic finder are necessary for establishing precise focus. The electronic finder is superior to most of the optical finders found on digital SLRs in that it provides a highly magnified, bright, detailed image of the subject. Today's optical finders for digital SLRs lack sufficient magnification and display optical defects that hide fine details, making it difficult to find focus. For this type of extreme photography, the Panasonic finder system does an excellent job.

This is not to say that the Panasonic G2 is the perfect camera. There are cameras that are better for low light conditions or that focus faster and are better suited for rapid-action sports photography. However, for the majority of photographic subjects, the Panasonic G2 camera serves admirably and for many, including us, its full photographic capabilities are more than adequate. This camera will provide enormous satisfaction for those interested in still and video photography. We found the camera's small size and light weight to be an advantage. It is the ideal vacation camera, perfect for the person on the go. For the family photographer, it is quick to set up and focus, and it can easily be switched from still to video photography.

This camera invites the user to explore different avenues of photography. It can be used by a point-and-shoot photographer who is uninterested in learning photographic terminology, yet it provides the whole gamut of manual controls for those who wish to take control of their cameras. In other words, the Panasonic G2 camera works well for either the neophyte or the experienced photographer, giving them both great results with minimal effort.

When writing this book, we enjoyed testing the camera's limits and capabilities. It is our hope that this book will allow you to find the same enjoyment as you use the camera and discover its capabilities.

1

Getting Started

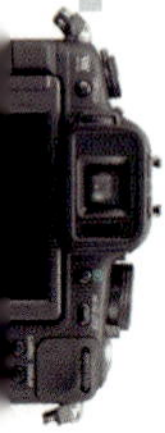

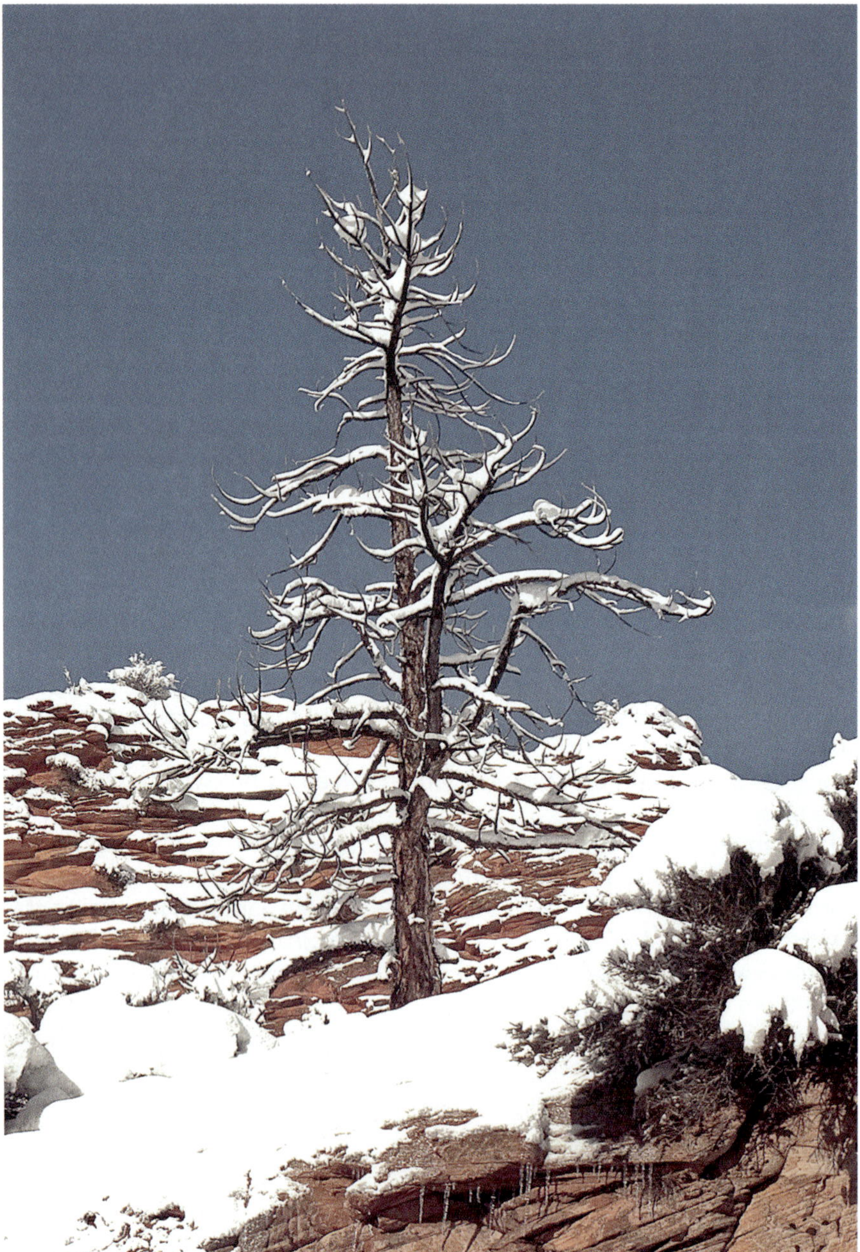

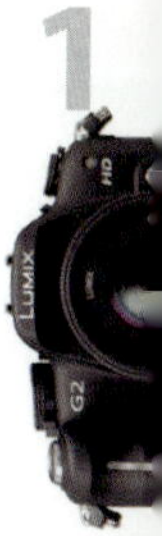

Introduction

The Panasonic G2 camera has a diverse range of functionality and controls, allowing it to be adeptly used by a beginner, an experienced camera user, and anyone in between. To help you learn what the camera can do, we have divided this book into three main sections tailored to the reader's level of experience and camera needs: the beginners (chapter 4), the intermediates (chapter 5), and the experienced crowd (chapter 6). Regardless of what group you fall into, this camera is the one for you. It has it all—or just about all. That is what makes it an exciting camera. But it also makes it potentially very confusing. Each section, starting with fully automatic, progressing to semi-automatic and culminating with going completely manual, will describe the camera's capabilities in simple descriptive terms to help you learn what the camera can do for you and how you can use it to capture memories and explore your artistic talents.

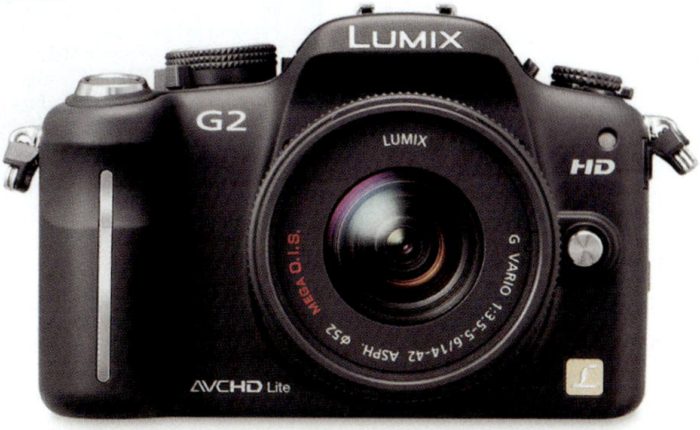

For beginners and those who wish to use the camera immediately, the Panasonic G2 has an Intelligent Auto (iA) Mode for both still pictures and videos. This mode automatically determines the camera settings needed to get quality results. For those who subscribe to the "point-and-shoot" approach, this is a great way to capture quality pictures and videos immediately. If you already have the battery and memory card installed, turn on the camera and switch on the Intelligent Auto Mode by pressing the iA button (top of the camera on the right). If the button's surrounding ring glows blue, Intelligent Auto Mode is initiated and all you need to do is find your subject and press the shutter release button. It is really that simple. The iA button acts as a toggle—pushing the button will turn this mode on or off—so the blue glow is your assurance that it has been activated.

The Intelligent Auto Mode attempts to identify the type of scene you are viewing and from this provides the settings to best capture the image. Unfortunately, scene identification is imperfect, so if the camera's intelligent software fails to identify the type of scene, it uses a generic setting that should still capture a technically good image—just not necessarily the best. As you gain experience, you can select from a set of predefined scene modes with assigned camera settings. The predefined scene modes have icons for such scenes as daytime and evening portraits and scenic, sports, baby, pet and close-up photographs. These modes automatically fine-tune the focusing, exposure, and light sensitivity for obtaining the picture. You will find these modes valuable and will most of the time be able to create better pictures than if you use the Intelligent Auto Mode.

Eventually, you may start using semi-automatic settings where the camera adjusts only some of the settings automatically and you select the rest. For the most experienced users, the camera provides the opportunity to manually set the camera controls to stage a picture themselves. This gives users the opportunity to fully exercise their artistic creativity to capture unique images.

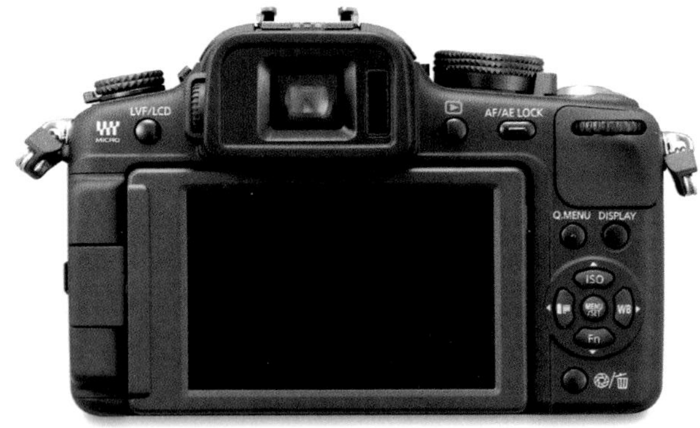

To control many options, the Panasonic G2 camera has many different menu commands and buttons, which you need to understand and manage. The Intelligent Auto Mode and predefined scene modes automatically control the camera settings and therefore need the least amount of input from you. You will control some of the commands when using the semi-automatic modes, although everything is available for you to change. While in the manual mode, you will have to rely on your experience and creativity to get the pictures and videos you want. In this case, all of the camera menu and button controls are at your disposal.

This book has two appendices covering the menu commands. Appendix C* contains a limited set of menu commands available when in the Intelligent Auto Mode. Appendix D* contains a list of the camera's entire main menu commands and their submenu commands and values along with some pointers about the commands and their options. There are so many available commands (many of them covering small details about the camera) that it would require a very large book to cover them all, which, quite frankly, would bore many of you. Appendix D* is a great resource for going through all of the commands and finding something that might pertain to just that one thing you want to experiment with.

* For more information on the Appendix see: http://rockynook.com/PanasonicG2

Viewing Images and Menu Commands

If you are just taking your new Panasonic G2 camera out of its box while you read this book, you might want to read Appendix A, "Setting up your Camera." It covers the camera components and proper installation of the battery, memory card, and camera lens. Once you have the camera properly assembled, you are ready to turn it on. The ON/OFF switch is on the top of the camera on the right side (figure 1-1). Switch the small lever to ON. A small green light next to the letters ON will glow.

If you have not done so, you should set the date and time settings, as this information is recorded with each picture and video. But before covering the setting of the camera's clock information, let's first examine how to navigate through and set values for the camera's extensive menu commands.

The Panasonic G2 camera has two methods to view the images and menu options. You can use either the LCD screen (Panasonic refers to this as an LCD monitor) in the center of the back of the camera or you can use the electronic viewfinder (Panasonic refers to this as the viewfinder) at the top of the back of the camera. To start using the camera's menu structure, we will work with the rear LCD screen—at the end of this section we will describe the electronic viewfinder.

Figure 1-1 shows both the iA button and the camera are turned on. The blue glow surrounding the iA button indicates that the mode is activated. The green light indicates that the camera is on and ready to take a photograph. The green light goes off when the camera is turned off or if it goes to "sleep" to conserve battery power. If this happens, a light pressure on the shutter release button (big silver button) will wake the camera up.

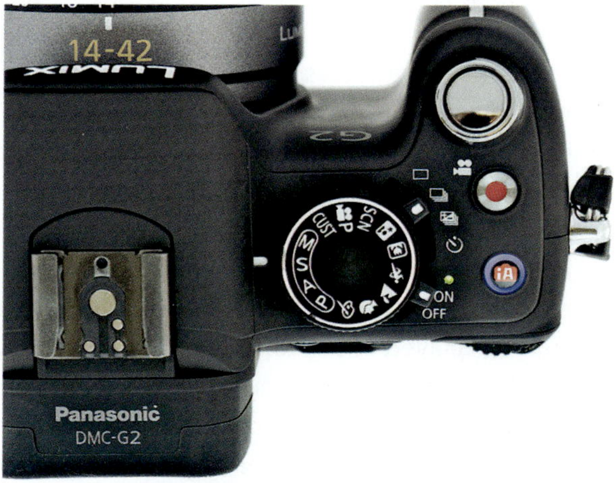

Figure 1-1: Top portion of the camera displaying the iA button and the ON/OFF lever

Menu Commands

You can view and change the menu command values by pressing the MENU/SET button (on the right side on the back of the camera, figure 1-2). Although the displayed menu screen structure and contents will vary depending on your selected mode, how you navigate the menu structure is the same.

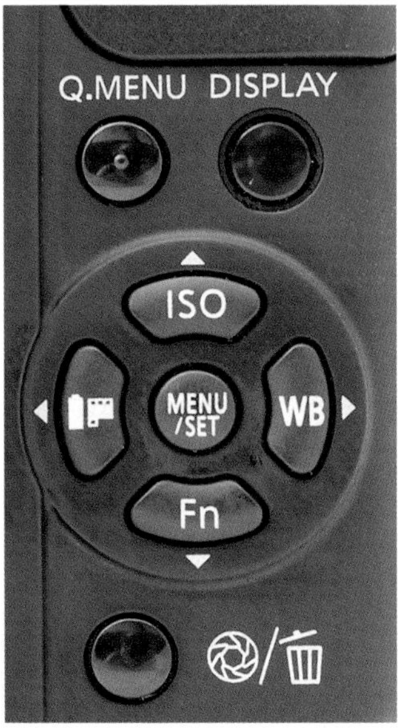

Figure 1-2: MENU/SET button

The MENU/SET button is positioned on the right-hand side surrounded by the directional arrow buttons. The MENU/SET button is used to review and set menu command options.

When you first enter the camera's menu structure, the main menu options are displayed as icons in a vertical bar on the left side of the screen (table 1-1). The main menu options that are displayed are dependent on the mode the camera is set to. Figure 1-3a shows a screen shot of the core set of main menu options (from top to bottom): REC, MOTION PICTURE, CUSTOM, SETUP, MY MENU, and PLAYBACK. Note that the selected option (REC) is a different color than the others, and its name is displayed at the top of the screen.

For some camera modes, such as Intelligent Auto and the predefined scene modes (covered in detail in chapter 4), the main menu options displayed are a bit different. Figure 1-3a displays the core main menu options in the vertical bar on the left side of the screen. When the camera is in Intelligent Auto Mode, the REC main menu option is replaced with the Intelligent Auto Mode's iA icon (figure 1-3b). For predefined scene modes, an additional main menu option is displayed at the top of the list signifying that a scene mode has been activated. Figure 1-3c displays the main menu options for the Night Portrait predefined scene mode.

All of the menus consist of a set of main menu commands, each with a separate set of submenu commands. Most of the submenu commands have values to choose from. Some of the submenu commands have menus of their own, each with a set of values. Most of the main menus have multiple pages of submenu commands. There are so many choices that it is impossible to display them all on a single screen.

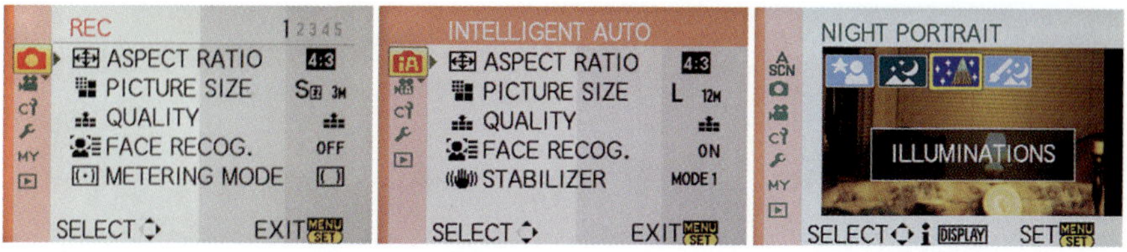

Figure 1-3 (a–c): Pressing the MENU/SET button displays the camera's menu

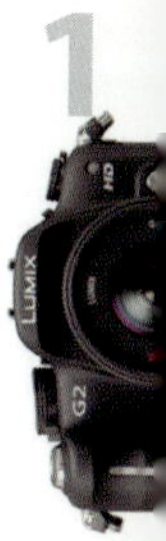

The selected main menu submenu commands' page numbers are displayed in the upper-right corner of the menu screen. To help you quickly find them within the Panasonic G2 camera's menu structure as we cover them in the book, menu commands are shown in the following format.

MENU/SET>***main menu name***>**(pg *submenu page #*) *submenu command name***>[***value1***], [***value2***]

The > separates menus and submenus and pg refers to the number of the screen page on which the submenu is found. No page number will be included for those commands displayed on page 1. If the submenus have subordinate commands, we will list them separated by > until we have reached the option we are discussing. We will include the values in brackets when appropriate to the subject being covered. We list the page number so you do not have to read each option to find the command. You can rapidly move through the commands to the page that you need.

For example, we will identify the AUTO BRACKET command's location as follows:

MENU/SET>REC>(pg 4) AUTO BRACKET

Figure 1-4 shows the menu flow for selecting the AUTO BRACKET command. Starting with figure 1-4a, within the REC main menu, AUTO BRACKET is selected. Pressing the right directional arrow button moves to STEP (figure 1-4b), and pressing the right directional arrow button again moves deeper in the command sequence to select a value for the command. Using this book's defined menu nomenclature, this command would be displayed as follows:

MENU/SET>REC>(pg 4) AUTO BRACKET>STEP>[3 1/3], [3 2/3], [5 1/3], [5 2/3], [7 1/3], [7 2/3]

Some menu commands have icons as values. In these cases, we will denote the value in upper and lower case italics.

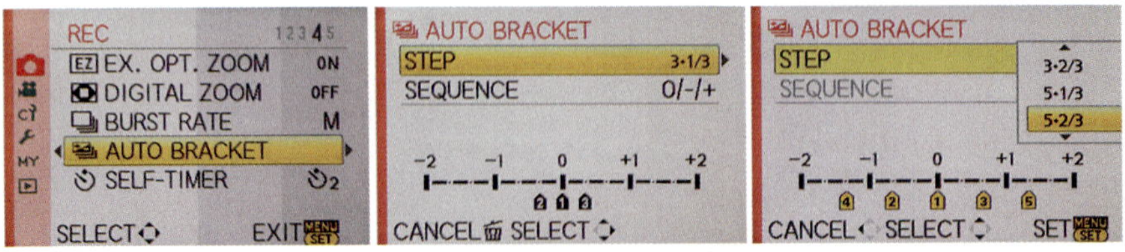

Figure 1-4 (a–c): Menu option display screen

When the MENU/SET button is pressed, the available menu command display is initiated. The last command within the selected menu is remembered and is highlighted in a yellow rectangle. If the menu was last positioned on the main menu list, the selected main menu command will have up to three gray triangles resting on the yellow highlighted rectangle, indicating which directional arrow buttons are available to use to move through the menu structure from the given point. If the last-viewed menu command was within a submenu command, the specific page containing the submenu option is displayed with the actual submenu command highlighted in yellow with two gray arrows—one on the left side of the option and one on the right side, representing available directions you can move (figure 1-4a). Moving to the right will take you deeper into the menu command structure to view the command's available settings or additional submenus (figure 1-4b).

In addition, the menu will display the current value of each of the submenu commands to the far right of the command (figure 1-4c).

Menu Navigation

The camera gives you many ways to navigate through available menus and select values. You can use the directional arrow buttons, the rear dial, or in some cases, the LCD Touch Screen function to move through the menus and their available values. You can also use them all interchangeability. All of these navigational options are available to you on the back of the camera. Play with all of them so you are comfortable with maneuvering through the list of menu commands and their values.

Icon	Menu Name	Icon	Menu Name
	REC Mode		Playback Mode
	Motion Picture Mode	iA	iA REC Mode
	CUSTOM	A SCN	Advanced Scene Mode
	SETUP	SCN	Scene Mode
MY	My Menu		

Table 1-1: Main menu icons and associated names

Using the Directional Arrows

Navigating through the camera's extensive set of menu commands is easy using the up, down, right, and left directional arrow buttons on the back of the camera with the MENU/SET button (center button, see figure 1-2) functioning as the "enter" key to select the yellow highlighted command or value. Once you have highlighted a menu command, moving the right or left directional arrow button will move the cursor in or out of the menus and their list of available commands or values. Using the up or down directional arrow button will move the cursor to scroll up or down through menu commands or a specific command's list of available values. The cursor's position is marked by the item being highlighted in yellow. Use the MENU/SET button to choose the value for the selected menu option.

Using the Rear Dial

In addition to using the directional arrow buttons, you can use the rear dial to navigate through the menu commands and their associated values. The rear dial works by rotating left or right, moving the selection cursor vertically through the list of menu commands. The commands are highlighted in yellow, just as they are when you use the directional arrow buttons.

When you want to move from the list of main menu commands into its list of submenu commands, press the rear dial to select the menu command and the cursor position moves to the first option displayed in submenu list. Again rotate the rear dial right or left moving through the list of submenu commands.

When you want to view the available values of the highlighted menu command, again press the rear dial inward and the sub-menu values will appear. Rotate the rear dial through the available values. Press the rear dial when you are positioned on the value you want. The list of available values disappear, and the selected value is now displayed next to the submenu option. As noted earlier, when you enter the first submenu level, there can be several pages of options.

We find using the rear dial a more convenient way of rapidly moving through a long list of commands that spans several pages than using the directional arrow buttons. Its only disadvantage is that it does not allow you to go to a higher main menu command (backwards).

Setting the Clock's Date and Time

The first request your camera is going to make of you is to set the camera's date and time. The "PLEASE SET THE CLOCK" message is displayed when you turn on your camera for the first time. The date and time stamp is a great way to keep track of when a picture or video was taken. Plus there are several camera functions that can use this date and time stamp to your advantage. You can always set it at a later time, but it is easiest at this point since you are prompted instead of having to remember on your own.

Setting the date and time is easy. Use the directional arrow buttons or rear dial to move through the options. You have the option to set the time as [24HRS] or [AM/PM], where 12:00 a.m. is midnight and 12:00 p.m. represents noon. If you decide to set the date and time later, you can do so from the SETUP menu (table 1-1). Select the MENU/SET>SETUP>CLOCK SET option in the camera's menu and push the right directional arrow button to advance into the menu's values. With the directional arrow buttons, enter the current date and time and press the MENU/SET button to accept (figure 1-5).

In addition to the clock date and time, you should set the Home settings in the WORLD TIME command. The WORLD TIME command (MENU/SET>SETUP>WORLD TIME) allows you to identify your time zone and whether daylight saving time applies.

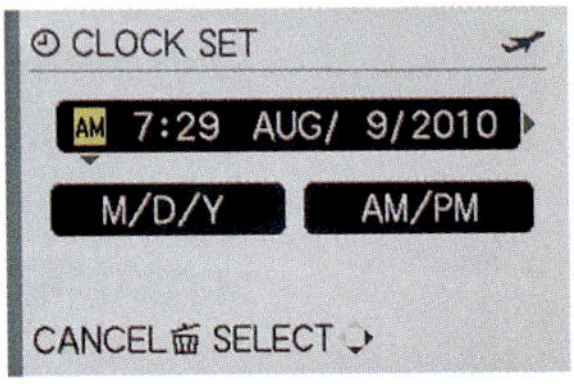

Figure 1-5: The CLOCK SET display screen with the clock's date and time set

The same information can be set for travel destinations. When you travel to another time zone, you can set the destination settings within World Time and the travel start and end dates within the Travel Date option (MENU/SET>SETUP>TRAVEL DATE). This way, the camera's clock date and time will be adjusted according to your location during the specified travel dates.

Quick Menu Option

The Panasonic G2 camera has a Quick Menu option, which displays the commands commonly used for the camera's current mode and display style. Rather than using the MENU/SET button and navigating through the camera commands, you can access the most-used ones by activating the Quick Menu option. The Quick Menu option is designed to save you time by simplifying your selection choices.

The Quick Menu option can be activated in two ways: by pressing the Q.MENU button (figure 1-2) on the right-hand side of the back of the camera or by pressing the Q.MENU icon (figure 1-6) displayed on the LCD screen. To activate the Quick Menu option, press either. When the option is activated, menu commands and available values are displayed in the viewfinder or on the LCD screen. To deactivate Quick Menu, either press the Q.MENU OFF icon on the LCD screen or press the Q.MENU button on the camera body a second time.

We will be covering the Quick Menu option further in chapter 4 when we discuss the different mode and display styles available.

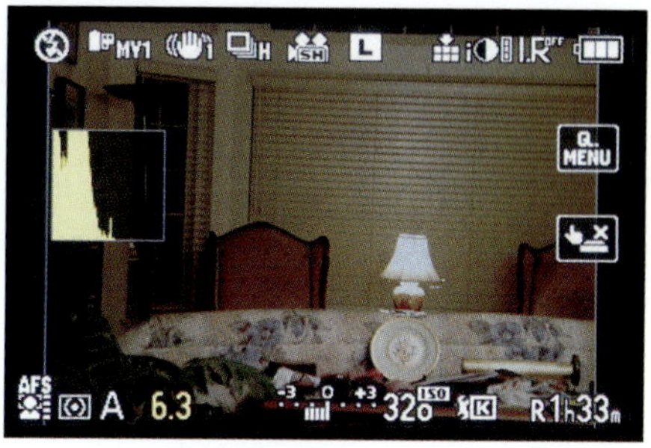

Figure 1-6: The camera's LCD screen showing the Q.MENU icon

Daylight Saving Time

Many areas within the United States observe daylight saving time. In the spring and fall, the time is set forward or backward 1 hour, respectively. Every year a big effort ensues to remind people of the time change and which way to set their clocks. The camera's World Time option allows you to specify if you reside in, or will be traveling to, a location that observes daylight saving time. If so, the camera will take this into account when calculating the current time. This way, you won't have to remember to change the camera's clock. Instead, it will be done automatically for you.

Intelligent Auto Mode

With minimum skill and effort, a photographer can produce excellent pictures with the Panasonic G2 camera by turning on its Intelligent Auto Mode. This activates the camera's interpretative intelligence, which determines the best settings for the subject the camera has in its view.

All you need to do is press the iA button on the right side on the top of the camera. When pressed, the button will glow blue. Once it's activated, find the subject in the viewfinder and press the shutter release button. The camera's intelligent software will quickly evaluate the scene and choose the camera settings it believes appropriate for the picture at hand. This goes beyond simple automatic exposure.

The camera's software determines if the framed subject should be photographed as a portrait, landscape, action picture, or close-up. Based on the type of picture, the available lighting, and the picture's mobility, the camera's intelligent software will determine where to focus, the white balance, and the best shutter speed, aperture, and gain to produce an optimal picture. We will cover the specific picture types and how you might want to utilize these settings to your advantage in producing the perfect picture in chapter 4.

What is Gain?

In terms of a camera, gain is controlled either by the camera automatically or by the photographer pressing the ISO button in back of the camera. Practically, it is used as a measure of the sensor's sensitivity, so raising the ISO or the gain results in generating a brighter image for a given light level. However, raising the gain magnifies the defects from the sensor's signal, and while the image appears brighter, its quality will be reduced.

Saving Your Pictures and Videos

When you push the shutter-release button to take a picture or initiate the recording of a video, the digital camera will save the image or video and store it on the memory card. Most likely you will eventually be transferring the saved files to your computer. The format (file type) of the saved image or video will help determine what you can do with it after transferring the file to another medium.

JPEG and RAW Defined

JPEG: A JPEG image file has been compressed using a method developed by the Joint Photographic Experts Group. There is a loss of information from the image file that cannot be restored. The file's name has the extension .jpg (commonly used on Windows machines) or .jpeg (commonly used on Macintosh computers).

RAW: A RAW file is a file that is from a digital camera and is minimally processed so it has all the data captured by the imaging sensor. For Panasonic cameras, a RAW file has the filename extension .rw2.

There are two different file types you can choose for your pictures and videos: JPEG and RAW. The one you select depends on what you are going to do with your pictures and videos after they have been saved.

When you start using your Panasonic G2 camera, you will find that JPEG is the default file type. The JPEG file format has the advantage of being readable and usable by almost any computing device. You can view these files on your cell phone and send them as email attachments, and viewing them on your personal computer is usually a simple matter of placing your mouse cursor on the file name and clicking.

In contrast, the RAW format is more cumbersome and occupies more space on the memory card as well as any place you move your images to, such as your computer hard drive. In addition, the RAW format is a proprietary format specific to the camera manufacturer and can require special software to open images saved in that format. With all these drawbacks, what could possibly be the benefit of saving your images in the RAW format?

These inconveniences are accepted because the RAW format minimally processes the data from the camera (hence the name RAW) and gives the knowledgeable user greater flexibility in processing their images on the computer. There are many software packages available that will allow you to enhance, clean up, change, and sharpen your saved images. These programs generally work best when the image has been saved in RAW format since there is much more data available to work with than in a JPEG image.

So what to use? Well, the simplest answer is to use both. The Panasonic G2 allows you to store your file in both RAW and JPEG at the time the image is saved. This gives you the best of both worlds: the convenience of using a generally accessible, small JPEG file and the capability of full image processing potential by using the RAW file format. To set the camera to store an image in both JPEG and RAW, press MENU/SET button and then proceed as follows.

If you are in Intelligent Auto Mode:

> **MENU/SET>INTELLIGENT AUTO>QUALITY>select one of the menu command values**

If you are not in Intelligent Auto Mode:

> **MENU/SET>REC>QUALITY> select one of the menu command values**

Choosing the resulting picture's QUALITY option (file format) will in part determine future file capabilities (table 1-2).

Value Options	QUALITY Descriptions
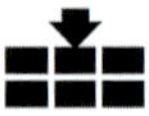	JPEG – Fine. Image is stored in JPEG format only. A high level of detail is captured.
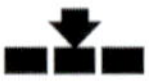	JPEG – Standard. Image is stored in JPEG format. Equivalent to the standard level of detail recorded.
RAW	RAW + JPEG – Fine. Two images are stored, one in RAW and one in JPEG – Fine with a high level of detail captured.
RAW	RAW + JPEG – Standard. Two images are stored, one in RAW and one in JPEG – Standard with an equivalent to the standard level of detail recorded.
RAW	RAW Only. Image is stored in RAW format.

Table 1-2: Available QUALITY command values

Although storing the images in both JPEG and RAW formats provides you with opportunities and flexibility, you will quickly find that you are filling up the camera's memory card. However, considering the low cost of cards, this is a minor disadvantage when using a large memory card. The Panasonic manual provides a chart showing the number of images that can be stored on a memory card.

If you use an 8 gigabyte (GB) card, you can store about 410 images total using the RAW and JPEG FINE QUALITY option. Admittedly, if you use just JPEG format, you can store thousands of photographs. So you must balance this

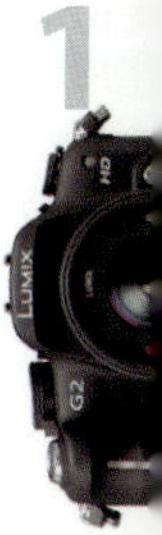

with the impracticality of handling this many pictures in a shooting session. If you make a practice of downloading your pictures at the end of the day, 410 pictures most likely will be adequate. If not, you can always carry more than one memory card and replace the card as the need arises.

When shooting videos, you have two versions in which the files can be saved: AVCHD Lite and Motion JPEG. Your choice is further defined by the recording quality level within the file type. This involves a combination of the REC MODE and REC QUALITY commands (table 1-3). Keep in mind that video files can be massive.

REC MODE Value Options	REC MODE Descriptions	REC QUALITY Value Options	REC QUALITY Descriptions
(movie camera icon)	AVCHD Lite—Best REC MODE for playing on a TV in HD	SH	High quality. High megabits per second recorded. 1280 x 720 pixels (approx. 17 Mbps).
		H	Medium quality. Medium megabits per second recorded. 1280 x 720 pixels (approx. 13 Mbps).
		L	Lower quality. Low megabits per second recorded. 1280 x 720 pixels (approx. 9 Mbps).
(film strip icon)	MOTION JPEG—best REC MODE for email and playing on a PC	HD	High Definition format. 1280 x 720 pixels (30 frames/sec.).
		WVGA	WVGA format. 848 x 480 pixels (30 frames/sec.).
		VGA	VGA format. 640 x 480 pixels (30 frames/sec.).
		QVGA	QVGA format. 320 x 240 pixels (30 frames/sec.).

Table 1-3: The REC MODE and REC QUALITY commands are tied together

One of the distinctions of these files is the extent to which they have been compressed and the ease with which they can be edited on your computer. The AVCHD Lite format is used if you intend to play back your video on your high-definition TV. Motion JPEG is a larger file, but its advantage is that it is easily edited on a home computer. You can use, for example, QuickTime to download and play back your video. As a file, it is easier to manipulate on the computer and does not require as powerful a machine in terms of CPU capability.

To define a video's type of recording, first assign a value to the REC MODE command:

MENU/SET>MOTION PICTURE>REC MODE>[*AVCHD Lite*], [*MOTION JPEG*]

After you select the type of video file, you then need select the file quality.

For ACVHD Lite:

MENU/SET>MOTION PICTURE>REC QUALITY>[SH], [H], [L]

For MOTION JPEG:

MENU/SET>MOTION PICTURE>REC QUALITY>[HD], [WGA], [VGA], [QVGA]

The REC MODE command you choose determines what value choices are displayed for the REC QUALITY command.

The Memory Card

An essential accessory for your camera is the memory card. Usually, when you order the camera online or in a store, you will receive a reminder that the camera needs a memory card, and this is the perfect time to buy one. This is good advice since the camera will not operate without one! But what should you buy? Well, the camera uses a type of memory card called Secure Digital (SD).

These cards come in many varieties, with different memory capacities and different speeds in transferring data. Your camera can read SD, SDHC, or SDXC cards—and as this book is being written, Panasonic sells a SDXC card that can hold 64 GB of data and costs about $480. We opted for a 16 GB card that cost only $85 and an 8 GB card, which cost $42. These are Panasonic cards and are rated as class 6 to be used with any of the camera's recording modes. However, if we are willing to sacrifice the AVHCD Lite movie mode, we can use a card that transfers data at a slower rate, and by using MOTION JPEG movie mode only, we can buy a Panasonic class 4 16 GB card for $50.

We recommend against getting an overly large memory card. You should get in the practice of transferring your images from your camera to your computer at the end of each shooting day.

Information and Error Messages

The Panasonic G2 camera helps you with a large number of descriptive information and error messages to guide you through setting up and using the camera. See Appendix B* for a compiled list of common information and error messages in alphabetical order for easy lookup.

Important RESET Command

Nothing is perfect. With that said, Panasonic has thought of just about everything, including the possibility that you will need to reset the camera's command settings back to its defaults. As you learn how to use the camera, you will be setting, changing, and resetting the camera command options frequently. Panasonic has added a RESET command in the SETUP menu to allow you to restore the default menu options and in essence start over.

MENU/SET>SETUP>(pg 4) RESET

* To view the Appendix, see: http://rockynook.com/PanasonicG2

This command has two options:

- Reset only the REC menu and FACE RECOG. command settings
- Reset the SETUP and CUSTOM menu command settings

There are drawbacks to doing a reset. Resetting the REC menu and FACE RECOG. commands deletes the saved registered face recognition data. If you have registered specific people's name and birth dates with their face, this information will be deleted. Resetting the SETUP and CUSTOM menu commands will erase saved World Time and Travel Date information along with Baby1/Baby2 and Pet name, birthday, and age information. However, if your camera commands do not work as described in the manual, you might need to execute the RESET command.

The Dual Viewing System of the Panasonic G2 Camera

The Panasonic G2 camera is unique in having two electronic displays. As mentioned earlier, there is an electronic viewfinder that has an eyepiece and there is the LCD screen at the back of the camera. Most users of digital cameras are familiar with the latter. But the electronic finder is unique in the Panasonic; unlike early versions of this type of viewfinder that appeared in Minolta, Sony, and Olympus digital cameras, this viewfinder is very sharp and has a good refresh rate. It enables you to use the camera at eye level, and it functions as the replacement to the optical viewfinder that users of digital single-lens reflex (DSLR) cameras are familiar with. Unlike with the DSLR, you can use this viewfinder to frame and compose your video while the camera is recording.

Both the viewfinder and LCD screen will work, but only one at a time. The viewfinder is enabled when the camera senses the presence of something near the viewfinder window. When something is detected, the camera assumes it is your eye and activates the viewfinder while deactivating the LCD screen. The LCD screen will reactivate when the sensed object has moved away, making both viewing modes unavailable at the same time. This thoughtful feature preserves battery life.

As with everything in life, there are both drawbacks and advantages to each of the viewing displays. The Panasonic G2 camera has many different settings for controlling what you see in the viewfinder or on the LCD screen. As you use the camera and become familiar with its settings and buttons, over time you will develop personal choices as to which method works best

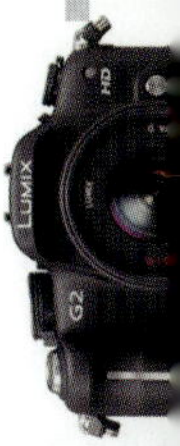

for you. We will be covering details about the LCD screen and the viewfinder and how to display information on them in chapter 3.

Diopter Adjustment Dial

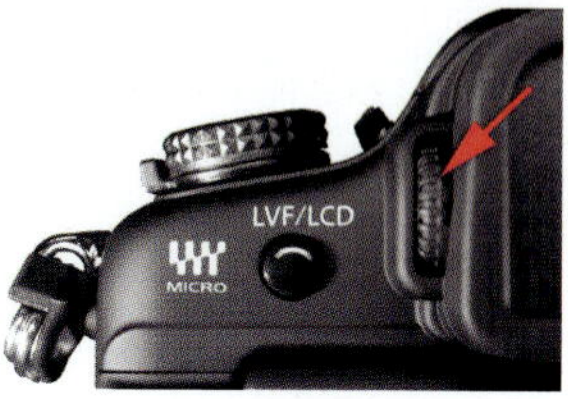

Figure 1-7: The Panasonic G2 camera's diopter adjustment dial

Before we move on, there is one more thing you need to know about the viewfinder. Its optics should be focused to the user's eye. There is a small wheel to the left of the eyepiece called the diopter adjustment dial. Rotate the wheel back and forth until the objects in the viewfinder appear at their sharpest.

Of course, if you share your camera with others, your setting may not be perfect for them. If your family and friends need to change the setting, you will have to readjust it for yourself when you take the camera back. It enables the user to tailor the viewfinder's magnification to their needs

Summary

As you become more familiar with the camera, you will want to try out your own setting combinations by overriding the camera's interpretive intelligence and setting its components yourself. As intelligent as the camera software is, it can make mistakes, and with experience you may find that you wish to control some of your pictures' settings yourself. Chapter 5 will cover how to combine your own settings with those of the camera's Intelligent Auto settings. You will be able to start creating more artistic pictures and interjecting specific moods into your pictures and videos.

Chapter 6 will cover going solo by setting your own controls, creating advanced options to formulate more artistic control over the resulting pictures. You will be able to format artistic pictures and capture the mood and unique qualities that otherwise would not be possible should you rely on the camera's built-in interpretive intelligence.

Basic Photographic Ideas and External Buttons

2

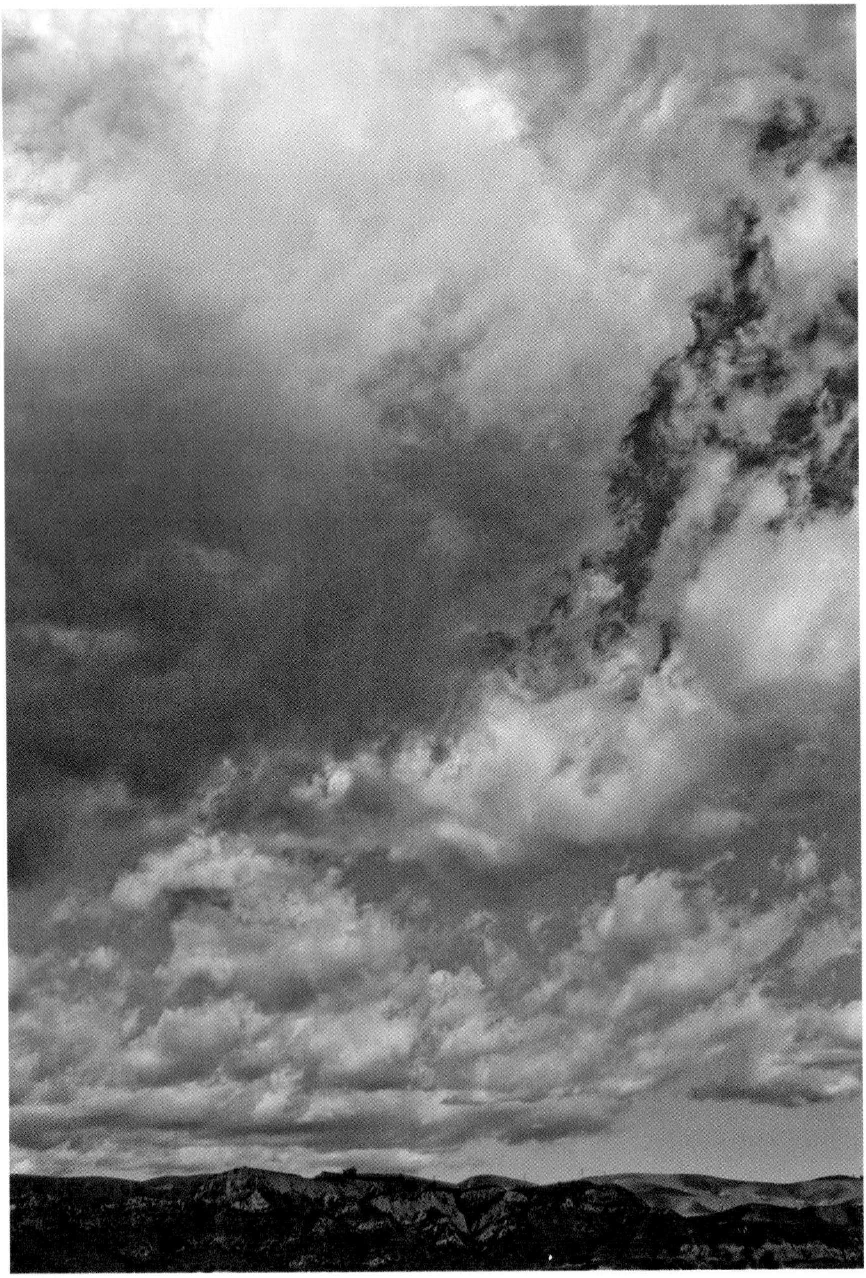

Introduction: Basic Photographic Ideas and External Buttons

The Panasonic G2 camera comes with a 200+ page manual listing scores of menu commands and options. Considering that recording a picture involves only two operations—focusing an image onto the camera's sensor and providing it with enough light to ensure that the image is recorded—having scores of command and option selections seems incongruous. This anomaly is explained by the multitude of technical and artistic controls that enable you to apply your own interpretation of the subject. The many menu commands reflect the diversity of subjects that can be photographed. Although the Panasonic G2 camera has several dials and buttons, these menu controls may be disabled so that the camera automatically sets its aperture, shutter speed, sensitivity, and focus to capture the image. This automation enables the novice to record professional-quality images with minimal effort.

This camera's design is unique in that it has an operational style that can be customized for everyone from the novice to the most expert photographer. At its most automatic, it sets virtually everything. Its internal computer identifies the type of subject and from this determines the combination of automatic controls needed to capture the photograph. Virtually all the external controls are overridden, and they cannot be used to modify the camera's settings. For example, if the camera identifies a face, it assumes that you will be photographing a portrait and sets the camera accordingly. Automation is imperfect—face recognition may fail when you're photographing a person's profile or if sunglasses cover the eyes, an error that a human operator would not make. So even in an automated mode, a camera's operation may require human intervention.

As you gain experience and wish to experiment, you may gradually assume greater control of the camera. While still operating in an automatic mode, the camera's settings can be partially overridden. Intelligent Auto Mode provides instant gratification in collecting images, but with experience, you can improve your photography by obtaining images under difficult lighting conditions that would fool this system. With the Panasonic G2, you can gradually move away from automation and assume control of your photography. Eventually, you may wish to use the camera in a manual mode and dispense with any automatic setting. The assumption of control requires an understanding of the basics of light's interaction with the sensor, making this knowledge increasingly important as you exercise artistic control. This chapter will describe photographic basics of exposure, depth of field, shutter speed, and sensitivity.

A photographic recording of a subject is complex, and it helps to understand how to operate the camera by understanding what happens when we record a picture. A photograph is a two-dimensional rendering of a three-dimensional subject. The camera's light detector, called a sensor, is flat, and light from the subject is projected onto it. If the distance of the lens from the sensor is not adjusted precisely, the subject will be blurred, causing a loss of definition.

Further, only one plane parallel to the sensor is rendered at maximum sharpness—in other words, the subject will be in focus only at one plane. Objects in front of or behind this plane are less sharp, a progression that increases until the most distant planes appear as a complete blur. This is unlike our vision, where the eye and brain interpret the entire view as sharp. In contrast, the camera and the photographer must decide how to record the single maximum plane of sharpness into a photograph that mimics the automatic control of the human eye.

We can take this analysis further. A human's visual system handles a broader range of brightness than can be recorded by an electronic sensor in this class of camera. When we look about a sunlit landscape, we see the blue sky, the white clouds, and details in the shadows cast by trees. In contrast, the camera sensor can record only a limited range, and when it photographs such a scene, only objects reflecting median light intensities are shown in detail. The blue sky with white clouds appears as featureless regions of white. Similarly, areas in the shadows are hidden and rendered as regions of black. Again, our visual senses automatically record the entire range of brightness while the camera sensor is limited to recording only a partial portion of the scene. To use your Panasonic G2 camera effectively requires an understanding of its limitations.

To record a subject requires two things: Its image must be focused onto a sensor and the intensity of light collected must lie within a prescribed range. Prior to digital cameras, when the recording medium was film, the photographer would control these two variables manually. Focusing was achieved by rotating a ring that varied the distance of the lens to the film. To obtain accurate focus, some cameras had optical aids. In the case of a single-lens reflex (SLR) camera, a mirror would reflect the light from the lens and project it onto a frosted screen placed at a distance equivalent to that of the film. By viewing the screen, the photographer could focus by adjusting the lens until the image was maximally sharp.

> **What Are Sensors and Images?**
>
> Digital cameras use a solid-state device composed of millions of individual photosites for converting light into an electrical signal. The individual photosite is the physical basis of a pixel, the smallest unit for sensing light. In the G2, there are more than 12 million pixels in a 3000 x 4000 rectangular array. Signals from these sensors are transmitted to the camera's viewing screen. Altogether, these will make up a mosaic of intensities and colors that will become an image. The viewed image is a numerical expression, which can be manipulated mathematically so that the camera's computer can alter its appearance. Recording the picture requires that these values are stored on a memory card from which they will eventually be downloaded to a computer.

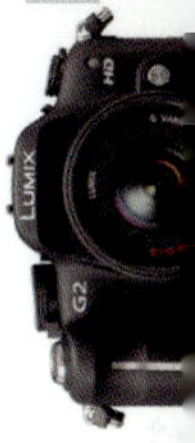

Focusing

Our eye and brain automatically see the world as being in sharp focus. For those with normal eyesight, it is only when using a microscope, telescope, or binoculars do they need to focus. With these optical instruments, we improve the image's definition by turning a wheel that moves a lens forward or backward toward our eye.

The same occurs with older SLR cameras—we looked through a viewfinder and turned a focusing ring surrounding the lens to bring a blurred image into sharpness. Things have changed with the modern camera; focusing is automated and a motorized lens brings the image to focus at a push of a button. Even so, to exploit this automation fully, an understanding of what is going on is necessary to optimize camera settings for fast accurate focusing.

Focus Mode

To determine if the subject is in focus, the Panasonic G2 camera uses contrast detection. The camera moves the lens closer and further from the sensor, comparing its changing appearance until it finds one that has the greatest range of brightness. This seems straightforward; however, one of the difficulties in designing an automatic system is identifying the subject to focus on. When you look through the finder, it is evident to you what you want to focus on, but an automatic focusing system has to be told what it needs to target. Usually, the entire scene is not usable for focusing.

For example, your friends are standing in front of a range of majestic mountains—do you focus on your friends, rendering the mountains a blur, or do you focus on the mountains and render your friends as a blur? For most of us, the decision is easy; we focus on our friends. Unfortunately, our camera has no friends, and it will not be able to distinguish between people or mountains. A solution to this dilemma is to have the photographer tell the camera what is important. This can be done by having a sight in the viewfinder and restricting contrast detection to that target. The photographer aims this sight at the object of interest. Pressing lightly on the shutter-release button, he initiates the focusing, and when the lens is adjusted and the area in the target is sharp, the camera signals that it has obtained focus and the photographer takes the picture by depressing the shutter-release button fully.

In this manner, assuming he aimed the sight on his friends, he is assured that they are recorded in splendid detail. For an automatic camera, this mode of operation is reliable and provides the user with maximum control. Locking into focus is a brief operation, but it can be prolonged if the chosen subject is dimly lit or lacks well-defined features.

For example, the camera may not focus on the surface of a wall in dim light. If this is the case, one finds something else with more detail at the same distance and uses that as the focusing target. So, a highly detailed picture hanging on the wall can be used as an alternate target. Once focus is locked in, the camera can be moved to the intended subject and you can take the shot.

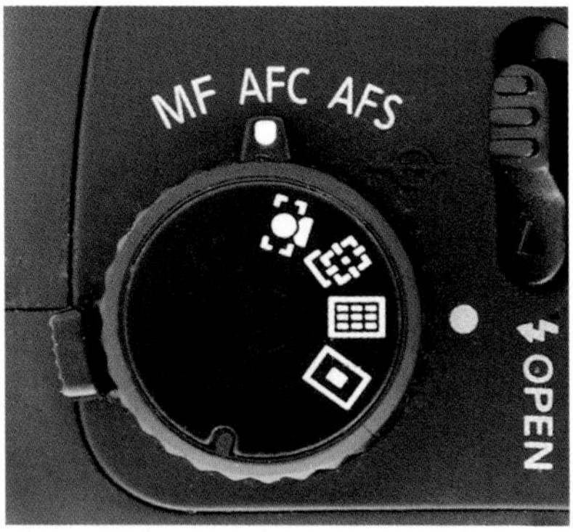

Figure 2-1: Auto focus mode dial

Figure 2-1 is looking down on the top of the camera at the auto focus mode dial where its four icons for identifying the regions to focus are found. A white dot on the camera body to the right of the dial indicates the selected command (in this case, 23-area-focusing is selected). The four icons from top down are Face Detection, AF Tracking , 23-area-focusing and 1-area-focusing modes. These modes are not recognized by the camera when using the Intelligent Auto Mode. The focus mode lever is pointing at AFC.

Menu Option	Display Screen Icon	Auto Focus Mode Dial
		Face Detection
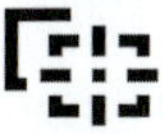	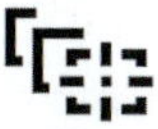	AF Tracking
		23-area-focusing
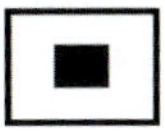	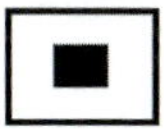	1-area-focusing

Table 2-1: Listing of the Auto Focus (AF) Mode icons and their corresponding display screen icons as they are viewed within the viewfinder or LCD screen.

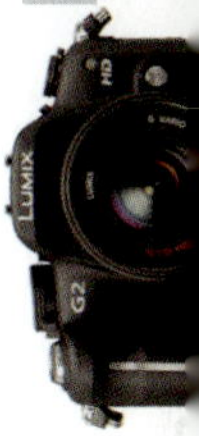

1-Area-Focusing

Turning the auto focus mode dial found on the left side of the top of the camera counter-clockwise to its left-most position sets 1-area-focusing (figure 2-1). The auto focus mode dial contains four icons one of which is 1-area-focusing, symbolized by a small rectangle in a rectangular border (table 2-1). It is selected by rotating the dial until it is opposite the selection white dot. In either the viewfinder or LCD screen, a white bracket is superimposed on the displayed image: This is the targeting sight and it identifies the object for focusing.

Nominally, it will be in the center of the screen, but it can be positioned anywhere on the screen. Moreover, the size of the square can be changed. These points will be covered later in chapter 5.

For now it is important to realize that it establishes a single region for focusing. A particularly convenient method of positioning the site is to use the touch screen. By simply touching the rear LCD screen, you will position the sight under your finger. When the camera is tripod mounted this is a convenient way of identifying the point of focus.

Keep in mind that when you're using the fully automatic modes, such as Intelligent Auto or the predefined scene modes, the camera will sometimes override what you set on the auto focus mode dial. For example, when you're using Intelligent Auto Mode, the camera will use an alternate Auto Focus (AF) Mode (the default is Face Detection).

To be guaranteed of getting 1-area-focusing mode, you will have to use the camera in a semi-automatic or a fully manual mode. If you use automation that employs a scene identification scheme (e.g., portrait, scenic), the camera determines the AF Mode.

23-Area-Focusing

1-area-focusing is the most accurate but slowest method for implementing automatic focusing. When you're feeling rushed, it may be desirable to use a shotgun approach and have the camera guess what points it should use for good focus.

This is accomplished by using what Panasonic defines as 23-area-focusing, where up to 23 regions may serve as focus points, freeing you from having to select and then aim your targeting sight. When focus is achieved, the camera may show what areas were chosen for focusing by displaying multiple rectangles on the targeted regions. This is not guaranteed; when you're shooting rapidly with the camera firing in bursts, like a machine gun, there is no such display. Selecting 23-area-focusing mode requires rotating the auto focus mode dial until the icon of a rectangle containing nine small rectangles is opposite the white dot (figure 2-1).

Pressing the shutter release button half way activates the focusing, and there may be a series of multiple green rectangles displayed, indicating where focus is being locked in. In chapter 5, we will discuss how you can limit the number of areas so that only portions of the screen are used for focusing. For now, we will take advantage of having all these focus points.

AF Tracking

It is possible to tell the camera to lock onto an object and track it—altering focus and exposure to ensure that it is accurately recorded as it moves within the display screen.

This mode is called AF Tracking and is selected by choosing the icon that has a border surrounding a crosshair (figure 2-1, table 2-1). The target can be selected by using either the shutter release button or the LCD touch screen.

When you're using the viewfinder, there will be a white targeting sight. If you aim the camera and press down on the shutter release button halfway, the camera will attempt to lock onto the target, and if it succeeds, the white targeting sight turns yellow. If it fails, it turns red. If the camera is successful, the target sight will follow the subject as it moves across the screen. When you use the Pet scene mode, AF Tracking is activated. Fully depressing the shutter release button captures the image. To cancel this mode, press the MENU/SET button or turn the auto focus mode dial to another mode.

Possibly an easier way of using AF Tracking is to take advantage of the touch function on the LCD screen. After selecting AF Targeting on the auto focus mode dial, touch the subject you wish to lock on and track when it's displayed on the LCD screen. If the targeting sight turns yellow, the camera is locked on the subject and will track it as it moves through the frame. To take the picture, press the shutter release button halfway to focus the lens. When focus is achieved, the tracking square turns green. Press the shutter-release button fully to take the picture. To cancel tracking, press the Trash Can button or change the AF Mode.

Surprisingly, if the object moves outside the border of the screen, AF Tracking will attempt to reacquire it if the subject returns within the screen. However, its success at this is unreliable.

Face Detection

When you're photographing friends and relatives, their faces should be recorded sharply. The Panasonic G2 camera can use facial identification software to achieve this goal. Setting the auto focus mode dial to Face Detection enables this feature. In addition, when you're using the camera in Intelligent Auto and several scene modes such as Portrait, Baby1, Baby2, and Night Portrait, the camera will use Face Detection to establish focus. If the camera fails to find a face, it goes to 23-area-focusing.

Face Detection can be used with either the electronic viewfinder or the LCD screen. When a face is detected, a yellow border appears surrounding it. The size of this border as well as its position varies depending on the size and position of the face. When several faces are in the scene and the camera identifies them, one square will be yellow and the remainder white. Each of the squares represents a detected face. One face, the one framed in yellow, will be used as the point of focus. The yellow square will turn green when focused when you press the shutter-release button halfway down.

Face detection is imperfect: It will not work on profiles and sometimes fails if the face is viewed at an angle. When this occurs, the camera shifts the AF Mode to 23-area-focusing to make a "best guess" on what should be recorded. So even if facial detection fails, automatic focusing is still in play and, fortunately, the alternate focusing mode is usually satisfactory.

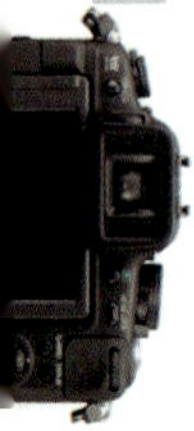

Face Detection vs. Face Recognition

These terms can be a source of confusion. Be aware that Face Detection is an automatic focusing mode and simply identifies a "generic face" to be used as a point of focus. Face Recognition refers to identifying a specific person's face. You have to register a face in the camera—once it's registered, a name and age can be associated to the face. This provides, on playback and future recordings, a means of identifying a specific person. This recognition software is fallible, and there are situations in which it fails to identify a registered subject correctly. Using facial recognition will be discussed in chapter 4.

Recommendations

If you use the camera solely in the automatic mode, such as Intelligent Auto or the scene modes, the AF Mode will not be under your control—the camera selects it. In part, the desire to exert greater control over the camera is based on the need to control focusing. On a personal note, we frequently use the camera in a manual exposure mode and usually use 1-area-focusing. It provides the greatest accuracy and precision. When we feel rushed and do not need to identify a specific area for focusing, we will use the 23-area-focusing setting. This sacrifices control but guarantees that the majority of the image is well focused.

Unfortunately, we have recorded shots whose composition was ruined because the wrong area was selected. This usually occurs when working with low ambient illumination with the lens "wide open." The narrow depth of field shows immediately if the wrong object was selected for focus.

In contrast, this is not so much a problem when the subject is brightly lit and the lens is stopped down, increasing the depth of field. Even if the wrong object is focused on, the chances are the subject is captured within the depth of field.

We seldom use facial detection—when a face is tilted or under unusual lighting conditions, this software may fail to recognize it. At this point, the camera shifts itself to 23-area-focusing mode to find a point of focus.

Again, we use 1-area-focusing to focus on a person's eyes and use this as our target. This is a trick portrait photographers use—they know that viewers are drawn to the subject's eyes and therefore, for an attractive portrait, it is important that this area is in sharp focus.

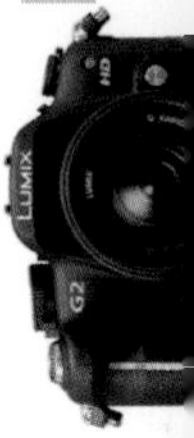

Focus Mode Lever

The Panasonic G2 camera has two automatic focusing modes, Automatic Focus Single (AFS) and Automatic Focus Continuous (AFC), and a single manual-focusing mode, Manual Focus (MF). The first two rely on the camera to establish focus with its own software; the latter requires the user to judge focus through the display screen and obtain it by turning the lens's focusing ring.

During automatic focusing, the camera must decide to either lock the lens in focus or to allow it to refocus if the subject moves. The former has the advantage of allowing you to move the camera while retaining your focus point. Frequently, when the camera is positioned for the best composition, the subject lies outside the target area used for focusing. When this occurs, it is necessary to aim the camera so the focusing site rests on the subject. Set the focus on the subject, lock focus, and then move the camera to frame the subject for the best composition.

Panasonic describes this style of focusing as Automatic Focus Single (AFS). Once the camera finds focus, the lens is locked into position and the camera will not refocus until after the camera is fired. You set it by moving the focus mode lever (figure 2-1) until a pointer is aimed at the letters AFS. A white sighting target is displayed within the camera's viewfinder. Move the camera to center the sighting target on the object you wish to focus on. At this point, pressing the shutter release button half way will focus the lens. You know the process is successful when the sight turns from white to green, a green dot appears in the upper-right corner of the screen, and, if the BEEP command is turned on, two beeps sound. At this point, depressing the shutter release button fully takes the picture. If the camera fails to find focus, the target sight turns red and there is no beep and no green circle; the camera will not fire when the shutter release button is depressed. This mode is used the most because it provides the photographer with precision when focusing. However, it is also the mode where potential photographic opportunities can be lost since the camera cannot be fired if it cannot determine focus.

To guarantee getting a shot during rapid shooting situations, there is a second mode, Auto Focus Continuous (AFC). The camera keeps its focusing motor on and the shutter can be fired rapidly. Between shots, the focus motor will continue operating. This mode is usually used when taking photographs of rapidly moving subjects and firing the camera in Burst Mode. Burst Mode will fire the camera repeatedly while the shutter release button is depressed, and during the intervals between shots, the autofocus motor keeps focusing the lens. To activate this mode, turn the focus mode lever to AFC. Find the subject in the viewfinder or on the LCD screen and depress the shutter-release button half way. The camera starts to focus and will fire when the shutter-release button is depressed fully. There is no targeting square and focus is signaled by the appearance of the green circle. However, this confirmation signal is not always visible. When the camera is set to fire in "bursts", it may not appear at all. We will discuss later how to fire the camera in Burst Mode, but suffice it to say, when the camera is firing three shots a second, it will attempt to retain focus when AFC is active.

The final setting is Manual Focus (MF). As the name implies, the user focuses by studying the display screen and turning the focusing ring of the lens until the image is sharp. After you rotate the focus mode lever to MF, the autofocus motor will not come on. You have to study the display and, by turning the focusing ring on the lens, determine when the image looks maximally sharp. Panasonic's electronic viewfinder is unique in that it provides a bright detailed image, so it is easy to judge when the object is out of or in focus.

For a modern camera, it may seem like manual focus is an archaic feature; however, its availability is a recognition that the most accurate judge of focus is the human eye and not an electronic sensor. Automatic systems can be fooled, and using nature photography as an example, manual focus can be superior. When an animal is being photographed from cover, there are often intervening branches and reeds between the subject and the camera. Automatic focusing may target this debris for focusing and the mistake may cost you a picture. To avoid this, shift the camera to manual focus. An additional benefit in this mode is the increased speed with which you can trigger a second shot. In AF Mode, there is a slight delay in firing the camera as it confirms focus. Even when using AFC there is a delay. The delays can be avoided by using MF. The increased speed in operation may seem trivial, but it can be critically important when photographing a skittish subject.

Exposure (Shutter Speed, Aperture, ISO)

Light intensity is controlled in one of two ways: regulating the amount of light falling on the sensor or regulating its duration on the sensor. The first method uses an adjustable circular opening called the aperture, which regulates the amount of light allowed to pass through the lens. The size of the aperture (or opening) can be varied continuously. For reproducible settings, it has indents with tactile clicks when a defined position is reached. These are marked with numbers, such as 1.4, 2, 2.8, 4, 5.6, 8, 11, 16, 22, and 32, which are called f-stops.

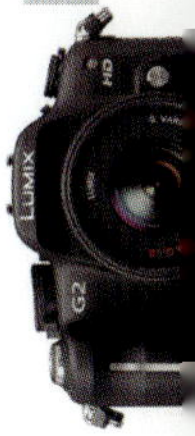

What Are F Numbers?

F numbers represent a ratio of the lens opening to its focal length. It provides a measure of consistency when using lenses of different focal length or magnifications. A telephoto lens with a focal length of 400 mm and a wide-angle lens with a focal length of only 14 mm will both pass the same intensity of light when they are set to f/16.

To put it simply, the f-stop number quantifies the amount of light passing through the lens, with each number signifying a doubling or halving depending on if it decreases or increases. Opposed to what you might assume, the amount of light increases as the numerical value falls and vice versa. So a setting of f/16 doubles the volume of light coming through the lens onto the camera sensor when the lens was set to f/22.

The second method of controlling light is to regulate the duration it falls on the sensor. A shutter opens and closes, regulating the time the sensor is exposed to light. An exposure to light for 1/30 second would allow twice as much light to fall on the sensor than a shutter speed of only 1/60 second.

Having two means for controlling light has advantages. For one, you can control exposure over a much broader range of intensities. Closing the aperture and shortening the shutter speed are additive and will reduce light's effect more than just doing one or the other. So the intensities you work with will range from using the longest shutter speed and most open aperture to the shortest shutter speed and the narrowest aperture.

Second, multiple combinations of the aperture and shutter speed settings can result in an equivalent exposure. For example, setting a lens to f/2 and a shutter speed of 1 second is, in terms of exposure, the same as setting the aperture to f/16 and the shutter speed to 60 seconds. Equivalent exposures can be obtained by the judicious selection of aperture and shutter speed.

It can be seen, then, that the dual controls, shutter and aperture, provide the photographer with multiple settings for controlling exposure. For a given condition, you can use a shutter speed of 1/15 second at f/16, or 1/30 second at f/11, or 1/60 second at f/8, and so on. By altering the aperture, you can use a different shutter speed for a given scene, and this provides artistic opportunities in rendering an image.

For example, flying birds can be rendered as tack sharp objects suspended in space, or their flapping wings can be blurred to give the impression of their movement.

A short shutter speed will freeze the appearance of a moving object onto the sensor. A long shutter speed allows the subject to move across the sensor's surface, but the subject will appear blurry in the final image. The ability to use shorter or longer shutter speeds is balanced by using a wider or narrower aperture.

Another advantage to having a combination of f-stops and shutter speeds is the ability to increase or decrease the depth of field. Earlier in the chapter, we mentioned that aperture controls the depth of field. Narrowing the aperture increases the depth of field, while widening the aperture decreases the depth of field. In a scenic shot, such as a broad landscape, it is often desirable for the entire scene to be in sharp focus—however, selectively blurred areas will work in some situations.

Portrait photographers use this feature to direct the viewer's attention to their subject. When the model is rendered sharp and the surrounding background and foreground blurred, the viewer's attention is focused on the subject. This is accomplished by opening the lens aperture and ensuring that the foreground and background structures are outside the depth of field while the subject's face is contained within it.

Again, the dual control of shutter speed and aperture comes into play. Narrowing the depth of field and limiting the zone of sharpness to a smaller region requires an open aperture with short shutter speed, and extending the depth of field requires a narrow aperture and a long shutter speed.

What Is ISO?

ISO stands for the International Standards Organization and in the world of photography, historically referred to the sensitivity of film. Today, it is associated with digital cameras and provides a measure of how much gain can be employed to generate a brighter image. In a sense, the sensor's sensitivity to light does not vary—it generates a signal that is proportional to the intensity of light falling on it. However, it has an amplifier whereby a weak signal can be increased. This gain is adjusted by setting the camera's ISO number. So a photographer has the option of capturing an image in dim lighting by raising the ISO. For the highest image quality, the lowest ISO number is used, and in the case of the Panasonic G2 camera, this value is 100. Many photographers use an ISO of 400 and claim that there is little degradation in the image. However, most agree that noise becomes apparent at an ISO of 800 and that it is greater at 1600. We prefer not using an ISO greater than 800 and tend to capture most of the images at an ISO of 100 to 200.

The final adjustment for exposure is the International Standards Organization (ISO) number. In film photography, this was the measure of the emulsion's sensitivity to light.

For digital cameras, it is viewed as an adjustment that enables the photographer to capture subjects in dim lighting. Raising the ISO increases the output from the sensor, but the "brightened" image suffers some degradation. Usually the range of light that the sensor can record is reduced and the image becomes "granular." Areas that should be rendered as smooth tones will become speckled with blotches of color.

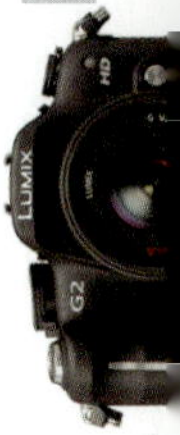

To get a feel for ISO, many film photographers used a rule for judging exposure. For a subject in open sunlight, you set a shutter speed that is the reciprocal of ISO and set the lens's aperture to f/16.

The Panasonic G2 camera's intrinsic sensitivity is ISO of 100, so under these conditions, its shutter speed is set at 1/100 second and its lens at f/16. For many photographers, increasing the camera's ISO 8x will generate an image of acceptable quality—so if the ISO is raised to 800, the shutter speed will be reduced to 1/800 while retaining a lens aperture at f/16.

An experienced photographer will set the ISO manually; however, the Panasonic G2 camera can be configured to sets its ISO automatically, depending on the subject matter. If there is plenty of light and the subject is stationary, the camera favors the lower ISO of 100 for maximum image quality.

However, for sports photography or photographing at night, the camera will raise its ISO setting to ensure that the photographer can capture the shot. When using Intelligent Auto Mode, the camera will automatically set its aperture, shutter speed, and sensor's sensitivity for capturing the optimum image.

Exposure Value (EV)

Even though the Panasonic G2 has an accurate exposure system, as the photographer, you may wish to take over and either add to or subtract from its recommended exposure. This capability is always available to you using the Exposure Compensation function. In this context, EV describes the difference between the indicated and the set exposure. The camera's scale starts at 0, so there is no compensation being applied. But by rotating the rear dial, it is possible to provide up to 3 f-stops over or 3 f-stops under exposure. Since there are two bars between each increment, you can set the exposure values by 1/3 f-stops. The effects of applying this compensation can be seen on the display screen, which gets progressively brighter when applying EV and darker when subtracting EV.

This introduction to exposure and describing the role of aperture, shutter speed, and sensor sensitivity provides a framework for understanding the rationale of some of the camera's automated settings and the need to have multiple commands to handle a variety of settings. We will discuss these controls in detail in subsequent chapters on semi-automatic and manual settings for photography.

However, for the sake of completeness, we should mention that the ability to override automatic exposure is always available. This is accomplished with the camera's rear dial. Depressing it activates Exposure Compensation, signaled by its icon changing color from white to yellow. This will make the view through the display brighter or darker as you vary the exposure from greater to lesser values.

One of the virtues of the electronic display is that when you're changing the camera settings, the effect is reflected in the changing appearance of the image. So if the image appears overly dark, you can compensate by increasing the camera's exposure using the rear dial. We will discuss how to evaluate and apply these changes in more detail in a later chapter, but for now, it is sufficient to know that it can be changed.

The ISO button allows you to set the camera's sensitivity. However, it is inactivated in Intelligent Auto and many of the scene modes. For most cases, to use this control you will need to set the camera to a semiautomatic or manual operating mode. This will be discussed in chapters 5 and 6.

White Balance and the Appearance of Color

We live in a world of color, with our eyes and brain working together so that we can identify hues correctly, no matter the lighting conditions. Our vision works so well it is inconceivable that an object's appearance should vary if it is sitting in direct sunlight, if it is in the shade, or if it is indoors and illuminated by a desk lamp.

But to a digital camera, its appearance would vary. The camera will record the changing appearance of the object under these lighting scenarios. If nothing is done to the image output, the object will be recorded with varying color shades depending on ambient lighting conditions. To match our visual impression of what the object should look like, digital cameras have an automatic white balance: a program that adjusts the balance of colors so an object's hues appear the same no matter the lighting condition.

For the most part, the Panasonic G2 camera does an excellent job of rendering the object's colors. Unfortunately, it is not foolproof, and the camera has a button at the back labeled WB (which stands for White Balance) to allow you to adjust the subject's colors.

When the Panasonic G2 camera is used in Intelligent Auto or in one of its scene modes, the camera disables the WB button and sets itself to Automatic White Balance (AWB) so it can compensate for the variations in lighting. For the most part, it does a good job to ensure that colors will appear natural.

However, if one goes into semi-automatic or fully manual exposure control of the camera, the WB button will be activated. There are some predefined scene modes, such as Close-up and Portrait, where this button is activated as well. We will describe this button's role and its menu structure in chapter 5.

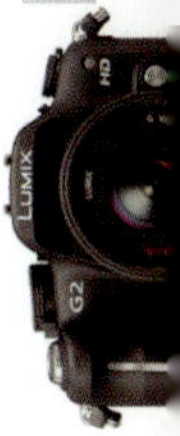

Drive Mode Lever

Menu Option	Display Screen Icon	Drive Mode Lever
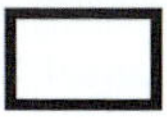	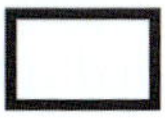	Single
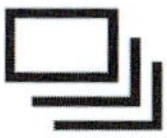	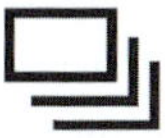 + burst rate set in MENU/SET>REC>(pg4) BURST	Burst
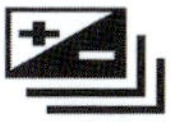	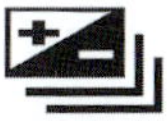	Auto Bracket
	 + no. of seconds set in MENU/SET>REC>(pg4) SELF-TIMER	Self-timer

Table 2-2: The drive mode lever icons and their corresponding display screen icons as they are viewed within the viewfinder or LCD screen.

The camera's shutter can be fired as a single shot or in a burst.

In Burst Mode, the camera can be made to alter its exposure using a range of shutter speeds or apertures to provide a series of over- and underexposed pictures surrounding a central value.

The drive mode lever resides on the top of the camera on the right side (figure 2-2 and table 2-2).

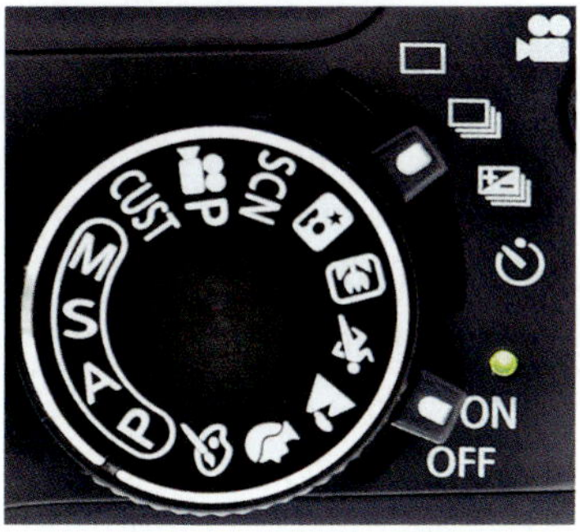

Figure 2-2: Drive mode lever set to burst mode

Single Mode

The camera fires once upon depressing the shutter-release button. Any automatic focusing done is for only that one shot.

Burst Mode

The camera can be made to fire automatically, like a machine gun, so that multiple shots are taken upon depressing the shutter-release button. Its rate of firing can be varied from 2 frames per second up to 3.2 frames per second (table 2-3).

BURST RATE Values	Description
H	High speed – 3.2 pictures per second
M	Middle speed – 2.6 pictures per second
L	Low speed – 2 pictures per second

Table 2-3: BURST RATE command values

Keep in mind that live view, where the display screen displays what the camera sees, will not be available when the camera is firing at the highest rate. This is obviously a disadvantage for firing live action; however, there are bracketing modes where the intent is to gather several pictures at slightly different exposure or white balance settings. For such, live view is not needed.

This rapid-fire capability can be advantageous for sports photography, but there are certain limitations. The image files must be transferred to the memory card, and this transference can be a bottleneck. To compensate for this, the Panasonic G2 camera has an internal memory of limited capacity that can rapidly take in the images.

However, when this memory is filled, the rate of firing decreases as images are offloaded to the memory card. So when the files are large, as when shooting in RAW format, the camera can only fire a burst of four to seven shots before the buffer fills and a bottleneck appears. When the buffer fills, the firing rate will slow until sufficient memory is cleared to take the next shot. This is where an expensive memory card with a high rate of data throughput is desirable. To improve the number of frames that can be captured in a burst, choose settings in the REC menu that will limit file size. Such strategies include shooting JPEG instead of RAW, choosing the more-compressed JPEG over the less-compressed file, and reducing the pixel array by shooting smaller size pictures.

It is difficult to predict how many files you can capture in Burst Mode; there are too many variables. The speed for acquiring the images places constraints on automatic focusing and exposure. In the case of focusing, sometimes only the first photograph can be focused and then the camera will stay

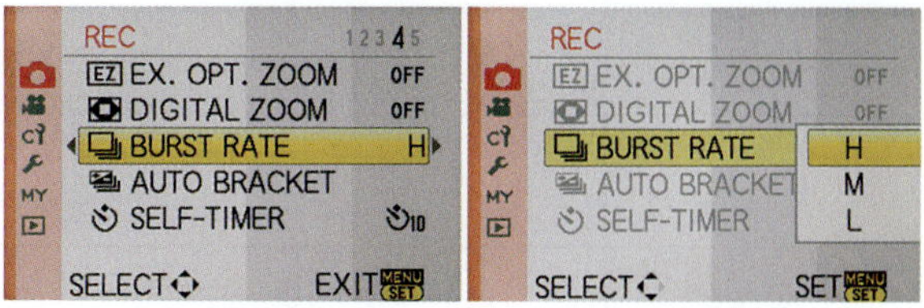

Figure 2-3 (a-b): Burst Rate menu screens

"locked" onto that focusing point. The actual Burst Rate is controlled by the value assigned to the BURST RATE command in the REC menu:

MENU/SET>REC>(pp 4) BURST RATE>[H], [M], [L]

The command sequence starts by pressing the MENU/SET button, entering the REC menu, and scrolling through four pages of commands (figure 2-3a). The Burst Rate setting is [H]. Going deeper in the menu allows you to change the Burst Rate setting (figure 2-3b).

Self-Timer

This setting is straightforward. When set, it disengages the shutter-release button from firing the camera immediately. Instead, there is a delay, usually of 10 seconds, so that when the button is pressed, you can move from the back of the camera to its front. This allows you to become part of a group shot. It is possible to set the Self-timer to a shorter delay of 2 seconds. This is commonly used when you do not have a cable release. This provides a means of firing the camera so that the motion arising from pressing the shutter release button subsides and a "vibrationless" picture is taken.

SELF-TIMER Values	Description
	10-second delay–single picture taken
	10-second delay–series of three pictures, each taken at about 2-second intervals
	2-second delay–single picture taken

Table 2-4: The selected delay will be utilized when the Self-timer option is selected on the drive mode lever.

The most curious setting is the Self-timer option that fires three shots after 10 seconds. Presumably, since it seems an inevitable consequence of group shots that someone blinks or turns away at the time of exposure, this provides a safety net of having three shots fired. Hopefully, one of the three will be usable. Table 2-4 contains the SELF-TIMER command options. The actual Self-timer delay is controlled by the value assigned to the SELF-TIMER command in the REC menu:

MENU/SET>REC>(pg 4) SELF-TIMER>[see table 2-4 for values]

Figure 2-4a displays the SELF-TIMER command highlighted on page 4 of the REC main menu option. Pressing the right directional arrow button displays the SELF-TIMER command's available options. Figure 2-4b shows the 10-second delay-single picture taken option highlighted.

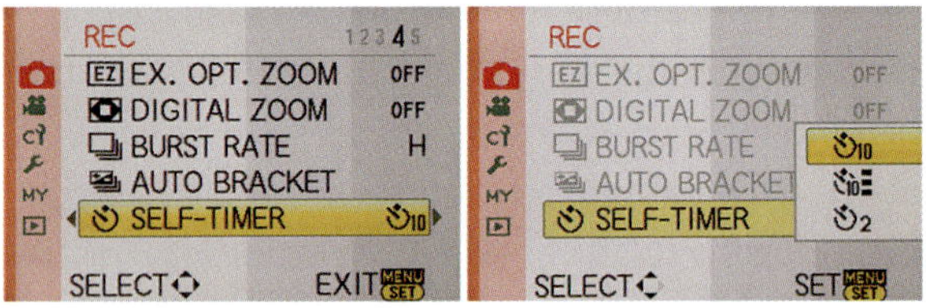

Figure 2-4 (a-b): Self-timer menu screens

Auto Bracket

Auto Bracket's function is to provide a series of shots for which one of the settings is varied to provide a range of effects. For example, the exposure may be altered between shots. However, this command can also provide variations in WB. Auto Bracket will be described more in chapter 6.

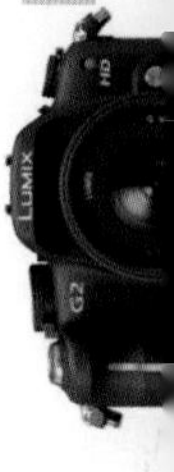
LUMIX
G2
HD

Previewing and Reviewing Images

3

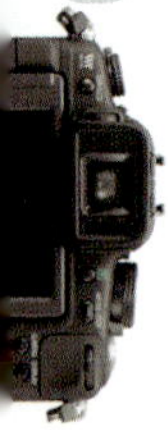

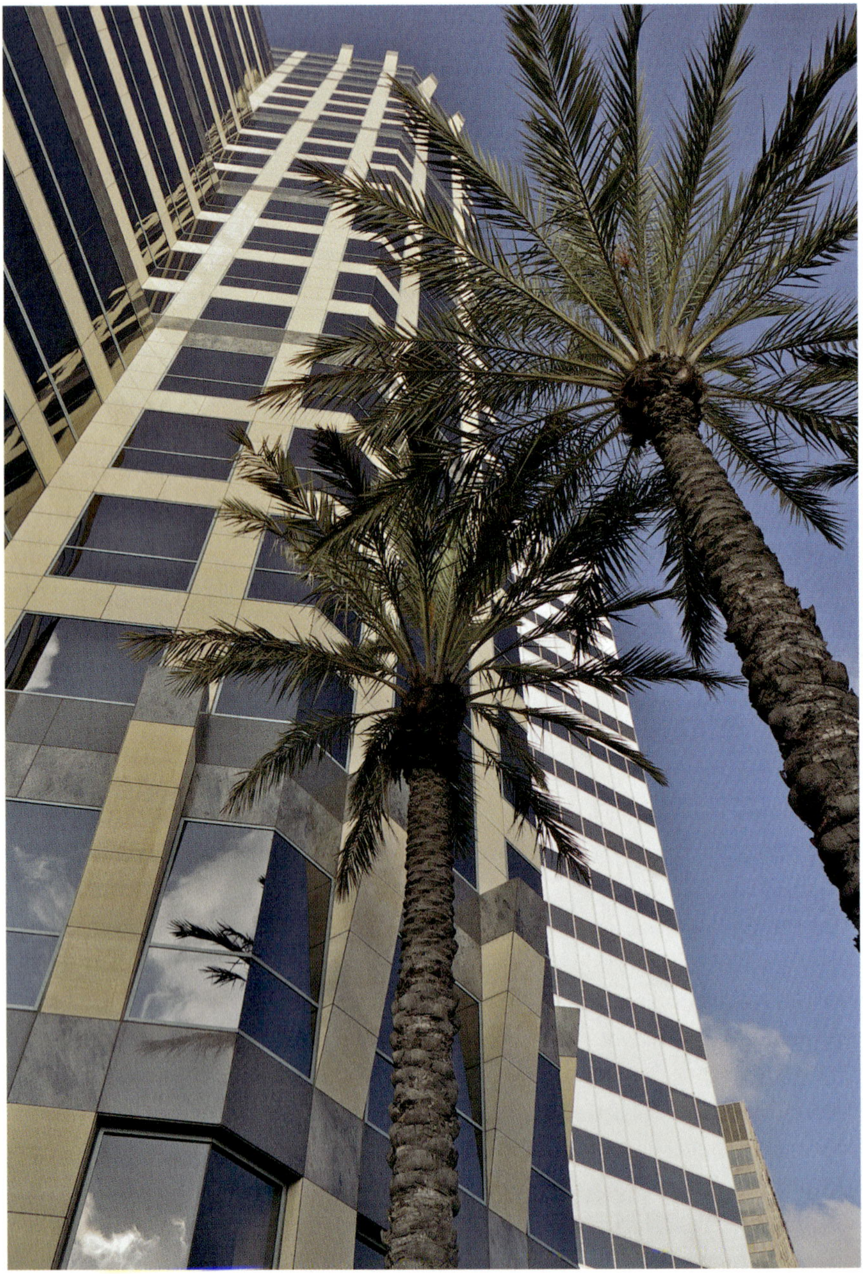

Two Electronic Viewing Methods for the Panasonic G2

The Panasonic G2 camera electronic display screens (viewfinder and LCD screen) serve two purposes. One is to frame the subject, helping the user to compose the image, check focus, and ensure that exposure and automatic modes are suitable for image capture. The second is to evaluate the picture after it is captured and fine-tune the camera settings to ensure that subsequent images are properly captured. If the captured image is flawed beyond redemption, you can delete it and reshoot with your new camera settings.

Both the LCD screen and the viewfinder will work but only one at a time. The viewfinder is enabled when the camera senses the presence of something near the viewfinder window. When something is detected, the camera assumes it is your eye that has approached and activates the viewfinder while deactivating the LCD screen. The LCD screen will reactivate when the sensed object has moved away from the viewfinder, making it not possible to use both viewing modes at the same time. This automatic switching of display screens, on and off, conserves battery power.

It may seem redundant to have two display screens, but having both is advantageous. Although they both serve the same purpose, there are differences between how they display data and images and how they provide access to camera controls. Both the LCD screen and viewfinder have their benefits—be flexible and use whatever gives you the best results for a given situation.

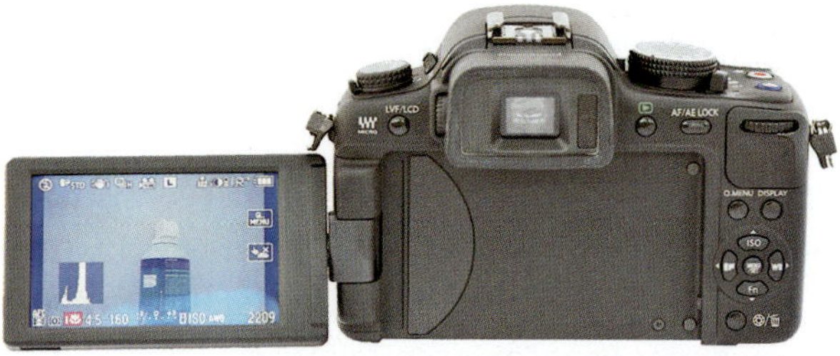

Figure 3-1: Panasonic G2 camera's LCD screen swung out for easier viewing in tight situations.

The LCD Screen

The Panasonic G2 camera has a more advanced LCD interactive system than the earlier G1 series models. The liquid crystal display (LCD) screen is large (approximately 460,000 pixels) and is found on the rear of the camera (figure 3-1). It has a diagonal measurement of 3 inches and is large enough to be viewed directly. Unlike with the viewfinder, you don't have to raise the camera up to your eye for viewing.

Instead, you can simply hold the camera, even at arms distance, frame the picture, and press the shutter release button. Indeed, you can even activate the shutter by pressing on the screen.

The LCD screen is hinged, so you will be able to position it at a variety of angles. The hinged display enhances the camera's usability by allowing the camera to be aimed at unusual angles. The LCD screen can be positioned at a convenient viewing angle when the camera is used in cramped locations. For example, to photograph a dandelion blossom, it may be necessary to rest the camera base on the ground. With the viewfinder, you would have to lie down behind the camera, positioning your eye against the camera body. But thanks to the tilting LCD screen, it can be adjusted so that the screen faces up. Now you can look down on it from a kneeling position and compose the photograph. It is even possible to take a self-portrait, by pointing the camera toward yourself and turning the LCD screen to face you. In addition, when you're setting menu commands, using the LCD screen allows you to look at the menu options and the camera buttons together, making it much easier to press the buttons and review the results at the same time.

Although you can navigate through the camera's menu structure, review stored pictures, zoom in and out of each picture, and play saved videos using the directional arrow buttons and rear dial, one of the new features introduced with the Panasonic G2 camera is its LCD touch screen. You can navigate and select commands almost entirely with the touch of your finger.

With these advantages, it would appear the large LCD screen would be all that is needed and you can forget about the viewfinder. This is not the case—the viewfinder has several advantages of its own.

The Electronic Viewfinder

The Panasonic G2's electronic viewfinder consists of a small screen of 1,440,000 dots with a magnifier; its function corresponds to the optical viewfinder of a DSLR. Some periodicals refer to this as an electronic viewfinder (EVF) or simply a viewfinder. Panasonic typically uses viewfinder but at times also refers to it as "Live View" or LVF, standing for Live Viewfinder. Unless necessary, we will be referring to this as simply a viewfinder. Its magnifier enlarges the image to make it more convenient for you to view fine details while holding the camera up to your eye. This is an excellent display, providing a large image for framing your subject. In comparison to some of the optical viewfinders, its image is much larger to the eye, making composition easy.

You will be able to display the camera's menu options in the viewfinder just as on the LCD screen. The directional arrow buttons and the rear dial both function in the same manner as they do for the LCD screen.

For example, when displaying saved pictures and videos, you will use the directional arrow buttons to move through the saved pictures or videos and rotate the rear dial to zoom in or out of an image. You will also see the camera's settings when framing and after taking the picture as you do when you use the LCD screen.

Although the camera has menu options to brighten the LCD screen for readability in bright settings, they can be inadequate in full sunlight. Using the viewfinder will be the way to go in these situations. Since it is placed against your eye, it cuts off almost all of the ambient light, allowing you to see menu options and the image clearly. Another advantage of using the viewfinder is the stability you gain when raising the camera to your eye and pressing it against your face. This is invaluable when working with a long telephoto lens where every tremor is magnified. Steadiness is even more critical when capturing videos since camera movement will be recorded.

I Only Want to View My Pictures on the LCD Screen

Some people find the automatic switching from the LCD screen to the viewfinder disruptive. If your hand passes close to the viewfinder's eyepiece while setting commands, it may register as an "eye" and turn off the LCD screen by turning on the viewfinder. This can be avoided by turning off the automatic switching between the two display screens and having the LCD screen enabled exclusively. To do this, set command MENU/SET>CUSTOM>(pg 5) LVF/LCD AUTO>[OFF]. You can then use the LVF/LCD button (on the left side of the back of the camera) to manually toggle between viewing on the LCD screen and viewfinder.

Framing Pictures

Data Display Formats

The camera has several features to control data displayed in the viewfinder and on the LCD screen. Two commands control the style or format of how the camera settings are presented when framing images. In addition, the DISPLAY button, located on the right side of the back of the camera, defines the types of data displayed both when framing images and reviewing stored pictures and videos. The following information covers the style and display structure. The selected mode dial option, command buttons, and menu settings determine the actual displayed data values.

The way in which you display the camera's data becomes a personal preference. We recommend you try out the different display styles and structures to see what works best for you.

Display Style Commands

There are two different styles or formats (table 3-1) available for displaying camera settings when framing images on the LCD screen or viewfinder: LCD Monitor Style and Viewfinder Style. Although the names may sound otherwise, you can set the LCD Monitor Style for the viewfinder and the Viewfinder Style for the LCD screen. Both display styles show the same data. The only difference is how the data is displayed. It is a personal preference as to which display style you use and where.

Value	Display Style Option Name
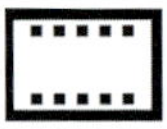	LCD Monitor Style
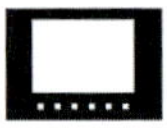	Viewfinder Style

Table 3-1: Menu value options available for setting both the camera's viewfinder and LCD screen's data display format through the LCD DISP. STYLE and LVF DISP. STYLE menu commands.

To set a display style for the LCD screen, use the following menu command:

MENU/SET>CUSTOM>(pg 4) LCD DISP.STYLE>[*Viewfinder Style*], [*LCD Monitor Style*]

To set a display style (figure 3-2a), press the MENU/SET button and select CUSTOM menu. You will have to scroll down four pages within this menu before you find LCD DISP.STYLE. Note the word CUSTOM at the top of the panel, the 4 in bold in the upper-right corner. The yellow bar indicates that the menu item LCD DISP.STYLE is selected. With the LCD DISP.STYLE command highlighted in yellow (figure 3-2b), press the right directional arrow button. The command's options are displayed for you to select from. Note the LCD Monitor Style icon is highlighted for selection in this screen shot.

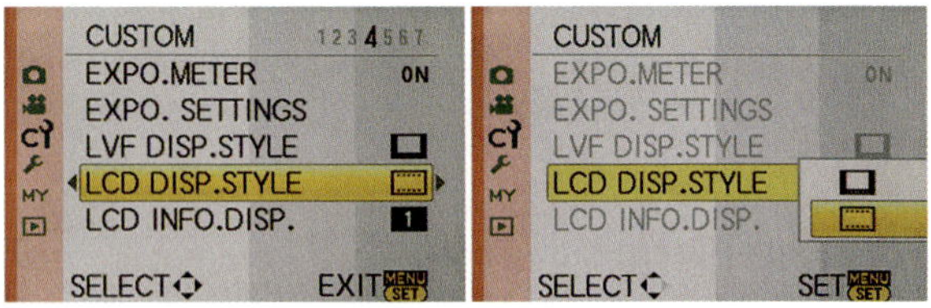

Figure 3-2 (a–b): Setting an LCD DISP. STYLE

To set a display style for the viewfinder screen, use the following menu command:

MENU/SET>CUSTOM>(pg 4) LVF DISP.STYLE>[*Viewfinder Style*], [*LCD Monitor Style*]

To set a display style (figure 3-3a), press the MENU/SET button and select CUSTOM menu. You will have to scroll down four pages before you find LVF DISP. STYLE. Note the word CUSTOM at the top of the panel and the number 4 in bold in the upper-right corner. The yellow bar indicates that the menu item LVF DISP.STYLE is selected. With the LVF DISP.STYLE command (figure 3-3b), press the right directional arrow button and you can select the display style. The command's options are displayed for you to select from. The Viewfinder Style icon is highlighted for selection in this screen shot.

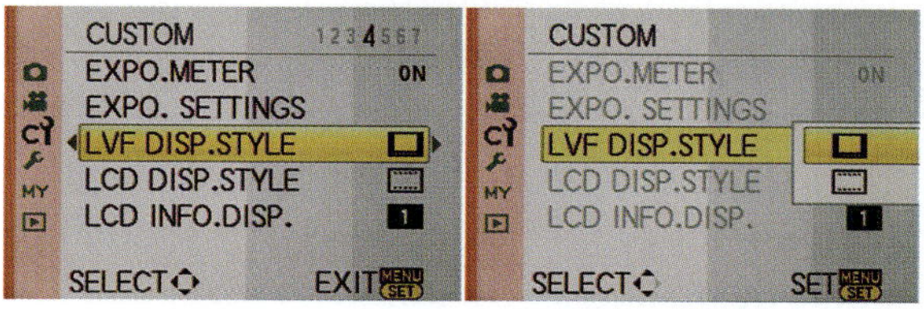

Figure 3-3 (a–b): Setting an LVF DISP. STYLE

In both cases, you have the LCD Monitor Style and Viewfinder Style formats available.

The Viewfinder Style display inserts a border around three sides (right and left sides and bottom) and displays the camera settings within the bottom border. Some data is superimposed on the top portion of the image in the viewfinder or on the LCD screen. Although the black borders emphasize the camera settings data, making them easier to see, it is at the expense of the display screen size

The LCD Monitor Style (figure 3-4) display obscures parts of the image by overlaying camera settings data on the displayed image. This is our preference because we like being able to see our framed image larger. Although this display style partially obscures the image along some of the edges, it is not enough to override our desire to have the image displayed larger for our viewing.

Figure 3-4 shows the LCD Monitor Style superimposing the data on the displayed image, obscuring a small portion of the image.

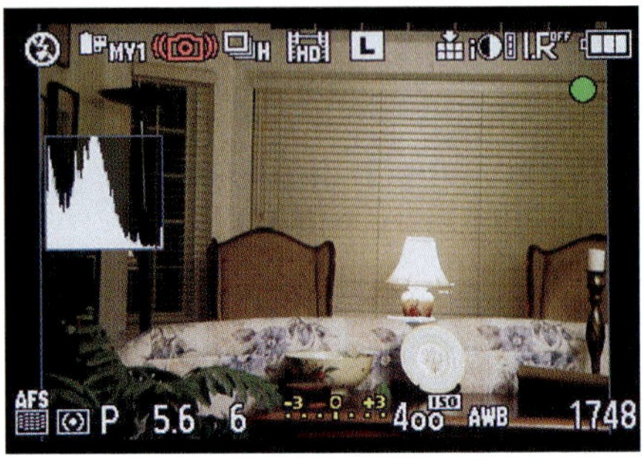

Figure 3-4: Image framed using the LCD Monitor Style.

In contrast, the Viewfinder Style will have a smaller image and the data will not be superimposed over the image. Red, yellow, and green icons alert the photographer of critical items.

Red is a warning signal and it colors the "jitter" warning icon, indicating that the shutter speed is too slow for shooting handheld and the camera should be mounted on a tripod for this shot.

Yellow indicates a control point: Here the Exposure Compensation marks are glowing yellow, indicating that the rear dial is controlling this function.

Green is the "go" signal, and the circle in the upper-right corner indicates that the camera has locked into focus.

Menu navigation is independent of the display screen's selected style except when using the Q.MENU button on the right side of the back of the camera. LCD Monitor Style displays the Quick Menu options with the selected option's available values in a drop-down list.

The Viewfinder Style displays only the Quick Menu options. To see the selected option's values, you will need to press the MENU/SET button or push in the rear dial. To navigate through the available options, use the up and down directional arrow buttons or rotate the rear dial.

Although the LCD screen and viewfinder can be set to different style values, we do not recommend you do this. There are several ways to navigate through this camera's vast number of controls, and it makes little sense to complicate things by varying how you view information or set command values.

Keep in mind that these styles will display only when you're framing images and will not display when you're reviewing saved pictures or videos.

Image Data Display Screen Formats

The DISPLAY button will present different data display formats depending on whether you are framing images or reviewing saved images.

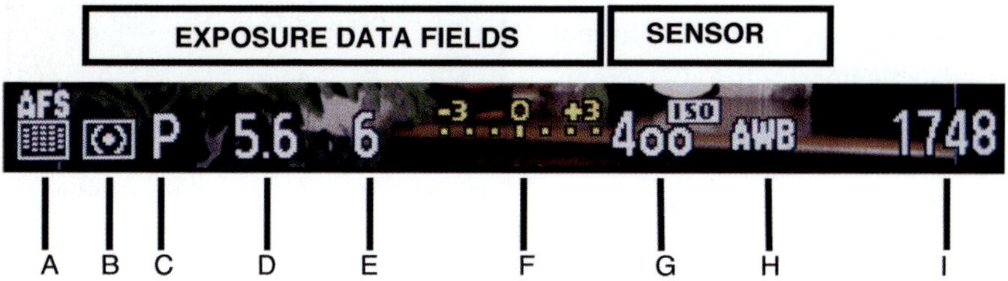

Figure 3-5

- A – Focusing Data
- B – Metering Field, Multimeter
- C – Program
- D – Aperture f/5.6
- E – Shutter Speed 1/6 sec
- F – Exposure Compensation
- G – ISO 400
- H – White Balance
- I – Frame Number

The critical data on focusing, exposure, and sensitivity is found across the bottom of the display (figure 3-5). This shot of the display shows only the bottom row icons. Starting from left to right is a description of the automatic focusing mode, the type of field coverage by the light meter, the exposure mode, f-stop, shutter speed, Exposure Compensation, ISO, White Balance. and frame number.

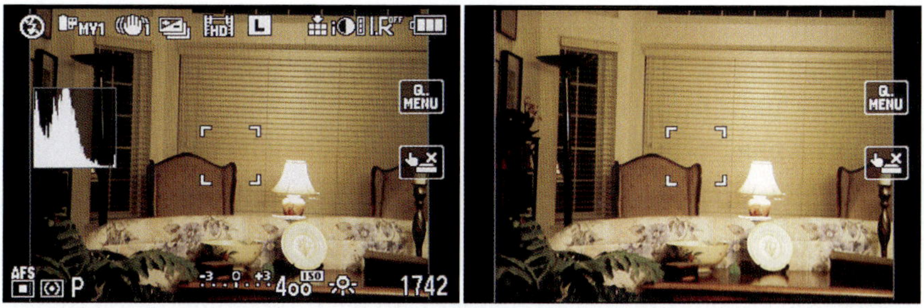

Figure 3-6 (a–b): Eliminating data clutter

Figure 3-6a displays the maximum numerical data with the subject and informs you of the camera settings. By pressing the DISPLAY button, you can eliminate the data clutter and have a clearer view of the subject (figure 3-6b).

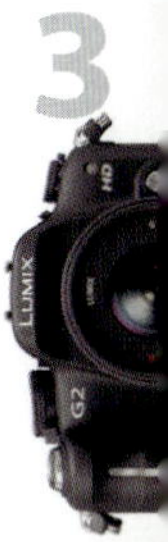

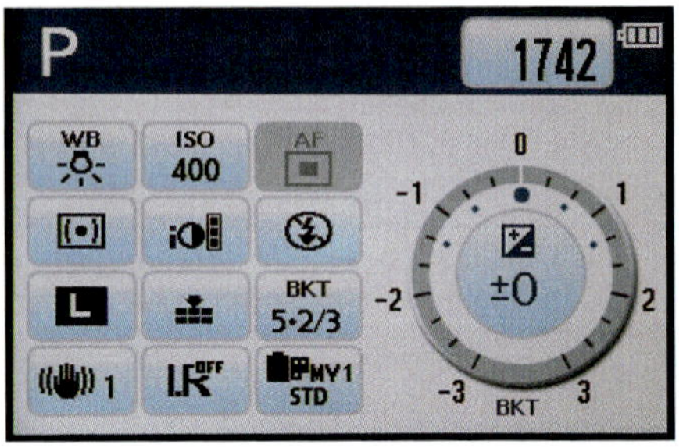

Figure 3-7: DISPLAY button shows settings

Another press of the DISPLAY button displays just the camera settings (figure 3-7). This can also serve as a control panel for adjusting camera settings. This display format is available only for the LCD screen. The viewfinder does not show this numerical data. Another press of the DISPLAY button blacks out the display. The blackened display conserves battery power. This display format is unavailable to the viewfinder. The last display, a black screen, is not shown.

As mentioned earlier, the Panasonic G2 camera has a large number of commands, recording modes, buttons, and settings, which can be displayed and maintained via the viewfinder or the LCD screen. When reviewing images prior to taking a picture or video, there are a maximum of four different data display screen formats to choose from.

- Display maximum image setting data (figure 3-6a)
- Display minimal image setting data (figure 3-6b)
- Display only control settings data (figure 3-7)
- Blank screen

While viewing from the LCD screen, you can cycle through the four formats by repeatedly pressing the DISPLAY button residing on the right side on the back of the camera. Selection is easy—just stop when you like the display format. The camera will remember the format you stopped on. To change, press the DISPLAY button again to cycle through and stop at a different display format.

The value of having a blank screen is to minimize battery drain. Additionally, having a blank screen is advantageous for theater work when the monitor's brightness may annoy members of the audience.

Note that what is displayed depends on what recording mode (mode dial) is selected. For the mode dial options P, S, A, M, CUST, Motion Picture P, and My Color, the selected data display format is displayed at the time you switch to the mode CUST will require that you select its own data display format instead of assuming what you had selected for the other modes. For the mode dial's predefined scene modes, the selected display format is presented after you have selected a specific scene mode.

In the case of the viewfinder, there are only two available data display format views: one displaying maximum data and the other displaying the subject with no overlying setting data.

Compositional Controls

In addition to data, the camera can project lines and grids onto the screen to aid in composition. Once set, these overlays are present during all image framing for both pictures and videos. You will not see the guidelines displayed when reviewing recorded pictures and videos. To set these lines, go to the CUSTOM menu:

MENU/SET>CUSTOM>GUIDE LINE>[OFF], [*3x3 grid*], [*diagonal grid*], [*crosshairs grid*]

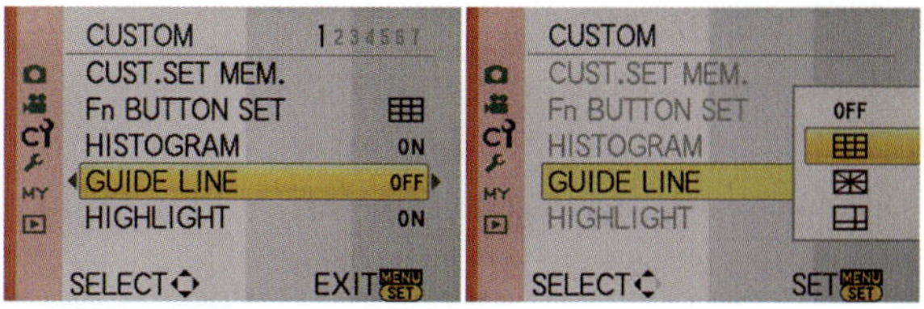

Figure 3-8 (a–b): GUIDE LINE settings

Figure 3-8a shows the menu commands for setting the guideline. With the setting off, guidelines are not displayed.

By going deeper into the menu, you can see the three guidelines that can be selected for display (figure 3-8b). Each pattern has benefits. The 3x3 matrix guideline pattern helps ensure that the picture is well balanced and not tilted (figure 3-9). The diagonal crosshair pattern separates the screen with 4x4 squares overlaid with diagonal lines radiating from the center to help you center the image in the frame. The final overlay, the movable crosshair pattern, consists of two lines—one vertical and the other horizontal—each of which can be positioned within the screen.

Value	GUIDE LINE Option Description
OFF	No guidelines displayed
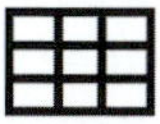	3x3 matrix
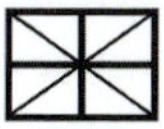	Diagonal (with 4x4 matrix) crosshair
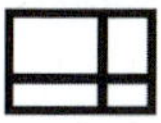	Movable crosshair

Table 3-2: The available values for the GUIDE LINE command and their descriptions

By taking advantage of the touch screen, it is possible to center the point of intersection of the two crossing lines. This guideline pattern can help you balance off-centered images.

All three guideline patterns are useful in architectural photography or scenic shots with a horizon. They can help you avoid canting the subject by providing an alignment guide for either a building or the horizon. Which one you use will depend on where you are positioning the subject within your picture.

Additionally, the 3x3 matrix guideline pattern comes in handy for employing the so-called rule of thirds, which recommends that you position compositional objects in regions that are 1/3 or 2/3 from the border of the frame. Since the grid pattern is a 3x3 array of rectangles, this will allow you to position the image's main subject to be 1/3 or 2/3 up from the bottom or from one side or the other within the screen.

Figure 3-9 shows the LCD screen with the 3x3 grid to help you position the image's subject according to vertical and horizontal lines. It also aids with the rule of thirds when composing the image. For many compositions, the subject should not be in the center of the picture but positioned 1/3 from the bottom or side of the display screen.

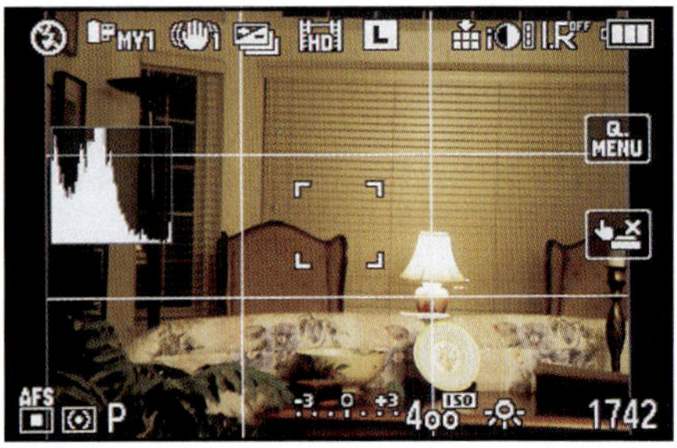

Figure 3-9: Guideline display in 3x3 matrix

Determine Image Exposure

This is a complicated subject and several factors determine the optimal exposure for a still picture or video. Although the camera's Intelligent Auto and predefined scene modes create excellent pictures, there will be times when their recommendations will need to be overridden. There are several tools to help you determine how to obtain the optimum image for your needs.

Histograms

The histogram is a graphical representation of the distribution of light intensities being recorded by the sensor. Intensities are displayed along the horizontal axis (black to white), while the vertical height represents the number of pixels at the x-axis's level of brightness.

Generally, a correctly exposed scene's histogram is in the shape of a classic bell curve whose maximum is near the center of the graph, indicating that most of the image's pixels have a brightness level in the middle—not too bright, not too dark. Figure 3-10 shows the recommended exposure for the image. An underexposed histogram graph would have the bell curve skewed to the left. An overexposed histogram graph would have the bell curve skewed to the right. Extreme over or under exposure would have the graph "piled up" on the right or left respectively.

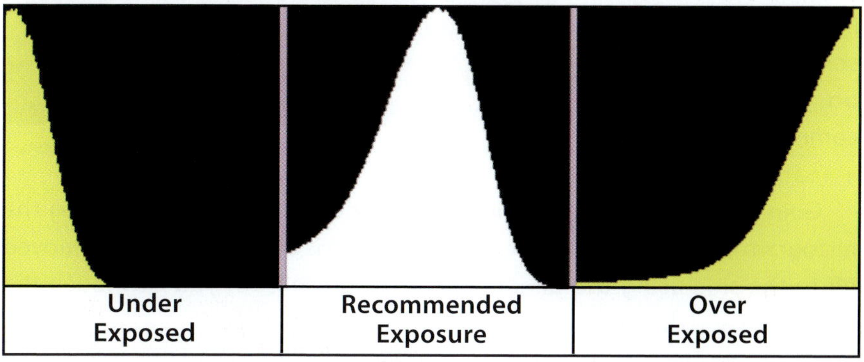

Figure 3-10: Histogram

The histogram plots shown in figure 3-10 represent a stylized look of the three different exposure situations. The middle histogram is white and is at the exposure setting recommended by the camera. When the Exposure Compensation is changed with the rear dial, you can underexpose the image. The histogram turns yellow and shifts to the left. If you decide to overexpose the subject with the Exposure Compensation tool, turn the rear dial in the opposite direction. Notice how the histogram's shape changes from underexposed to recommended, and then to overexposed.

With experience, you will notice that many histograms will consist of multiple peaks, typically two, neither of which is centered in the histogram. Although this does not look like a classic bell curve, it usually yields a well-exposed picture if the averaged intensity value falls in the center of the graph. You should be concerned if there is an excessive exposure spike piled up at one end of the histogram. In this case, there is an out-of-balance lighting situation at one end of the spectrum, which will need to be fixed to get a properly exposed picture.

Without intervention, the Panasonic G2 camera displays a histogram in white—a signal that its software considers this an optimal exposure. Overriding the camera's recommended settings will cause the graph to change color to yellow, signaling that the camera thinks the setting is not optimum.

You can display the histogram when viewing an image by using the following menu command:

MENU/SET>CUSTOM>HISTOGRAM>[ON]

The HISTOGRAM command is executed in the CUSTOM menu screen. It is found on page 1 of that command set (figure 3-11a).

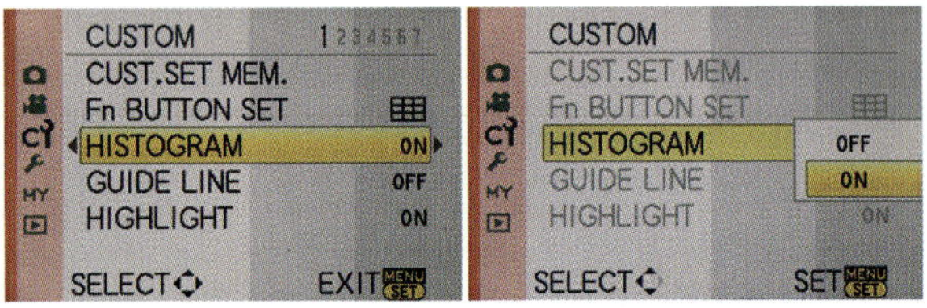

Figure 3-11 (a–b): HISTOGRAM command on Custom menu

Going deeper into the menu shows the toggle switch for turning the histogram display on or off. Once the histogram is displayed, it can be moved off to the side using the directional arrow buttons, or you can touch the histogram and drag it to a new location (figure 3-11b).

A Histogram in Intelligent Auto Mode

The histogram display is activated by the MENU/SET>CUSTOM>HISTOGRAM option being set to [ON]. But when the camera is in the Intelligent Auto Mode (iA button activated), the CUSTOM menu does not show this command. While the iA button is activated, the camera assumes much of its settings from the already set menu options. If you would like the histogram displayed while in Intelligent Auto Mode and it is not, deactivate the iA button and press the MENU/SET button. Then navigate to the CUSTOM menu. The HISTOGRAM command should display on the CUSTOM menu's first page. Set the option to [ON] and press the MENU/SET button to save the setting. Reactivate the iA button and the histogram should now appear.

Camera Exposure Control

When used in the automated modes, such as Intelligent Auto or the predefined scene modes, several elements go into controlling the camera's optimal exposure for the image displayed on your LCD screen. The camera uses the shutter speed, lens aperture (f-stop), and focus approach (1-area-focusing or 23-area-focusing averaging) to calculate the image's exposure.

The results are displayed via the histogram and the camera's suggested exposure is shown as a white histogram's curve. As mentioned earlier, the histogram will be recalculated and changes to yellow* if the f-stop or shutter speed setting is overridden from the camera's recommendation. The camera has a couple of tools you can use to obtain an optimally exposed image even when the camera's computer is fooled by unusual lighting conditions or you wish to change the camera's automatic settings. The beauty of the Panasonic G2 electronic display is that it shows you in real time the effects of the camera's recommended exposure and the effects of your overriding the camera's recommendations.

Exposure Compensation

Use this function when you suspect that the camera's exposure recommendation may not be the best. You might feel that darkening or brightening the image provides a better "mood" to the scene. Or, it may be that the lighting situation is so extreme that you have to decide what area, the bright highlights or the dark shadows, have to be sacrificed in order to capture the image.

The Exposure Compensation tool is displayed at the bottom of the display screen (figure 3-12a). It consists of a scale with a 0 in the center and three sets of three dots on either side of center, ending with a -3 to its left and a +3 to the right. The tool provides a guide on the extent you have overridden the camera's recommended optimum exposure, represented by the 0 position. You can provide up to 3 f-stops over or under exposure, with a 1/3 f-stop precision, by rotating the rear dial (figure 3-12b).

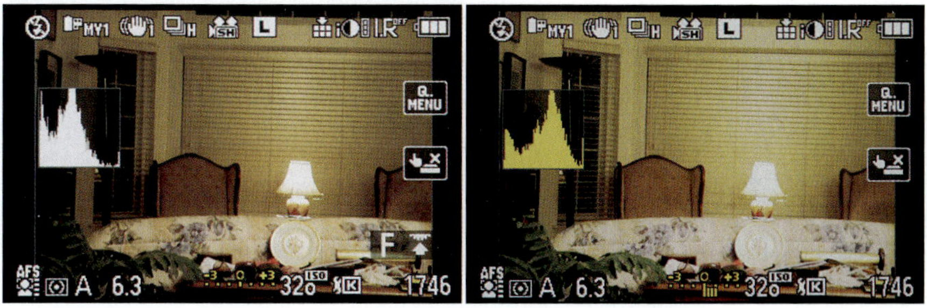

Figure 3-12 (a–b): Exposure Compensation

* The Panasonic G2 manual states that the color is orange, but it looks more yellow to us. Either way, it is no longer white.

When using the camera's suggested exposure setting, the Exposure Compensation tool will be white with the indicator tick positioned on the scale's 0. If you decide that your picture looks better either darker or lighter, you can obtain that effect by pressing the rear dial. This activates the Exposure Compensation tool and the scale turns yellow. Turn the rear dial and you will generate a tick mark with each click as you move away from the centered 0. Each mark represents a 1/3 f-stop change.

Turning the rear dial to the left reduces the exposure and adds tick marks to the left of center. Turning the rear dial to the right increases the exposure and adds tick marks to the right of center. In both cases, the maximum exposure change is three f-stops or nine clicks of the rear dial away from the centered 0 point. The shutter speed and/or focus settings will change as you add or subtract ticks on the Exposure Compensation scale. The Exposure Meter allows you to see the validity of the compensated exposure. Without it you will have to rely on pressing the shutter-release button halfway to see if the exposure is acceptable.

Exposure Meter

Contrary to its name, the Exposure Meter tool does not set exposure directly. Instead, it lets you see the available shutter speed and aperture values surrounding the camera's currently set shutter speed and aperture values (figure 3-13).

The Exposure Meter consists of two rows of numbers: the top row contains the available shutter speeds (SS) and the bottom contains available aperture settings (F). As you change aperture or shutter speed, their numbers change in the Exposure Meter. Directions on how to navigate and toggle between the two rows are also displayed on the screen.

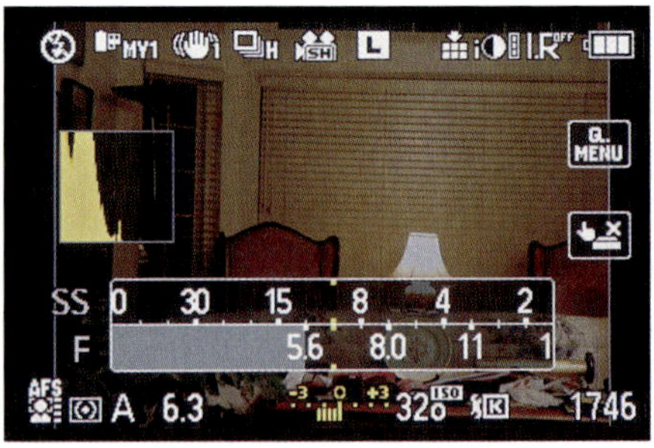

Figure 3-13: Exposure Meter Scale

At times, sections of the Exposure Meter's shutter speed and/or aperture numbers are displayed on a red background. The settings in the red section are not usable settings given the camera's range of shutter speeds or lens apertures.

Without the Exposure Meter, you can inadvertently enter an aperture setting beyond the range of the lens—those Exposure Meter values displayed in red.

Similarly, when adjusting the shutter speed, the Exposure Compensation can suggest settings that are beyond the shutter range of your camera. This is a rare event because the Panasonic G2 camera has a vast shutter range that spans 1/4000 sec to 60 seconds, but it can happen.

If you rely solely on Exposure Compensation, you can select settings that are outside the aperture and, although rarely, the shutter range of the camera. You will be able to fire the camera, but the exposure will not be what you expect. That is, when you press the shutter-release button halfway, a brief indication that you are using impossible settings is shown when the aperture and shutter speed numbers blink and flash red. You can anticipate and prevent this problem by enabling the Exposure Meter.

There are two commands involved in the displaying of the Exposure Meter.

Enable Exposure Meter:
MENU/SET>CUSTOM>(pg 4) EXPO.METER>[ON]

This command enables your ability to display the Exposure Meter. Setting this option to [OFF] means the Exposure Meter will not display. Setting this option to [ON] activates the Exposure Meter when you request it to be displayed.

Activate Exposure Meter:
MENU/SET>CUSTOM>(pg 4) EXPO. SETTINGS

This command lets you decide how you will activate the Exposure Meter (assuming you have enabled it. You have two choices for activating the Exposure Meter: pressing the rear dial or pressing the LVF/LCD button. Select the one most convenient for you.

Depth of Field Preview

As mentioned in chapter 2, the lens aperture controls the image's depth of field. Using a larger f-stop, more of the region surrounding the subject appears sharp. This increase can be evaluated directly by using the Preview button (figure 3-14) on the lower-right corner of the back of the camera. The button has two functions. If you are viewing a scene, it stops down the lens aperture and you see the depth of field. If you are reviewing a saved picture, it can delete the picture. Hence, this button is labeled with two icons: an aperture diaphram and a trash can.

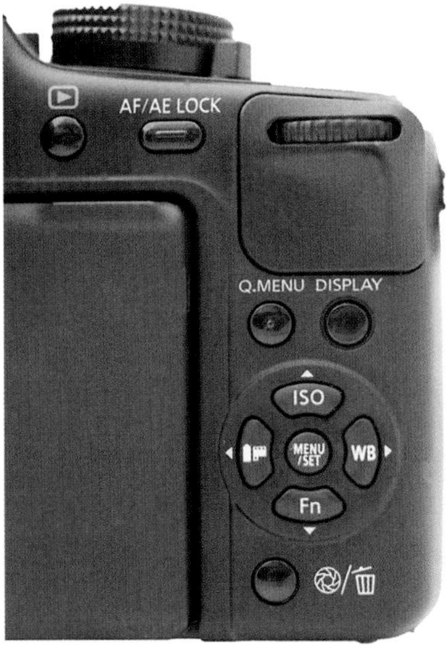

Figure 3-14: Rear panel Preview button

When you're viewing the image, the Preview button will allow you to preview the effect of the depth of field. Press the button and the lens is stopped down to the set aperture, and the depth of field can be evaluated on the display screen. Press the rear dial to change the aperture and the depth of field will change with its focusing effect on the subject displayed on the screen. You may not notice much difference in the focus for images that are at a normal distance away from you, but if you are shooting macro work, this becomes an invaluable aid where the depth of field is critical to obtain a well-focused image.

An additional benefit of the Preview button is that it provides an approximation of the effects of slow shutter speed on moving subjects. Press the Preview button and the DISPLAY button, and you will see the effects of your shutter speed on a moving subject. You can get an idea of how much blur will result when you select a slow shutter speed on a moving object.

> **Evaluating Depth of Field: DSLR vs. Panasonic G2**
>
> The lens aperture controls the depth of field of the recorded image—the smaller the aperture, the greater the depth. In the old days of photography, when we worked with mostly single focal length lenses and controlled the aperture with a ring surrounding the lens, the lens would have a depth of field scale. This would show the zone of sharpness in feet or meters. If our subject fell within this zone, we would be confident that it would appear reasonably sharp in print.
>
> Today, the modern camera lens lacks an aperture control ring and a depth of field scale. To gauge whether the subject will be blurred or sharp at a given distance and aperture, we have a depth of field Preview button. Pressing this control closes down the lens's aperture and you can see its effects on the DSLR screen.
>
> Unfortunately, this control darkens the screen, making it difficult to see the increase in depth of field. In contrast, the Panasonic's electronic display automatically compensates for this by brightening the image, allowing the photographer to better view and judge the depth of field.

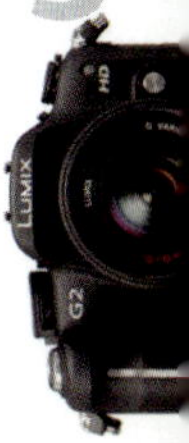

Navigating through Exposure Compensation Controls

Although the EXPO. SETTINGS command determines how you activate the display of the Exposure Meter, it is the rear dial that allows you to navigate through the Exposure Meter's shutter speed and aperture scales and adjust Exposure Compensation. Depending on the camera setting, the rear dial may have one of two functions. One is always available, and that is Exposure Compensation—press the rear dial and you will see its scale change color. If it becomes yellow, you are changing the exposure from the camera's recommendation. The screen will lighten or darken, depending on the direction you turn the dial.

The degree to which you change the exposure is seen by the lengthening of the bar extending from 0. In some modes, pressing the rear dial controls the aperture or shutter speed. You will know which is selected by the yellow highlighting of the shutter speed or aperture number. Changing these values will not change the exposure—there is a commensurate change of the shutter speed if the aperture is changed or a change in the aperture if the shutter speed is changed. In one mode, both values change simultaneously, but in all cases, the exposure remains a constant. This will be discussed in greater detail in chapters 5 and 6.

Exposure Summary

How does this all come together when taking a picture? In all cases other than the Manual Exposure Mode (mode dial = M), the camera will generate a shutter speed, aperture, and/or focus setting based on the selected mode. Generally, the camera does an excellent job in determining exposure. Regardless, there are times when you will want to change its settings to better conform to your artistic interpretation of the final photograph or video.

Review the image's histogram. The displayed graph ideally should have its light intensities concentrated in the center. If the histogram has its light intensities concentrated on either the left side (underexposure) or the right side (overexposure), you should consider making changes to the camera's settings. These conditions indicate that either shadow or highlight details are not being recorded. Under extreme lighting conditions, you have to decide which has to be sacrificed. If you desire details in these regions, you need to apply some exposure compensation to shift the histogram to either the left or the right.

As you change the exposure, the histogram and the view through the camera will change accordingly. Remember, simply changing the aperture or shutter speed by itself will not alter exposure in the automatic exposure modes. As mentioned earlier, your image could be properly exposed, even if its histogram is not a classic bell curve. You might have a multiple peak histogram due to multiple locations within the image having different brightness. Depending on your subject, this could create the perfect picture.

Reviewing Pictures and Videos

Unlike a DSLR, the Panasonic G series cameras allow you to review pictures in two areas—the LCD screen and viewfinder. Most people use the LCD screen because it is larger and the controls for scrolling through saved pictures, enlarging them, and, if needed, deleting the unsatisfactory ones can be easily operated. However, keep in mind that there may be instances where the viewfinder would be a better choice, such as in direct sunlight situations when the ambient light makes it difficult to view the pictures on the LCD screen.

Evaluating Pictures

So you have taken a picture or a video and you now want to review it and make sure you are happy with the outcome. You can review your saved files (pictures and videos) and determine if they are the quality you want or if they should be taken again. Whether you are a point-and-shoot enthusiast or set your camera manually, reviewing your pictures and videos before you leave the scene is a good practice. There are a few tools that will enable you to determine the quality of your pictures after you have taken them and determine if you need to do a redo.

Reviewing Pictures Immediately

The camera has the ability to display the picture immediately after it is taken and before you take the next picture.

The following command allows you to set the amount of time a picture is displayed after it is taken:

MENU/SET>SETUP>(pg 2) AUTO REVIEW>[OFF], [1 SEC], [3 SEC], [5 SEC], [HOLD]

You have the choice to display the picture for 1, 3, or 5 seconds or indefinitely until you execute another command. Many people like being able to briefly see the recorded picture so they can quickly determine if it is a "keeper." For example, are the subject's eyes open or did he blink just when you clicked the shutter release button. You will be able to review this quickly if AUTO REVIEW is set to a value other than [OFF].

Another example is if you have activated the HIGHLIGHT command:

MENU/SET>CUSTOM>HIGHLIGHT>[ON]

Blown-out highlights will be shown blinking black and white, and you can decide whether these regions are unimportant for the composition or if they are important, biasing the exposure on the next shot to ensure that details are recorded in the highlight regions.

The brief display of the recorded picture may disrupt the flow of photography if you are taking a series of shots in rapid sequence. A slight press on the shutter release button will cancel the review and return the camera to live view. You also have the option to not display the picture at all by setting the following command:

MENU/SET>SETUP>(pg 2) AUTO REVIEW>[OFF]

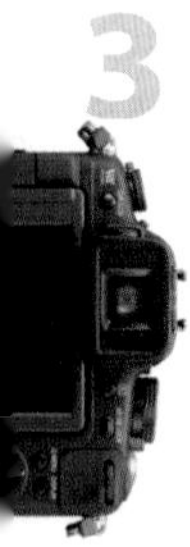

Reviewing (Playback) Pictures and Videos Later

To provide a leisurely examination of a picture or video requires that the review be done manually by pressing the green arrow Playback button at the back of the camera. Using this Playback button allows you to take your time to review the saved files. The Playback button is shown at the top of figure 3-14, next to a green arrow near the viewfinder.

The Playback button functionality is very extensive. You can play back single pictures and videos or review multiple pictures at one time. You can zoom in up to 16x and zoom back out of a picture. Plus, once you have zoomed in, you can move around the picture viewing different portions. You can also review your pictures and videos by the calendar date they were taken unless you have not set the camera's clock. In that case, each file's saved calendar date will be January 1, 2010.

To do all of this, you will use a combination of the LCD touch screen, directional arrow buttons, and rear dial functionality. Fortunately, the Playback button functionality helps you out by displaying some instructions on the LCD screen to prompt you when navigating through its many steps and capabilities.

Like the data display screen formats available when framing images, the Playback button functionality also has a set of data display screen formats geared to display pertinent information to better determine the picture's and video's quality.

Playback Data Display Screen Formats

When you're playing back images, the DISPLAY button has a new set of display screen formats. You can use the displayed information to help determine your picture's quality and decide if you should reshoot it to get better results. These data display screen formats are independent from the set of data display screen formats available when framing your images.

There are a maximum of five different data display screen formats to choose from. When in Playback Mode, press the DISPLAY button to cycle through the screen formats, stopping at the format you wish to display. The camera will remember the chosen format and display the next reviewed picture or video using the saved display screen format.

To change, press the DISPLAY button again to cycle through and select another data display screen format.

When viewing from the LCD screen, pressing the DISPLAY button four or five times will cycle you through each of the different available views.

The following lists each view in display order:

1. Display full-size picture with data superimposed on image. (figure 3-15a)
2. Display small picture insert with detailed information data (figure 3-15b).
3. Display small picture insert with histogram chart. (figure 3-15c)
4. Display full-size image with highlight data (figure 3-15d). Note that if you do not have the HIGHLIGHT command [ON], this screen will not appear and you will go directly to #5. Also, if the HIGHLIGHT command is [ON], the screen will show the overexposed region by flashing between white and black, except in Intelligent Auto Mode or #5 format.
5. Display picture only.

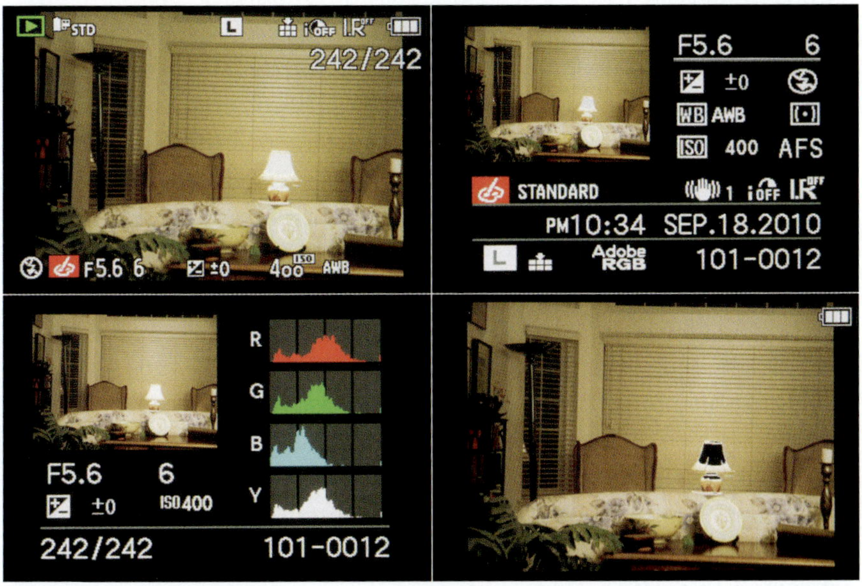

Figure 3-15 (a–d): Different image views from pressing the DISPLAY button multiple times

Figures 3-15a, 3-15b, 3-15c, and 3-15d illustrate the changing appearance of the image when using the Playback button and repeatedly pressing the DISPLAY button.

Figure 3-15a shows camera data superimposed over the full-sized image. Pressing the DISPLAY button provides a smaller image with the data shown in detail (figure 3-15b). Press the DISPLAY button again and the image's histogram is displayed. The three color channels are shown as well as the luminosity (figure 3-15c). In this example, a small peak can be seen at the extreme right within the histogram, which indicates there is some overexposure.

Figure 3-15d displays overexposed highlights. In this example the lampshade is overexposed. The overexposed areas are represented by flashing from black to white. This flashing can be distracting, so an additional press of the button will provide a view without marking the blown-out areas (this screen is not shown).

Execute the following command to turn on highlights:

MENU/SET>CUSTOM>HIGHLIGHT>[ON].

For both the first and second display format, the picture's camera settings are displayed. The second format includes more information, such as the date and time the picture was recorded. The third display format contains the histogram, showing the color channel and luminosity values.

Remember, the highlight display format will be available only if the HIGHLIGHT option is enabled. This display will show a full-sized image with blinking areas where the intensity is too high to be recorded by the camera. The last format displays only the recorded picture—the highlights will not be blinking. This allows you to evaluate the overall image without the distraction of the periodic blinking of highlights. Again, experiment with the different display formats.

You may find you will want to vary the formats depending on the type of pictures you plan to review. Keep in mind, if you want to know which file is a still picture and which is a video, you would be able to see the indicators on only the first three data display screen formats. Each video file will have recorded elapsed time and the mode dial icon that was set when the video was recorded will be displayed in the upper-left corner of the display screen. In addition, "PLAY MOTION PICTURE" will be displayed briefly when the file is first displayed on the screen. The last two data display screen formats will not contain this information.

Altering the Playback Display

Pressing the Playback button initiates displaying your saved files for your review. You will initially be presented with either the last picture or video played back or the last picture or video saved if this is the first time you pressed the Playback button since turning on the camera. Again, the saved file will be displayed in the selected data display screen format. In the case of a video, you can play it by pressing the up directional arrow button. The display will then shift, showing you prompts for using the cursor key to control the video and the rear dial for adjusting the video's volume. The data display screen will disappear and you will see the actual video with the number of seconds played displayed.

You have several options at this point. You can move through the individual saved files (pictures and videos) by using the left or right directional arrow buttons or by sweeping your finger across the LCD screen. Each sweep of your finger will take you to the next picture in your stored memory card. Pressing the left directional arrow button or sweeping your finger from left to right will display the previous stored picture or video. Conversely, pressing the right directional arrow button or sweeping right to left will move forward through your stored pictures.

Note that continued requests to view the next saved image wraps around and cycles through them again. You can also zoom in for a better view of your picture by turning the rear dial to the right or by touching the LCD screen up to four times total. Each turn of the rear dial to the right or touch of the LCD screen will enlarge the image further (2x, 4x, 8x, 16x).

Once you have enlarged the picture at least once, directional arrow buttons will display at the edges of the image so you can move right or left or up or down through the image. You can use the directional arrow buttons or your finger to view areas of the image. A box is displayed in the upper-right corner of the LCD screen representing the level the picture has been enlarged.

Zooming in can give you an idea of the picture's quality and how well it will hold up to being enlarged in a printed format. For example, you took a picture of a bird at your backyard bird feeder. Looks good, and you want to make a large print, frame it, and hang it on your wall. Will the picture hold up when it is enlarged? Although not ideal, by zooming in you can view how well the image is focused and determine if the detail withstands being enlarged.

There may be times when you want to find a specific image to review and will need some way to find it. Turning the rear dial to the left gives you some options to find a specific image or set of images to review. You can turn the rear dial up to three times to the left to cycle through different ways to find saved images to review.

- Turning the rear dial to the left once displays up to the last 12 saved images plus a vertical sliding bar representing all of the saved files on the memory card. Drag the vertical sliding bar's position box up or down to move through the complete number of saved files. Releasing the position box will display up to 12 saved images with the selected file positioned as the first saved image. You can either use the directional arrow buttons to move through the images and press the MENU/SET button or simply touch the saved image on the LCD screen to display the image using the selected data display screen format.

- Turning the rear dial to the left a second time displays up to the last 30 saved images plus the sliding vertical bar. Again, you can move through the complete number of saved files using the vertical sliding bar.
- Turning the rear dial to the left for a third time will display the last saved file and a corresponding calendar positioned on the last saved file's date. Only those dates that have saved files are bolded and available for selection. You can select only one date and cycle through the associated saved files and videos.

Note that if you turn the rear dial to the left more than three times, nothing more changes—you are left with the final review option. You can also cycle back through the list by turning the rear dial back to the right.

Playback Button, Playback Mode, PLAYBACK Menu, and PLAYBACK MODE Command

The Playback button is a tool for you to review a picture or video. It has methods to locate a single recorded file and then display it along with information about how it was recorded. You use this to determine if the picture or video is to your satisfaction.

Playback Mode is the state the camera is in when you have initiated playing back pictures and/or videos.

The PLAYBACK menu is an option within the camera's main menu structure. It has an elaborate system of command options to allow you to chain together and play back multiple pictures or videos for your pleasure.

The PLAYBACK MODE is a command within the PLAYBACK menu. This command enables you to play back a selected group of pictures and/or videos one at a time.

We will be discussing both the PLAYBACK menu and the PLAYBACK MODE command in chapter 10.

Evaluating Exposure

The histogram and highlight data display formats help you evaluate a picture or a video's exposure and determine if you were on "target" or whether you need to reshoot. The histogram display screen format shows the intensity range of the color channels as well as the overall luminosity. You will be able to see if the overall light intensity or one or more colors (red, green, blue) are under- or overexposed. Look to see if there are pixels whose values "spike" at the borders of the graph. Underexposed images show all the intensity values lying on the left half of the graph with a flat region to the right. This is easily corrected by increasing exposure.

As more light is collected in subsequent exposures, the intensity values in the image will be pushed to the right until they start reaching the far end of the graph. This is the point to stop increasing the exposure. Ideally, you do not want the histogram to shift to the right so much it "piles up" against the right graph line. When too many pixels are in this area, it means that some of them will be fully saturated by light. A few pixels affected this way will be unnoticed if they are isolated and well separated. However, if a large number of pixels are so affected, then the chances are that they will be clustered in the same region. If this area is sizeable, it will be noticed in the picture as a region that lacks fine details. If one of the color channels piles up in this manner, it will result in a color shift—and fine details having that color will disappear. For example, if broad areas of sky are overexposed, you might reshoot and use less exposure to bring out the details in these areas.

On the other hand, if you have several small specular spots in the picture, you may decide to accept this exposure. Thus, we usually turn on the HIGHLIGHT command and use it in conjunction with the AUTO REVIEW command. Together, we see the captured image right after we press the shutter release button and can evaluate the overexposed areas immediately. This allows us to reshoot quickly and capture the scene before something has changed.

Playing Back Videos

When you have recorded a video, its first frame will be visible as you cycle through your stored files in Playback Mode. Once you have found a video to play back, press the up directional arrow button to initiate the playback. Additional informational icons will be displayed in the lower-left corner, reminding you how to turn up the audio volume. You can pause, fast forward, rewind, and so on while playing back your videos. Table 3-3 contains the available video playback operations to allow you to get the most out of reviewing your saved videos from your camera.

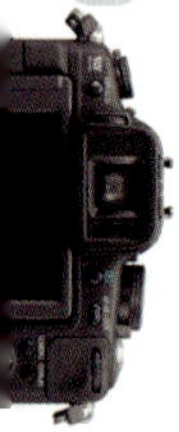

Function	Key	Process
Play/pause	Up directional arrow button	Toggle between the play and pause functions.
Stop	Down directional arrow button	Stop playing the video.
Fast forward	Right directional arrow button	Increase the playback speed. Push the right directional arrow button again (up to two additional times) to increase the fast forward speed. Press the up directional arrow button to return to the normal playback speed.
Rewind	Left directional arrow button	Increase the rewind speed. Push the left directional arrow button again (up to two additional times) to increase the rewind speed.
Frame-by-frame forward	Up directional arrow button (pause), then right directional arrow button	Play back one frame at a time.
Frame-by-frame rewind	Up directional arrow button (pause), then left directional arrow button	Rewind one frame at a time.
Reduce volume level	Rear dial	Turn rear dial to the left.
Increase volume level	Rear dial	Turn rear dial to the right.

Table 3-3: Video playback operations

Deleting Saved Pictures and Videos

Not every picture or video is going to be a keeper. As you play back the saved files on the camera, you may want to delete one or more at review time. You can delete a single saved file, a group of up to 50 saved files, or all saved files at one time. The Delete function is activated when you press the Trash Can button in Playback Mode.

The Delete function pertains to only the saved files (pictures and videos) that are on the memory card inserted in the camera at the time the function is activated and that are not protected. The PROTECT command will be covered in chapter 10 when we discuss the PLAYBACK menu commands. The Delete function walks you through each step to ensure that you do not make any mistakes. Once you delete a saved file, it is permanently gone from the memory card.

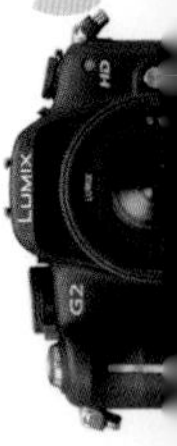

When deleting a single file, the camera will assume the one you are currently reviewing is the one you want to delete. Press the Trash Can button, select [DELETE SINGLE] and [YES]. Pressing the MENU/SET button will immediately delete the reviewed file.

If you wish to delete multiple files at one time, select the [DELETE MULTI] option from the Delete function screen. You will be presented with the six most-recently saved files organized on your screen with the cursor positioned on the last file and its file number highlighted in yellow. To select one for deletion, press the DISPLAY button while the cursor is positioned on the file. A red Trash Can icon will display in the upper-left corner of each file you have indicated you want deleted. Use the directional arrow buttons to scroll through your saved files and the DISPLAY button to select those for deletion. Once you have finished identifying what you want deleted, press the MENU/SET button to activate the delete.

Remember, all deletions are permanent! If you are not sure you want to delete a file, keep it and download it later to your computer to save. That way you won't be disappointed later if you realize you deleted the wrong picture or video.

You can also delete all of your saved files at one time by selecting the [DELETE ALL] option. When you select this command, you will be given one more time to confirm your request. Selecting [YES] will delete all of the unprotected files off of the memory card. Remember that this is permanent.

There are benefits to deleting files off of your memory card as you are using it. If you are approaching the memory card's limit and you are not near your computer to off-load the files, you will need to delete some of them to make more space available on the memory card to take more pictures. It is a good practice to review your pictures and videos periodically just to clean out those you don't want. This way your camera will always be ready to take that impulsive picture or video.

Recommendations

When out in the field, actively taking pictures, we make sure that this command is active:

MENU/SET>CUSTOM>(pg 5) LVF/LCD AUTO>[ON]

It is a setting that minimizes battery drain and conveniently allows us to switch between the two display screens. The only time we turn it off is when we are only reviewing pictures and do not want to inadvertently turn off the rear LCD screen. This command is usually set at the factory; however, it is good to check and ensure that it has not been altered in the course of shooting the camera.

We also like to make sure the following commands are on:

MENU/SET>SETUP>(pg 2) AUTO REVIEW>[3 SEC]
MENU/SET>CUSTOM>HISTOGRAM>[ON]
MENU/SET>CUSTOM>HIGHLIGHT>[ON]

Once turned on, the histogram will display on all images before the image is saved and when reviewing, including in the Intelligent Auto Mode. If you are not seeing the histograms while in the Intelligent Auto Mode, here is a little trick to turn this command on:

1. Turn off Intelligent Auto Mode.
2. Press MENU/SET button.
3. Using the down directional arrow button, navigate to the CUSTOM menu icon in the vertical bar on the left side of the screen.
4. Use the right directional arrow button to enter the CUSTOM menu and proceed down to the HISTOGRAM and HIGHLIGHT commands.
5. Set them both to [ON].

When you return to Intelligent Auto Mode, these commands will be remembered and kept on.

Normally, if you press the MENU/SET button while in the Intelligent Auto Mode, these commands are invisible—but you can use the aforementioned trick to make them active.

The HIGHLIGHT command works differently. First, it affects only saved images. Second, it does not work in Intelligent Auto Mode.

Therefore if the HIGHLIGHT command is set to [ON] and the camera is not set to the Intelligent Auto Mode, a saved image's overexposed portions will flash between black and white during the Auto Review process and the playback mode. If the camera is set to the Intelligent Auto Mode, the overexposed portions of the saved image will not be identified regardless of the HIGHLIGHT command's setting.

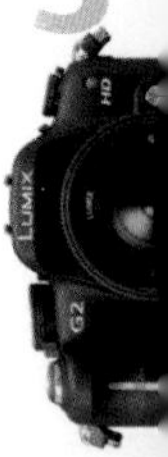

Automatic Settings

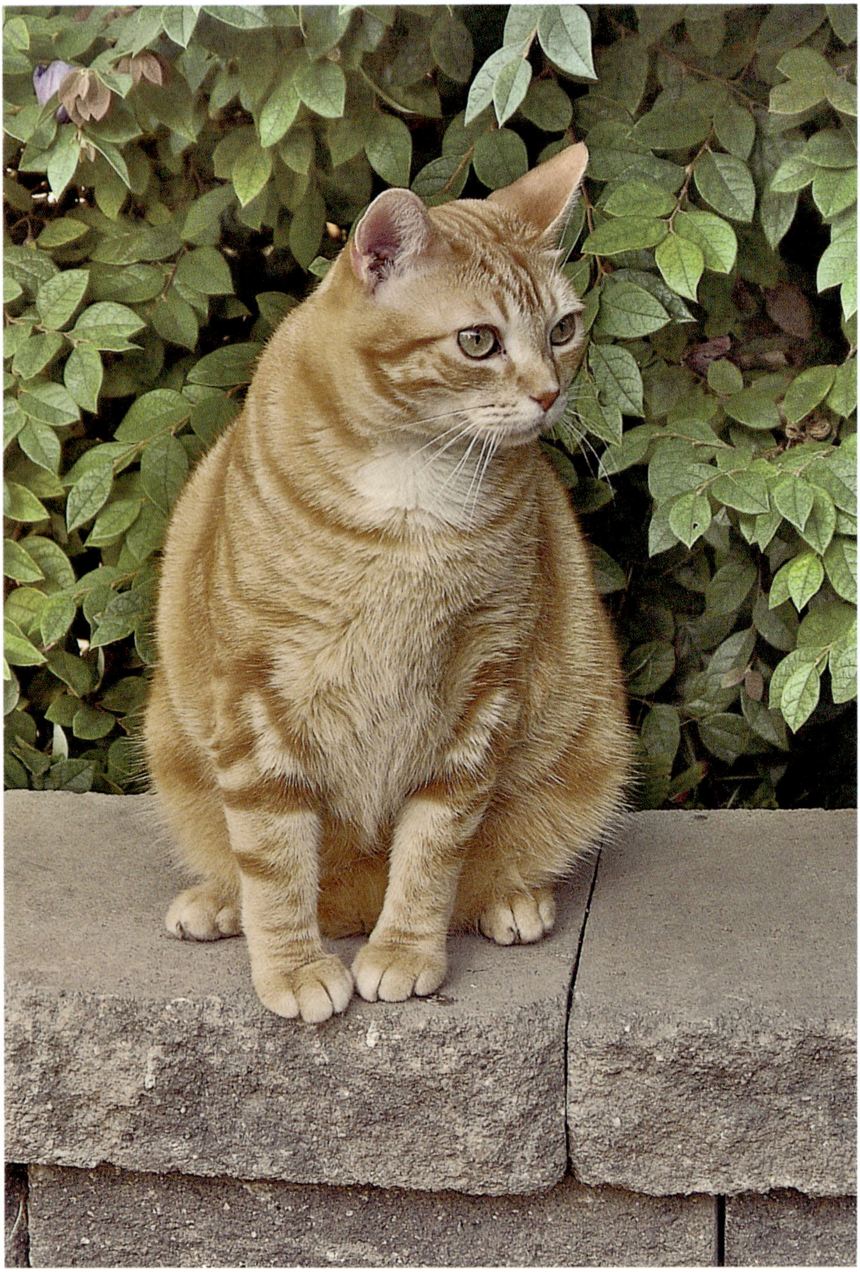

Introduction: Automatic Settings

As mentioned in chapter 1, the way in which you use the Panasonic G2 camera depends on your level of expertise, your desire to control different aspects of your picture taking, and the degree of creativity you want to introduce. You can start taking technically excellent pictures and videos using the camera's Intelligent Auto Mode with minimal knowledge and prior picture taking experience. The camera's software allows the user to point and shoot while the camera determines if the subject belongs within a list of image types (categories) and selects the most efficient aperture, shutter speed, ISO, and auto-focusing mode.

Essentially, the camera identifies the scene type to optimize camera settings so that a rapidly moving subject will be photographed with an elevated ISO and fast shutter speed to freeze the action while a scenic shot will have a slow ISO, small aperture, and slow shutter speed to record a panoramic view with maximum fidelity. It is amazing to see that the camera will identify a person's face in the frame and use it as the preferred object for focusing.

The Intelligent Auto Mode will do its best, but scene recognition is not 100 percent accurate and you may decide to take over. Instead of using the Intelligent Auto Mode, you can utilize the camera's predefined scene modes. They allow you to identify your image's type of scene or category rather than have the Intelligent Auto Mode determine it through software. There are two groups of predefined scene modes: advanced scene modes and the Scene Mode. There are multiple predefined scene modes to choose from covering a wide range of both picture and video scenarios.

In this chapter, we will cover the camera's Intelligent Auto and predefined scene modes, their options, and how they might work best for you. We will also cover Quick Menu as an easy way to view and modify these automatic modes' camera settings. But first we must cover one more camera feature that can be utilized throughout your use of the camera: Face Recognition.

This feature allows the camera to go past just identifying that there is a face within the image; the camera is able to assign a name to the face. It is activated in the Intelligent Auto Mode and in several of the predefined scene modes and you should be aware of how it works so you can determine its value to you when using the automated modes.

Face Recognition

Face Recognition functionality is unique to cameras such as the Panasonic G series that have live view sensors. It is only available for pictures and can slow down your camera's operating time. It is such an interesting feature that we think you will want to play with it—even if it is at a later date after you have gained more familiarity with the camera. It seems uncanny when you raise the camera to your eye, it has correctly identified a specific person. You will see this even before you take your picture. The camera will have the recognized person's name on display as you frame the image. If you determine at a later time you don't need Face Recognition functionality, you can always turn it off. Also, if you do not think you need to use Face Recognition with the camera, feel free to jump to the Intelligent Auto Mode section.

Remember that Panasonic distinguishes between facial identification and facial recognition. The former describes the identification of a generic face. If a face is detected, the camera will prioritize its action to make sure the face is the point of focus. Face Recognition goes a step further in that the camera executes software to determine if the detected face is stored among the registered faces. If the camera recognizes the detected face, you will be informed of it while framing the image and the person's name and age will be stored with the saved picture.

For the software to work, you will have to compile a library of images of a person's face and associate those images with a name and birth date. There are limitations. You can register only up to a total of six people for Face Recognition. Each person's registration will include their name, age, and up to three different sample images of their face. These images should all be different but cover typical looks for the person. In addition, the images must be of the subject's full face. The software bases its determination on recognizing two eyes, a nose, and a mouth at typical human proportions and locations. So, if the registered person is not facing the camera, but instead presents his profile to be photographed, facial recognition will fail. Also, certain conditions, such as being too distant from the camera (face appears too small) or harsh shadows falling on the persons face, may interfere with correct recognition.

To make the image library, you will have to decide whom you wish to register and place images of them in the Face Recognition system. Suppose you wish the camera to recognize your best friend. This is accomplished by taking up to three different sample images of her full face, showing a range of typical facial expressions, such as a big grin outdoors, a serious contemplative look while indoors, and a subtle, Mona Lisa smile taken with an electronic flash. This way the camera's software will have a variety of your best friend's typical facial expressions under different lighting conditions for reference. We recommend that you take the maximum of three sample images for each person you register. This improves the software's accuracy in recognizing and identifying the person.

The Face Recognition software works in group shots, recognizing up to three people in a single picture, even when they are scattered among a group of people. Of course, to be recognized, each registered person must be facing toward the camera so that his or her facial features are clearly presented. Also, if a group is too large and, as a result, a registered face occupies too small an area on the sensor, it may not be recognized.

When you raise your camera to take a picture, the camera software will determine if it can identify the face belonging to any of the six Face Recognition registered people. If so, the saved registered name will be superimposed on the image below the framed face. In addition, in the case of Intelligent Auto Mode, an R will be displayed in the category icon (table 4-2), which is displayed in the lower-left corner of the display screen.

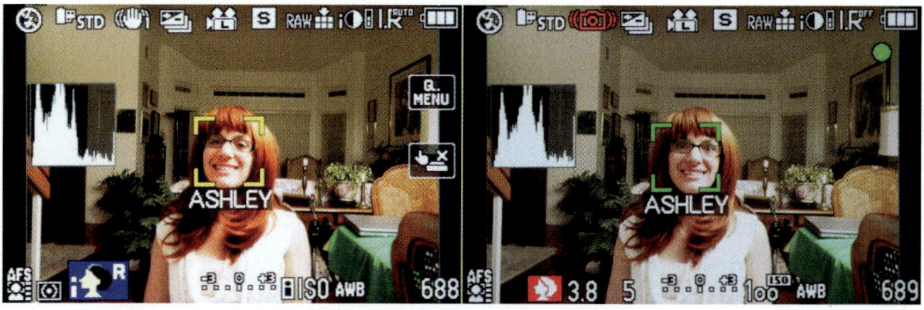

Figure 4-1a: Subject's face recognized while in Intelligent Auto Mode;
Figure 4-1b: Subject's face recognized while in Intelligent Portrait Mode

In the first picture (figure 4-1a), you can tell by the display of the subject's name and the Intelligent Auto Mode's R icon that the subject's face has been recognized by the camera's software. In the second picture (figure 4-1b), the subject is similarly recognized but there is no R icon because the camera is not in Intelligent Auto Mode.

The person's registered name and calculated age in years, months, and days are stored with the saved picture and displayed on the screen when the picture is played back on the camera and when you are printing the picture. In addition, the person's registered name will download with the picture to your computer when you use the supplied PHOTOfunStudio 5.0 HD software.

Where is Face Recognition functionality enabled? It is enabled in many of the predefined scene modes, in several of the iA categories, and when Face Detection is turned on for the modes. The following is a list of where Face Recognition function is not enabled even if the command is set to [ON] in the menu:

- When the focus mode lever is set to MF
- Motion Picture Mode
- Pet and Peripheral Defocus predefined scene modes within the Scene Mode
- Night Scenery and Illuminations predefined scene modes within the Night Portrait Mode
- Food predefined scene mode in the Close-Up Mode

Note that Face Recognition is automatically set to on when choosing any of these predefined scene modes:

- All of the predefined scene modes within the Portrait Mode,
- Night Portrait and Creative predefined scene modes within the Night Portrait Mode
- Party predefined scene mode within the Scene Mode

Face Recognition requires the auto focus mode to be set to Face Detection and in the above predefined scene modes this is the default setting. All other modes have a different default auto focus mode and to use Face Recognition in them, you must manually set the auto focus mode dial to Face Detection.

The Delay in Displaying a Person's Age When a Saved Picture is Reviewed

There is a delay in displaying the recognized person's age. The name displays first with the person's calculated age displaying soon after. The name disappears after a few seconds, but the age continues to display with the picture on the screen.

Activating Face Recognition

Getting the Face Recognition software to work is very simple. You must have three items in place:

a. You must have Face Detection functionality enabled:

Turn the auto focus mode dial to the Face Detection setting

b. You must enable the Face Recognition software:

MENU/SET>REC>FACE RECOG.>[ON]

c. You must have a Face Recognition registered face in your framed image.

Keep in mind that items 1 and 2 are automatically covered if any of the following conditions are enabled:

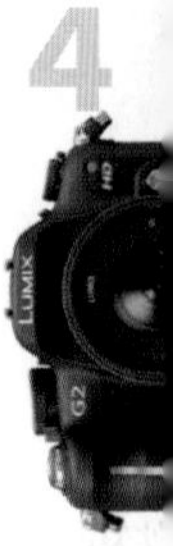

- Intelligent Auto Mode by selecting the iA button
- A mode dial scene that allows Face Recognition

Registering Faces

There are two different times you have the opportunity to register faces for future face recognition: prior to taking the picture and when you are actually taking a picture. The actual face registration is the same in both cases; just how you enter into the process is different.

Registering Faces Prior to Taking Pictures

The Face Recognition registration system is pretty extensive but fortunately simple to follow. The camera gives you plenty of help along the way.

First, to register a face, you will need to have your subject available for picture taking. Once the subject is available, execute the following steps.

1. Ensure MENU/SET>REC>FACE RECOG.>[ON].
2. Select MENU/SET>REC>FACE RECOG.>[MEMORY].
3. Six boxes are displayed on the screen. Each box represents a slot to register a person. The first available slot will have [NEW] superimposed. Once registered, the person's image will be displayed in the box with the [NEW] superimposed on the next available slot. Select the box labeled [NEW]. You can navigate through the screen either

with the rear dial or the directional arrow buttons. Once the [NEW] box is selected, press the MENU/SET button (figure 4-2a).

Note that if you already have six registered faces, you will have to delete one first before you can add a new one. We cover deleting registered faces in the section "Keeping Face Recognition Up-to-Date" later in this chapter.

4. The following message displays on the screen:

POSITION FULL FACE WITHIN GUIDELINE AND PRESS SHUTTER

The message is displayed for about 2 seconds, after which a yellow box-shape frame is displayed on the screen. Here is where you start to take the three sample images of the person you wish to register. Choose carefully. You want to make sure the images represent a good sampling of the person's appearance and facial expressions. Use indoor and outdoor settings to vary the lighting. The Face Recognition software recognizes only a frontal view—in other words the subject should look directly into the camera. Anything that obstructs the face or prevents both eyes, the nose, and the mouth from being clearly seen will prevent Face Recognition from working. Therefore, have the subject remove dark sunglasses and make sure both eyes are in clear view (figure 4-2b).

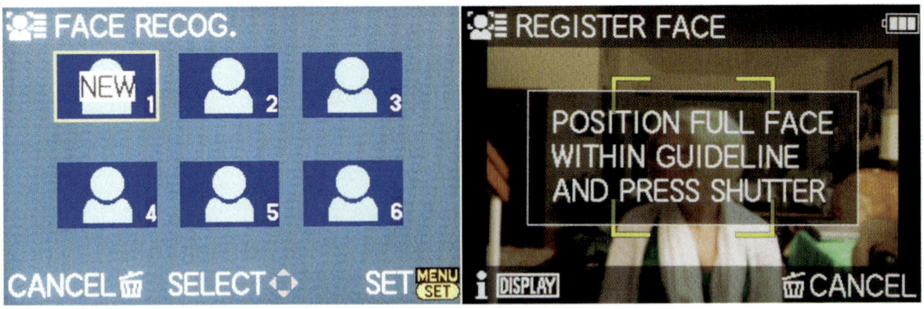

Figure 4-2a: The FACE RECOG. screen when you first enter it without any one being registered (Step 3) ; Figure 4-2b: Instructions to take the first image to register a new person (Step 4)

5. Press the shutter-release button to take an image of your subject (figure 4-3a).

a. If the camera's software could not identify the subject in the yellow frame as a face, you will receive the following error message:

REGISTRATION FAILED

Reframe and reshoot the image until the camera identifies a face in the framed image.

b. If the resulting image was identified as a face, you will receive the following question:

REGISTER THIS PERSON? [YES] [NO]

6. Select [YES] if you like the image and want to save it. Press the MENU/SET button. The camera will take a few seconds to save the image into its registration memory (figure 4-3b).

   Select [NO] to reject the image and return to step 5.

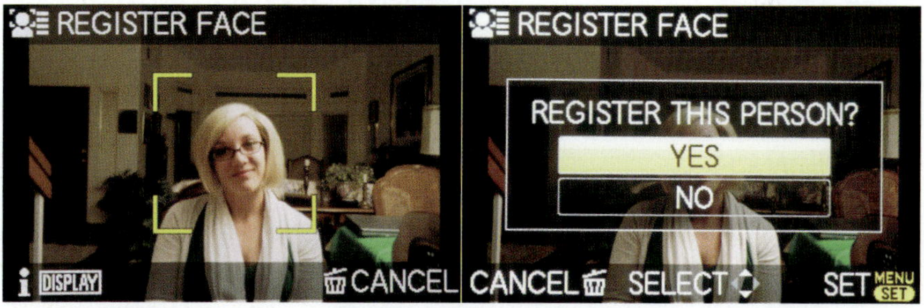

Figure 4-3a: The subject's face is framed looking forward into the camera (Step 5);
Figure 4-3b: Since the image is acceptable, [YES] has been selected to register the person (Step 6)

7. Once you have saved the image, a screen appears with the image you just took along with the following menu options: NAME, AGE, and ADD IMAGES.

a. To enter in the person's name (up to nine chars), select NAME>[SET] and press the MENU/SET button. The resulting text data screen may look complicated, but it is really quite simple. The DISPLAY button controls the keyboard pad. Pressing the DISPLAY button will cycle through a capitalized alphabet, lowercase alphabet, and number/symbol keyboards as indicated by the three icons in the upper-right corner of the screen (figure 4-4a, figure 4-4b).

Use the directional arrow buttons to navigate through the screen and the MENU/SET button to enter selected values. Once you have entered the name, highlight the SET icon in the upper-left portion of the screen and press the MENU/SET button to accept your entered name (figure 4-4c, figure 4-4d).

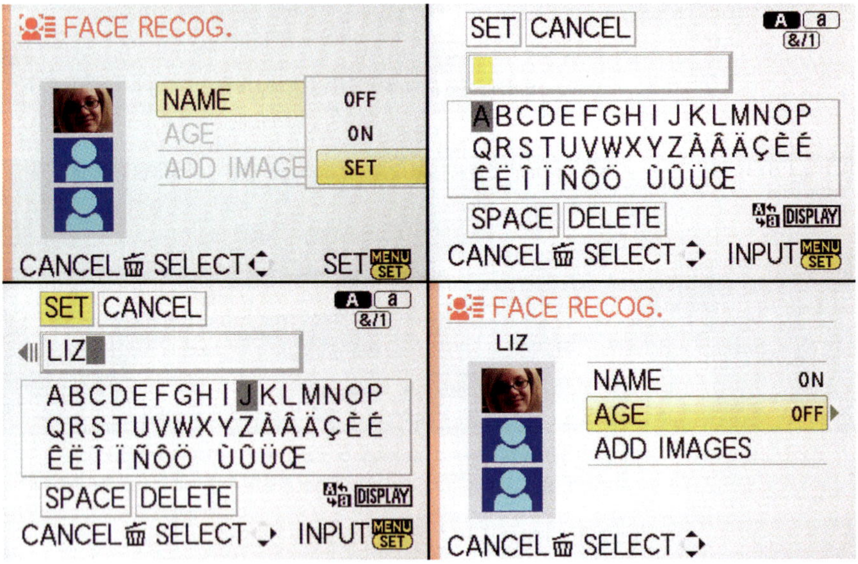

Figure 4-4a: NAME>[SET] has been selected.; Figure 4-4b: The text data entry screen; Figure 4-4c: Entering the name. Note the SET icon is highlighted; Figure 4-4d: The name has been accepted and is now displayed next to the saved image on the FACE RECOG. screen

b. To enter the person's age, select AGE>[SET] and press the MENU/SET button. You will be presented with a screen to enter in the person's birth date (in the date format selected when setting the camera's clock). Use the directional arrow buttons to navigate through the date components and their values. Press the MENU/SET button to accept the subject's birth date (figure 4-5a through figure 4-5d).

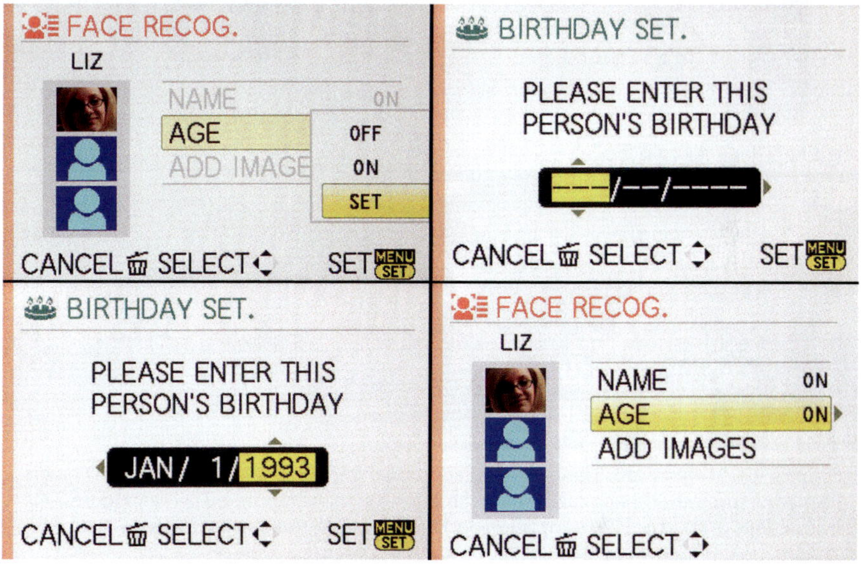

Figure 4-5a: AGE>[SET] has been selected; Figure 4-5b: The empty BIRTHDAY SET screen; Figure 4-5c: The directional arrow buttons are used to navigate through field values and between fields; Figure 4-5d: Age has been accepted. Note AGE now displays [ON]

c. To add another sample image, select the ADD IMAGES option and press the MENU/SET button (figure 4-6a). The returned screen will be the same as in step 3 but will have the recently saved sample image (figure 4-6b). Highlight the [NEW] box and press the MENU/SET button. The following message will be displayed (figure 4-6c):

PLEASE REGISTER FACE WITH DIFFERENT EXPRESSIONS AND SITUATIONS.

To take another picture of the subject, repeat steps 5 and 6 and then this step until you have reached the maximum of three sample images (figure 4-6d). Although you can stop with only one image, we recommend you take the time to use three different facial images as it improves the accuracy of facial recognition. You can go to step 8 once you have added all the sample images.

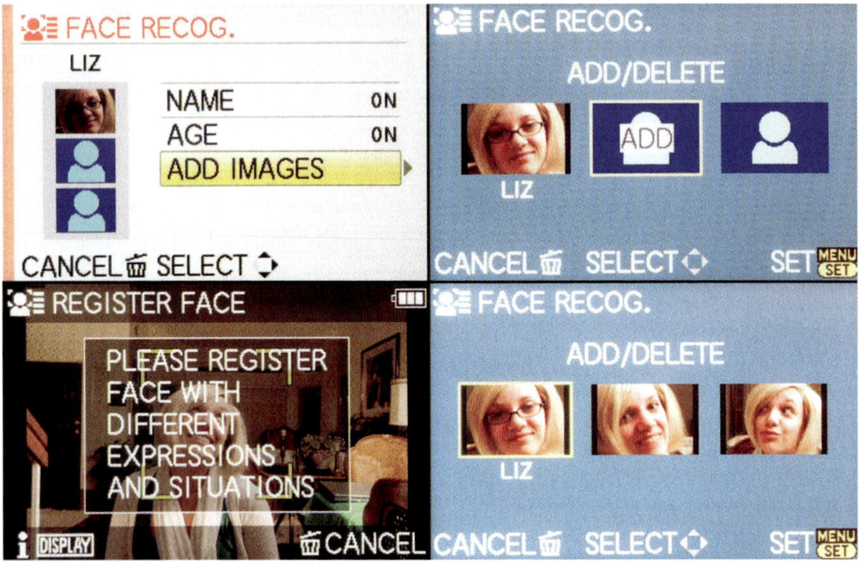

Figure 4-6a: Screen is positioned to add additional images; Figure 4-6b: The ADD box is displayed, so another image can be taken and saved with the registered person; Figure 4-6c: Instructions to take the next sample image; Figure 4-6d: All three sample images registered

8. Review the images and make sure they cover a diverse representation of how the person typically looks (figure 4-7a).

    a. If you are not satisfied with one of the sample images, select it and press the MENU/SET button.
    b. You will be prompted to select whether or not to delete the image. Select [YES] to delete or [NO] to retain the selected image. Once you have selected an answer, press the MENU/SET button.
    c. If you selected [YES], the remaining saved images will be displayed with an open image slot with [NEW] superimposed appearing on the far right (figure 4-7b). You can return to step 5 to add another sample image or decide that the ones you have are sufficient.

9. Press Trash Can button to exit the Face Recognition system.

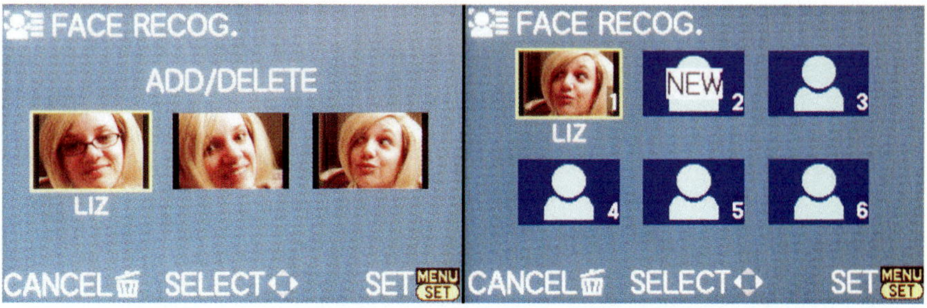

Figure 4-7a: Three sample images have been taken and stored in the Face Recognition system; Figure 4-7b: The FACE RECOG. screen with the first two images deleted

How is a Person's Age Calculated?

As part of Face Recognition, the camera's software will calculate the person's age based on the date the picture was taken (camera's CLOCK SET value) and the birth date entered when registering the person. The age, along with the name, will be stored with the saved picture. So when you take a picture of your best friend one day and then another the next day, the camera will calculate her age as a day older.

So, if you registered your subject with the wrong birth date, all of the saved pictures prior to making the correction will be based on the original birth date and all of the pictures saved after the correction will be based on the corrected birth date.

Registering Faces as You Take Pictures

Being in a mode that does face detection, such as Intelligent Auto, and having MENU/SET>FACE RECOG.>SET>AUTO REGISTRATION>[ON] selected will automatically cause the FACE RECOG. screen to be displayed after taking several pictures of the same face in succession. When this happens, the camera will ask if you wish to register the person's face at that time. Select [YES] and follow steps 3 through 10 in the section "Registering Faces Prior to Taking Pictures" earlier in this chapter. If you already have all of the six slots filled, you will have to replace one of them with this new person. The software will walk you through that process. Note the camera will not prompt you to register the person's face when Burst Mode, Auto Bracket, White Balance Bracket, and Multi Film Bracket functionality is enabled or when AUDIO REC. command is set [ON].

All Six Slots in Face Recognition are Filled But I Want to Add More

There are only six slots. You can replace one of the existing registered faces or you can handle the face recognition outside of the camera by downloading your pictures to your PC and using third-party face recognition software.

To replace a sample image within the Panasonic G2 camera, you can delete one of the existing registered people and then add the new person. Another way is to start adding a new person while the six slots are already filled and the camera will ask if you want to replace a registered face. Answer yes and the system will walk you through a series of screens to replace an existing registered person with someone new.

Keeping Face Recognition Up-to-Date

Keep in mind that you can always change a registered face's sample images and still retain the registered information both in the Face Recognition system and on the previously saved pictures stored on your memory card. As time goes on, you will need to do this. Everyone ages, and their faces will change over time, especially if the person was a preteen when you registered him and he is now moving into his teenage years. You can delete old sample images that no longer reflect how the person looks. (See step 8 in the section "Registering Faces Prior to Taking Pictures".) You can also delete the registered face if you no longer plan to take pictures of them. In doing so, the three associated sample images will also be deleted.

Here's how to delete the registered face along with its three sample images:

1. Select MENU/SET>REC>FACE RECOG.>[MEMORY].
2. Six boxes are displayed on the screen. Each box contains an image representing a person you have registered. Select the box you wish to delete and press the MENU/SET button.
3. Select [DELETE] option and press the MENU/SET button.
4. Select [YES] and press the MENU/SET button.
5. You can either register another person or press the Trash Can button and exit out of the Face Recognition system.

Change Sample Images

To change sample images, follow these steps:

1. Enter MENU/SET>REC>FACE RECOG.>[MEMORY].
2. Six boxes are displayed on the screen. Each box represents a person you have registered. Select the box representing the person for which you wish to change sample images and press the MENU/SET button.
3. Select [INFO EDIT] and press the MENU/SET button.
4. Select the [ADD IMAGES] option and press the right directional arrow button.

   At this point you will be executing the same steps you took when setting up the Face Recognition registration prior to taking pictures. We will repeat those steps here so they are easily available but with minimal detail. For more information, go back and reread the section "Registering Faces Prior to Taking Pictures." Also note that if you have all three boxes filled with images, you will need to delete one before you can add a new image. Select the one you wish to delete, press the MENU/SET button, select [YES] to delete, and press the MENU/SET button again. Now you will have an available image box with [NEW] superimposed. Highlight it and press MENU/SET button.

5. The following message will be displayed on the screen:

   POSITION FULL FACE WITHIN GUIDELINE AND PRESS SHUTTER

   The message is displayed for about 2 seconds, after which a yellow box shape frame is displayed on the screen. Frame your subject's face.

6. Press the shutter-release button to take an image of your subject.

   a. If the camera's software could not identify the subject in the frame as a face, you will receive the following error message:

      REGISTRATION FAILED

      Reframe and reshoot until the camera identifies a face in the framed image.

b. If the resulting picture was identified as a face, you will receive the following question:

REGISTER THIS PERSON? [YES] [NO]

7. Select [YES] if you like the image and want to save it. The camera will take a few seconds to save the image into its registration memory site.

   Select [NO] to reject the image. The camera will redisplay the frame for you to take another image. Return to the beginning of step 6 to take another image or go to step 8 to exit the process.

8. Press the Trash Can button to exit the Face Recognition system.

Enhancing Face Recognition Capability

Since you have a total of six slots for registering people, you can register up to six different people or use all for the same person or somewhere in between. The choice is up to you and dependent on whom you intend to take pictures of. As mentioned earlier, the Face Recognition software does not always recognize a person's face. Since you have only three sample images per person registered and your best friend might be a very expressive person, three sample images might not be enough for her. You might want to register your best friend twice using two of the six registration slots. This way you can have a total of six sample images for the person—three for each of the registrations.

Along with ensuring that you have selected sample images of your subject, which cover the most likely facial expressions you will encounter when taking his or her picture, you have the option of setting the Face Recognition Sensitivity command.

MENU/SET>REC>FACE RECOG.>SET>SENSITIVITY>[HIGH], [NORMAL], [LOW]

This command can increase or decrease the Face Recognition software's sensitivity—unfortunately not without a downside. Increasing the software's sensitivity can cause additional false matches, and decreasing the sensitivity can cause a low number of matches. We recommend that you set this value to [NORMAL] to start with and if you are having problems obtaining matches, review your subject's sample images first. If they appear to be good choices, then consider changing the SENSITIVITY value.

Intelligent Auto Mode

As mentioned in chapter 1, the Intelligent Auto Mode is activated by pushing the iA button on the right side of the top of the camera. Once pushed, the button will light up blue and an iA icon will appear in the lower-left corner of the display screen to indicate that Intelligent Auto Mode is activated. The Intelligent Auto Mode will stay in effect as long as the iA button is activated. Keep this in mind if you wish to change some camera settings. The Intelligent Auto Mode will set many of the camera commands and settings for you automatically (see table 4-1 on the next page). Note that these values cannot be changed unless they are listed in the INTELLIGENT AUTO menu.

While in Intelligent Auto Mode, you can view and maintain the available menu command options. Press the MENU/SET button to enter in the main menu screen. INTELLIGENT AUTO will appear in the screen's title bar and an iA icon menu option will be at the top of the main menu list on the left side (figure 4-8). The displayed screen contains only the available main menu commands, with paths to their associated submenu commands and values. The list is only a small subset of the total list. Don't be surprised when you realize many of the commands you might have seen when surfing the menu structure outside of Intelligent Auto Mode are not there. It isn't that most of them are not being used; it is that Intelligent Auto will determine their values automatically for you when presented with a framed image.

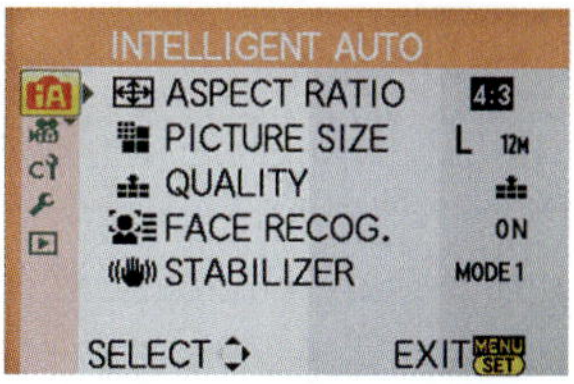

Figure 4-8: Intelligent Auto Mode's MENU/SET screen

Once in Intelligent Auto Mode, find and frame your subject. The camera quickly sets aperture, focusing, color balance, and exposure. You can press the shutter-release button halfway to apply the Intelligent Auto Mode's decisions and have them posted on the display screen—of course, what you see depends on your chosen data display screen format. This will give you advanced information on how the camera interprets the image.

There may be times when the camera cannot obtain focus for your framed subject. The preset Intelligent Auto command **MENU/SET>REC>FOCUS PRIORITY>[ON]** will prevent the camera from taking the picture until the subject is in focus. Typically this occurs when there is too little contrast or light in the image.

Intelligent Auto Preset Command and Setting Values	
Value	**Command**
5 MIN	MENU/SET>SETUP>(pg 2) ECONOMY>SLEEP MODE
Auto or Flash off	MENU/SET>REC>(pg 2) FLASH
1ST	MENU/SET>REC>(pg 2) FLASH SYNCHRO
H (High speed)	MENU/SET>REC>(pg 4) BURST RATE
3 1/3	MENU/SET>REC>(pg 4) AUTO BRACKET>STEP
0/-/+ -	MENU/SET>REC>(pg 4) AUTO BRACKET>SEQUENCE
Intelligent ISO with the maximum sensitivity = ISO 800	MENU/SET>REC>FACE RECOG>SET>SENSITIVITY
Multiple metering	MENU/SET>REC>METERING MODE
ON	MENU/SET>REC>(pg 2) RED-EYE REMOVAL
STANDARD	MENU/SET>REC>(pg 3) I.EXPOSURE
ON	MENU/SET>REC>(pg 3) LONG SHTR NR
sRGB	MENU/SET>REC>(pg 5) COLOR SPACE
Q-AF Quick AF	MENU/SET>CUSTOM>(pg 2) PRE AF
ON	MENU/SET>CUSTOM>(pg 2) FOCUS PRIORITY
ON	MENU/SET>CUSTOM>(pg 3) AF ASSIST LAMP
Value	**Setting**
Face Detection	AF Mode = AFS or AFC and face is detected
23-area-focusing	AF Mode = AFS or AFC and face is not detected
AWB	White Balance button

Table 4-1: The commands and settings Intelligent Auto Mode sets automatically

4

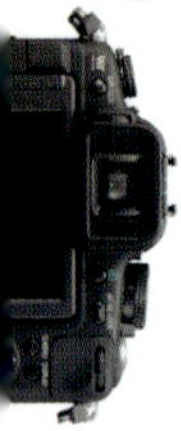

It can also occur when the subject is too close to the camera. When this happens, reposition your subject so there is greater lighting—or if too close, you need to back away. You cannot alter the contrast of the subject—however, increasing the light intensity helps the sensor, and it can usually find focus if the ambient intensity is raised sufficiently. There are additional solutions once outside of the Intelligent Auto Mode. They will be covered in chapter 5 when we cover taking your camera usage semi-automatic.

Keep an eye out for any icons highlighted in red, as these are your warnings. For example, if the shutter speed is too slow to take a handheld exposure, you will see the "jitter warning" icon in the upper-left side of the display screen (figure 4-9). This is your signal to raise the flash so the shutter speed can increase or to mount the camera on the tripod. This warning helps prevent taking pictures when the chances are high that they will be blurred. The Intelligent Auto function generally makes excellent camera setting decisions for your image, and for many people it will be sufficient for recording pictures or videos.

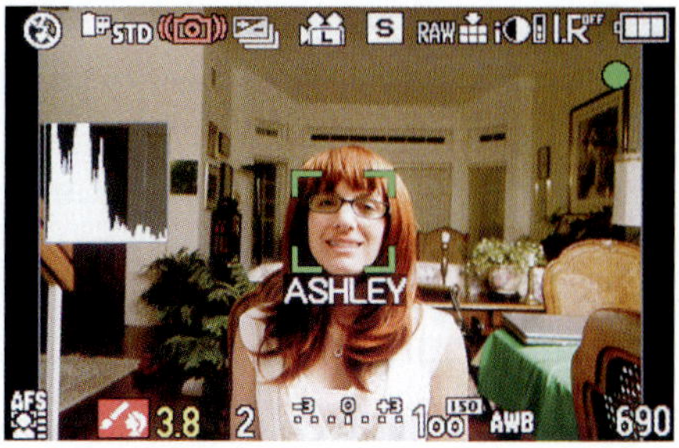

Figure 4-9: The red jitter warning icon indicates too much movement of the camera

Changing Intelligent Auto Settings

You have the option to modify some of the camera's Intelligent Auto settings. There are a couple of ways to do this. By viewing the potential picture, you can use the Q.MENU button on the back of the camera or the Q.MENU icon on the LCD screen to review and possibly change the camera settings selected for your image. You can also review the resulting camera settings by pressing the DISPLAY button when playing back the picture or video using the Playback button. In doing so, you may decide to change camera settings and reshoot.

4

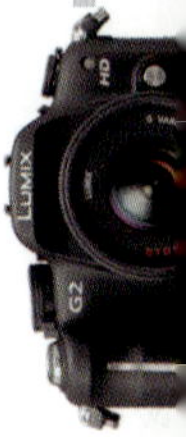

Note that most of the available adjustments will have nothing to do with the exposure, focus, or aperture—the Intelligent Auto Mode controls those functions listed in table 4-1. You can also view the settings and make changes by pressing the MENU/SET button and going through the menu structure. (See Appendix C* for a list of available Intelligent Auto Mode MENU/SET commands.) Last but not least, you can also make changes to the image's shutter speed and aperture using the Exposure Compensation tool as described in chapter 3.

Intelligent Auto Scene Detection

As part of the Intelligent Auto Mode, the camera will quickly evaluate the scene and attempt to assign it to a category from the following list: i-Portrait, i-Baby, i-Nighttime Portrait, i-Scenery, i-Nighttime Scenery, i-Low Light, i-Macro, and i-Sunset (table 4-2).

This is significant, because this is more than automatic exposure—it is automatic exposure biased to provide the best settings for a particular subject. Once determined, the camera displays the selected category's icon (figure 4-1) in the lower-left corner of the display screen in blue for 2 seconds and then changes its color to red.

* To view the Appendix, see: http://rockynook.com/PanasonicG2

There are times when the camera's software is unable to determine a specific category and the iA icon is displayed on the screen with the camera choosing a generic set of settings.

In addition, the software will save the category with the picture or video so you can later select it based on category for printing or playback purposes. As you can see from table 4-2, there are fewer available categories when taking videos. Nighttime scenarios fall into the i-Low Light category. So nighttime categories for portraits and scenery will be assigned the i-Low Light category for videos.

Display Screen Icon	Intelligent Auto Category	Available for	
		Pictures	Videos
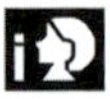	i-Portrait	X	X
	i-Baby	X	
	i-Nighttime Portrait	X	
	i-Scenery	X	X
	i-Nighttime Scenery	X	
	i-Macro	X	X
	i-Sunset	X	
	i-Low Light		X
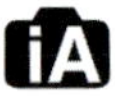	General	X	X

Table 4.2: Intelligent Auto Mode available categories and icons

Each of the Intelligent Auto Mode categories has predefined camera settings to optimize the resulting picture or video per the software's interpretation. For example, the camera is capable of detecting when there is a human face in the image by looking for two eyes, a nose, and a mouth at typical human proportions and location. This combination enables the camera's software to differentiate between a human face and the person's pet.

When a human face is identified, the camera's intelligent software will assign the appropriate scene category depending on the ambient light intensity and whether you're taking a picture or a video.

In both cases, the focus and exposure is automatically set for the face. When you're taking pictures, if **FACE RECOG.** = **[ON]**, the software will also check to see if the face has been registered.

Why Isn't an Image of My Cat Identified as a Portrait?

Yes, your cat has two eyes, a nose, and a mouth, and we are sure it is very cute. Face identification and recognition software relies on not only identifying that there are two eyes in the image, but that the mouth appears to be human. That means it is looking for something that resembles two lips and is positioned proportionally in the right location relative with the eyes and the nose. A cat's "portrait" has the eyes, but the mouth is uniquely feline and its position relative to the eyes or nose differs from a mouth located on a human's face.

Intelligent Auto Categories

i-Portrait (Daylight and Nighttime)

The Intelligent Auto Mode assigns a portrait category when the camera's software detects a human face in the image. The software goes a step further and determines if the image setting is daytime or nighttime. In both daytime and nighttime portraits, if there is insufficient light, you will be prompted upon pressing the shutter-release button with the message PLEASE USE THE FLASH. You will not be able to take the picture without adding light to the subject. Therefore, you should either pop up the flash unit or supply additional lighting to the image.

For still pictures only, when the face recognition option is enabled (**MENU/SET>INTELLIGENT AUTO>FACE RECOG.>[ON]**), the camera's software will search for a registered face. If found, the camera's software will display an R within the category icon and display the registered name beneath the face on the display screen. In addition, the camera will determine if the registered subject is classified as a baby (i.e., if the saved age is 3 years old or less). If so, the resulting picture will be categorized in the i-BABY category for future playback and group selection identification.

If the subject's identified age is greater than 3 years old, the resulting picture will be categorized as an i-Portrait or i-Nighttime Portrait, depending on the camera's software.

Why Doesn't the PLEASE USE THE FLASH Message Always Display in the Same Situation?

We found that while in Intelligent Auto Mode, when we were taking a portrait picture with insufficient lighting, the message PLEASE USE THE FLASH was displayed when we pushed the shutter-release button halfway after the camera's software had recognized that there was a face in the framed image. We also noticed with subsequent pushes of the shutter-release button halfway, the message did not display again.

We discovered that you need to point the camera somewhere else and then reinitiate the focus on the face for the message to reappear. Note: In Intelligent Auto Mode, just because the message does not display with subsequent halfway presses of the shutter-release button, you still will not be able to press the shutter-release button fully to take the picture until there is more light on the subject.

i-Scenery (Daytime and Nighttime)

The Intelligent Auto Mode determines an image to be in a "scenery" category based on a combination of what it is and what it is not. It is unclear what parameters are important for this function because we have noticed when taking multiple pictures of the same scene within seconds of each other that one would be categorized as i-Scenery and the next picture's category was undetermined and therefore assigned iA. Some of the parameters used for classifying a picture are based on what is lacking. Failure to identify a face means the scene is not categorized as i-Portrait. Failure to focus on a close subject—i.e., within about 1 foot—means the scene is not categorized as i-Macro. Frequently, the camera may identify a distant shot as a scenic shot, but as we mentioned earlier, this is not always the case. In other words, scene identification as practiced by Intelligent Auto is imperfect. It should be viewed as a convenience, and as you become more comfortable with using the camera, you can categorize the subject yourself and select the appropriate mode dial predefined scene mode.

As with portraits, the software goes a step further and determines if the image setting is daytime or nighttime scenery. We have run tests with indoor and outdoor scenes and have found, as in the case of portraits, that the software can differentiate between daytime and nighttime outdoor sceneries. However, time was not the deciding factor since the camera did not differentiate daytime or nighttime indoors shots. In this case the camera always selected daytime scenery category. In the case of videos, the category classification will be between i-Low Light and i-Scenery. Videos recorded in dim lighting, regardless of the time are assigned the i-Low Light category. Videos recorded with sufficient lighting are assigned the i-Scenery category.

i-Macro

This category is assigned when the Intelligent Auto software determines that the subject appears to be significantly close to the lens and the camera obtains focus on the subject. This second point is very important. If the camera cannot obtain focus on a close-up subject, the Intelligent Auto category will not be set to i-Macro and the shutter-release button will be disabled from being fully pressed to take the picture. How close is close? It ends up that in order for the picture to be considered in the macro category, the subject should be about 0.3 meters or about 1 foot away from the camera when using the standard 14-42 mm f/3.5-f/5.6 lens included with the G2 camera.

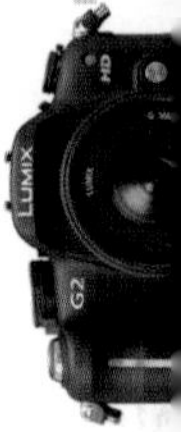

When the camera obtains focus on the subject, its software will attempt to close down the aperture to increase the depth of field and ensure that the subject and its surroundings appear sharp. In close-up work, the depth of field is very narrow, so objects rapidly lose sharpness as their distance from the plane of focus increases or decreases. When a close-up of a butterfly is photographed, its body may be recorded in detail, but its wings become blurred. Because of this, i-Macro will bias its setting to prioritize maximum depth of field. This may require a long shutter speed, and it may be necessary to steady the camera by using a tripod or placing the camera on a solid surface.

i-Sunset

The Intelligent Auto software has the ability to identify rich red- and orange-hued sunset (and sunrise) scenes. Unfortunately, we were unable to capture this category during our testing of the camera and we presume this was because our local sunsets and sunrises lack sufficient coloring to generate this category. If you intend to take a picture of a sunset and it is not registering in Intelligent Auto Mode, switch over to the Scene Mode option on the mode dial and set the specific scene type to Sunset. This will ensure that the camera is set to capture the scene and emphasize the rich reds and oranges commonly displayed in beautiful sunsets.

i-Baby

This is a three-step process. As in the case of i-Portraits, the camera must be able to first identify that it there is a face in the image and obtain focus. Then the camera must recognize that the face is registered within the camera's memory. The third step is to check the registered face's age by using the stored birth date. This is the same process as what occurs with Portraits. If the person's calculated age is 3 years old or younger, she is classified as a baby and will be assigned the i-Baby category.

This category causes the camera to adjust for a softer flash—less disturbing for the baby. As with i-Portrait, the camera's software will display an R within the i-Baby icon along with both the baby's registered name and age on the display screen. This information will be stored with the picture for use in future playback, printing, and downloading to your PC (with the latter two depending on the software used).

i-Low Light

This Intelligent Auto category is chosen only when videos are recorded in low-light environments. While the camera's software can adjust its settings to capture more light for still pictures, videos do not have the same flexibility. As an example, the i-Macro category may be identified when you're framing a picture, but when you switch over to video and the lighting that was sufficient for a Macro picture in Intelligent Auto is not sufficient for the video, the camera will display the i-Low Light icon instead. So i-Low Light is a common Intelligent Auto category for video recording.

General

If the Intelligent Auto Mode was unable to determine a specific category for the image you intend to record, it will set the camera to a general exposure (shutter speed and aperture), select 23-area-focusing mode, and assign the iA icon as the picture's and video's category.

Mode Dial

The mode dial contains 13 different modes for the user's selection (figure 4-10). The dial rotates 360 degrees in either direction. Turn the dial and line up the chosen mode to the white line on the camera body to the left of the dial. You will hear a click when each selected mode is in position. The mode dial is the starting point for exerting more control in your photographs and videos. It provides additional artistic features and a mixture of automatic and semi-automatic settings for the user.

For this chapter, we will discuss six of the mode dial options (table 4-3). Each option contains predefined scene modes that go a step further than Intelligent Auto Mode by allowing you to specify the type of scene and then having the camera automatically tailor its settings to the image and the selected scene type.

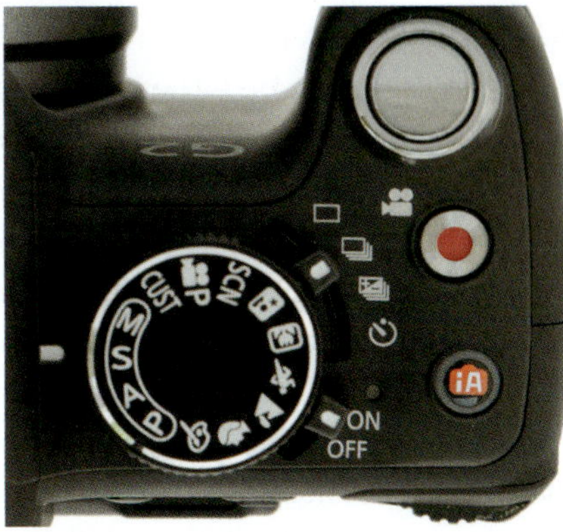

Figure 4-10: Mode dial is set to S Mode

The remaining seven mode dial options work differently and will be covered in later chapters.

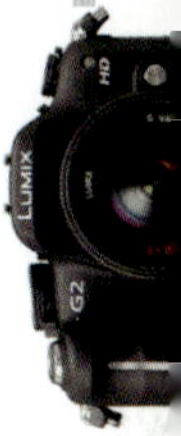

Figure 4-10 shows the mode dial, which is on the right side on the top of the camera.

Mode Dial Icons – Predefined Scene Modes		
Mode Dial Icon	**Mode Name**	**Short Description**
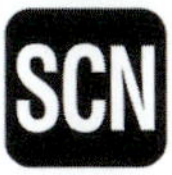	Scene (miscellaneous scene mode)	This mode gives the user a selection of miscellaneous scene scenarios. Generates specific camera settings for the selected scene.
	Night Portrait (advanced scene mode)	This mode gives the user a selection of nighttime portrait scenarios. Generates specific camera settings for the selected option.
	Close-up (advanced scene mode)	This mode gives the user a selection of close-up scenarios. Generates specific camera settings for the selected option.
	Sports (advanced scene mode)	This mode gives the user a selection of action sports scenarios. Generates specific camera settings for the selected option.
	Scenery (advanced scene mode)	This mode gives the user a selection of scenery scenarios. Generates specific camera settings for the selected option.
	Portrait (advanced scene mode)	This mode gives the user a selection of portrait scenarios. Generates specific camera settings for the selected option.

Table 4-3: The mode dial contains a total of 13 options. These six options cover the predefined scene modes.

Predefined Scene Modes

For a new camera user, the Intelligent Auto Mode is a convenient means to take pictures. But occasionally, it will fail to categorize a scene correctly, making the camera's settings non-optimal. For example, a scene identified as a Macro picture can be either an indoor shot of a two-dimensional subject, such as a paper receipt, or an outdoor shot with three dimensions, such as a flower. The scenery shot might be a shot of the mountain peak or a picture of a building. The Intelligent Auto Mode will make its best guess based on the brightness, speed, and contrast, but you may find that it doesn't take the picture you want because your subject is incorrectly identified. To remedy this, the Panasonic G2 camera allows you to provide scene identification. It has icons representing predefined scenes you match to your subject. Essentially, you match the subject to an icon that most closely mimics the conditions under which you are shooting.

Each of the six mode dial options (table 4-3) operates the same way. They each act as a classification holding a specific group of scenes with one important distinction. Five mode dial options (Nightly Portrait, Close-up, Sports, Scenery, and Portrait) are each a general themed scene category and when selected, each mode provides a group of subcategories for the scene. For example, the Close-up mode dial option contains a group of four related scenes: Flower, Food, Objects, and Creative Close-up. Panasonic calls these five themed mode dial options advanced scene modes and will also refer to their subcategory scenes by the same term. You can see how this allows you to fine-tune the classification of your subject. The mode dial option marked with the letters SCN is the Scene Mode option, which contains a group of unrelated scene modes. The Scene Mode option could just as easily have been described as miscellaneous. To simplify things, we refer to all of the individual scenes as predefined scene modes. This covers their function exactly and, hopefully, removes some of the confusion in Panasonic's rather arbitrary distinction between the Scene Mode and the advanced scene modes.

To use the predefined scene modes, you must disable the Intelligent Auto Mode, so make sure the iA button is not glowing blue. Move the mode dial to the desired predefined scene mode. Its associated scene menu will display automatically. Use the rear dial or directional arrow buttons to navigate and select the predefined scene that will best reflect the scene for the picture or video you are about to take. The camera will apply its settings based on the selected scene mode and the image's characteristics.

One more tip to cover before we move on to describing each of the predefined scene modes. The Panasonic G2 camera has a Help function represented by a bold lowercase *i* (figure 4-11a). Press the DISPLAY button and a helpful explanation about the selected predefined scene mode appears (figure 4-11b). To exit, press the DISPLAY button again and you will be returned to the selected predefined scene mode screen.

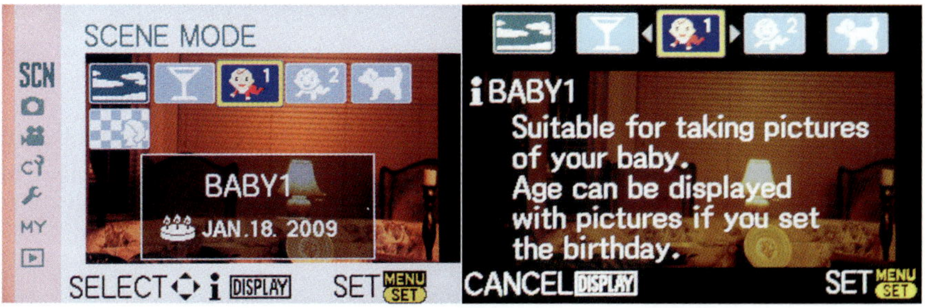

Figure 4-11a: The lowercase *i* means information is available by pressing the DISPLAY button; Figure 4-11b: i BABY1's information screen

4

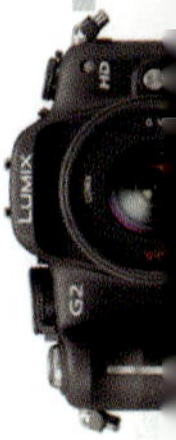

What Menu Commands Are Automatically Adjusted in the Predefined Scene Modes?

The camera's software will adjust the following commands automatically to the optimal setting based on the selected predefined scene mode and the image's brightness, contrast, movement, and interpretive content:

MENU/SET>REC>FACE RECOG.>SENSITIVITY

MENU/SET>REC>METERING MODE

MENU/SET>REC>(pg 2) FLASH SYNCHRO *

MENU/SET>REC>(pg 3) I.RESOLUTION

MENU/SET>REC>(pg 3) I.EXPOSURE

MENU/SET>REC>(pg 3) ISO LIMIT SET

MENU/SET>REC>(pg 4) DIGITAL ZOOM

Film Mode options other than [STANDARD] and [STANDARD] (B&W)

* FLASH SYNCHRO can be modified for Scene Mode's PERIPHERAL DEFOCUS scene mode.

The following sections cover each of the predefined scene modes. Remember, the camera will set its shutter speed, aperture, exposure, and other criteria to best record the selected scene. As mentioned earlier, you will still have the option to override the camera's selected values using the Exposure Compensation function. In addition, you can make changes to command settings within the main menu. But in most cases, the settings applied will give you a quality picture or video for the subject you desire to record.

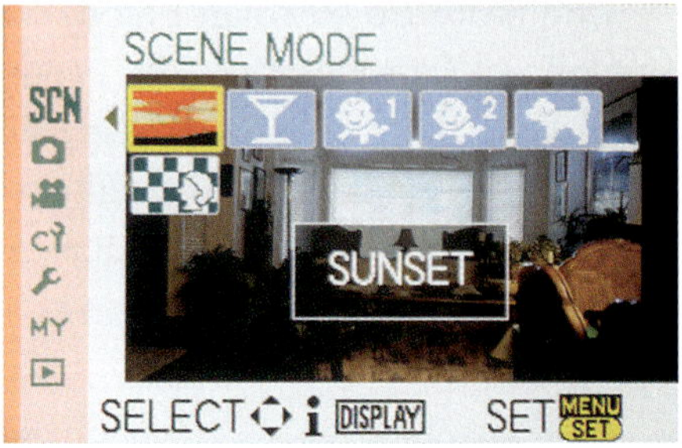

Figure 4-12: The Scene Mode options with the SUNSET predefined scene mode selected

Scene Mode

The Scene Mode sets the optimum exposure and hue to obtain the desired picture (figure 4-12). Select the Scene Mode by selecting the SCN icon on the mode dial. For this mode, you can choose from the scenarios listed in table 4-4.

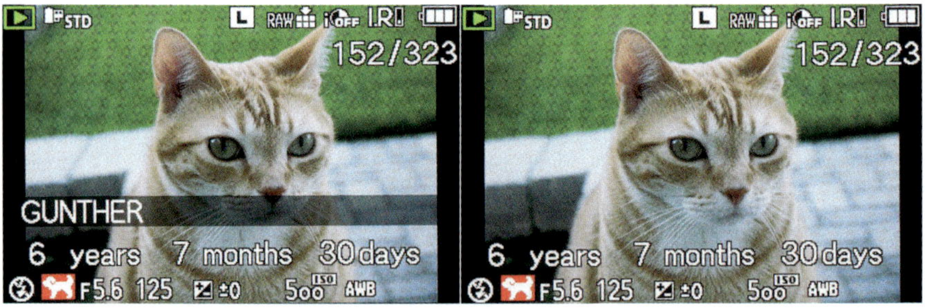

Figure 4-13a: Pet's name initially displayed;
Figure 4-13b: Pet's name no longer displayed after a few seconds

Screen Icon	Predefined Scene Mode	Description
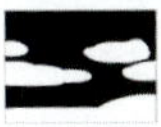	SUNSET	This mode captures the rich red hues featured in sunsets. Can also be used for sunrises. Use this mode if you are unable to get i-Sunset to register in the Intelligent Auto Mode.
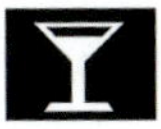	PARTY	This mode captures the natural hues for people and objects in both the foreground and background. Great for weddings, parties, and other indoor activities.
	BABY 1	This mode offers you an opportunity to enter the child's name and birth date. Once they're entered, each time BABY1 Mode is selected, the child's name and calculated age is displayed on the screen and will be stored with the picture for playback and print purposes. When required, the flash's strength is reduced. The camera automatic focus is set to AF Tracking so the camera can maintain exposure and focus as the baby moves. Note: This is not the same as Face Recognition and does not identify the baby through the software. The subject could actually be of anything, but the purpose is for the user to group all of one baby's pictures together under BABY1 and another baby's pictures under BABY2. Use this choice when Intelligent Auto Mode was unable to recognize a specific baby in the image or you have not registered the baby's face in the Face Recognition software.
	BABY 2	This mode is the same as BABY1. BABY2 Mode offers you an additional opportunity to enter in another child's name and birth date. See BABY1 for additional specifics.
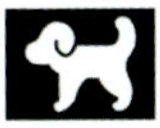	PET	This mode offers you an opportunity to enter one pet's name and birth date. Once they're entered, each time PET Mode is selected, the pet's name and calculated age is displayed on the screen and will be stored with the picture for playback and print purposes. The camera's automatic focus is set to AF Tracking so the camera can maintain exposure and focus on a rapidly moving pet. Note: As with BABY1 and BABY2, you can assign the PET predefined scene mode to anything. The camera software does not recognize the pet, only that you have selected the PET mode.
	PERIPHERAL DEFOCUS	This mode allows the focus to be set on the subject and the background to be blurred to further enhance the subject. This uses 1-area-focuing auto focus. The user can position the location of the area to be focused via the directional arrow buttons or touching the screen.

Table 4-4: The predefined scene modes available for the Scene Mode

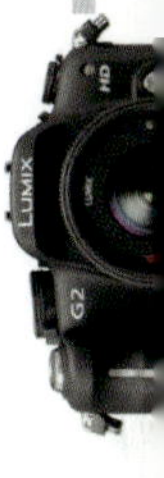

Advanced Scene Modes

Each of these mode dial advanced scene modes act as a classification or theme containing a group of predefined scene modes pertaining to the parent mode. Each of the predefined scene modes will determine camera settings, although the CREATIVE option gives you additional opportunities to set some of the camera settings yourself.

Depending on the predefined scene selected, you can control the shutter speed so you can create blur in a moving subject or vary the depth of field to limit sharpness to the plane encompassing just your subject or expand sharpness to encompass a much greater area. Here you will start moving into the realm of controlling the outcome of the camera yourself. This, in fact, becomes an intermediate step toward semi-automatically operating the camera and exerting your own creativity toward creating pictures and videos.

Figure 4-14a shows the Portrait advanced scene mode's screen. The Portrait Mode has five predefined scene mode options all related to recording images of people. One of Portrait Mode's predefined settings is to have the FACE RECOG. command set to [ON]. Figure 4-14b displays the playback of a picture taken using the Portrait Mode's NORMAL option. Note the red Portrait icon in the lower-left corner of the screen along with the Face Recognition results.

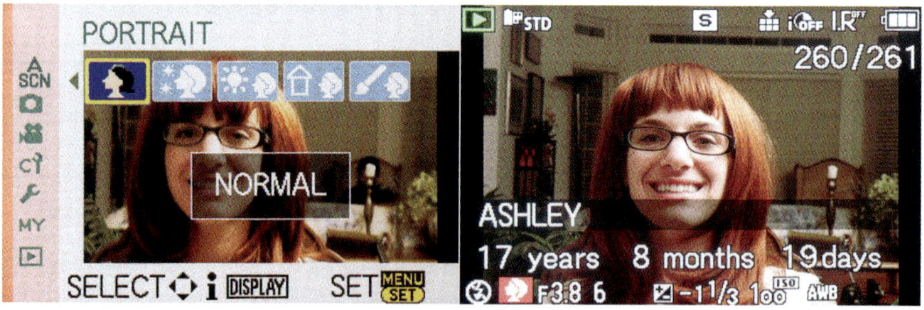

Figure 4-14a: The Portrait Mode menu options with the NORMAL predefined scene mode selected; Figure 4-14b: Picture taken using Portrait Mode's NORMAL predefined scene mode

Night Portrait Mode

Night Portrait Mode (figure 4-15) allows you to take pictures of a subject in a nighttime setting. Select this scene mode by selecting the Night Portrait Mode icon on the mode dial. For this mode, you can choose from the scenarios listed in table 4-5.

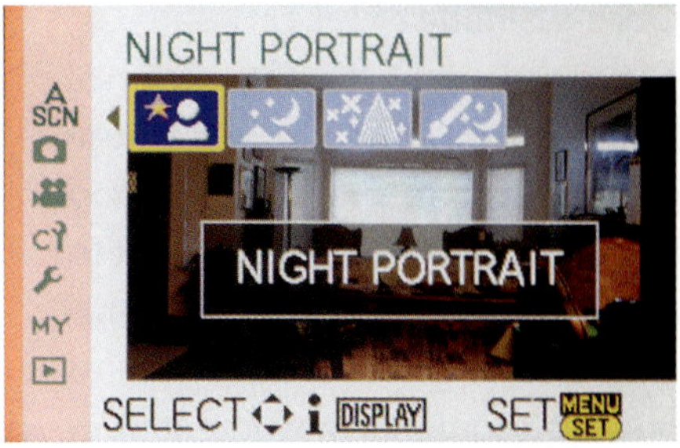

Figure 4-15: The Night Portrait Mode options with the NIGHT PORTRAIT predefined scene mode selected

Screen Icon	Predefined Scene Mode	Description
	NIGHT PORTRAIT	This mode is used to take photographs of people in a nighttime setting. The exposure and shutter speed are set to capture enough light falling on the subject to create an accurately colored and detailed portrait. Both Face Detection and Face Recognition functionality are enabled with this selection. The camera will focus on a face using 1-area-focusing. For pictures, the camera's software will also search through its maximum six registered faces to see if there is a match. If so, the person's registered name and age will be displayed with the image and resulting picture. The flash's intensity will be reduced if the recognized face is determined to be of a person 3 years old or younger.
	NIGHT SCENERY	This mode is photographed with a slow shutter to allow for the camera to capture enough light to vividly record the total scene.
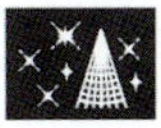	ILLUMINATIONS	This mode is used when there are points of illumination within the image.
	CREATIVE	This mode is initially set for nighttime portraits but allows the user to change the camera's aperture to control the depth of field to blur or sharpen the background from the subject.

Table 4-5: The predefined scene modes available for the Night Portrait Mode

Close-up Mode

The Close-up Mode (figure 4-16) selection is sensitive to camera movement and therefore a tripod is recommended. You may want to also consider using the optional remote shutter release DMW-RSL1 to prevent additional movement from pressing the shutter-release button. This mode has the scenarios list in table 4.6 to choose from.

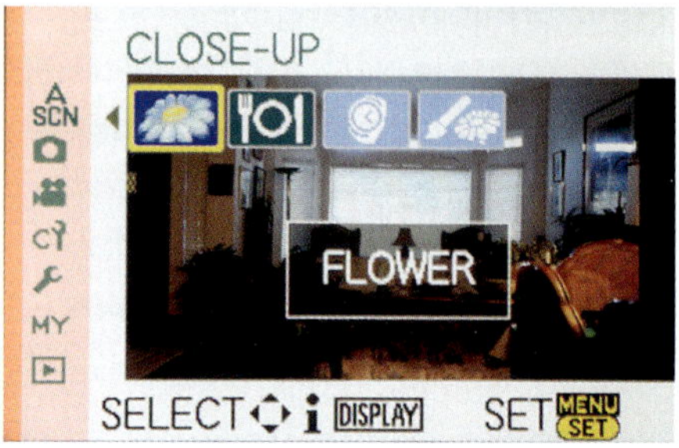

Figure 4-16: The Close-up Mode options with the FLOWER predefined scene mode selected

Screen Icon	Predefined Scene Mode	Description
	FLOWER	This mode helps record outdoor flowers' natural colors. Note: Guidelines will be displayed according to the MENU/SET>CUSTOM>GUIDE LINE command setting.
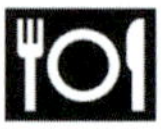	FOOD	This mode helps record pictures of food with their natural hues without being affected by restaurant ambient light.
	OBJECTS	This mode is tailored for taking close-up pictures of small objects, maintaining focus and accurate colors.
	CREATIVE	This mode allows the user to change the camera's aperture to increase or decrease the depth of field.

Table 4-6: The predefined scene modes available for the Close-Up Mode

Sports Mode

The Sports Mode (figure 4-17) allows the user to capture a subject in motion. Sports-related pictures need a fast shutter and proper exposure to ensure that a fast-moving subject is captured. This mode uses 1-area-focusing, so you will have to set the location the camera should use to determine proper focus. Remember, you can enlarge the 1-area-focusing box or shrink it depending on how broad or narrow you want the camera to focus on. The Sports Mode has several sports-related scenarios to select from to help you capture the picture. This mode has the scenarios listed in table 4-7.

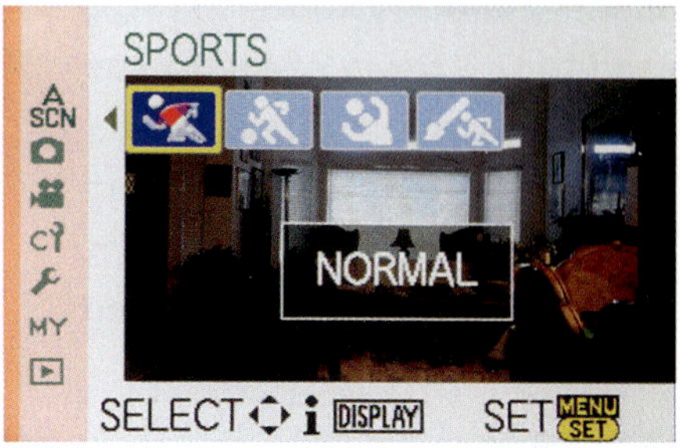

Figure 4-17: The Sports Mode options with the NORMAL predefined scene mode selected

Screen Icon	Predefined Scene Mode	Description
	NORMAL	This mode sets the ISO sensitivity and high shutter speed to stop the subject's movement.
	OUTDOOR	This mode is used for photographing outdoor action pictures. Picture will be taken with a fast shutter speed and assumes outdoor lighting.
	INDOOR	This mode is used for photographing indoor action pictures. Both the ISO sensitivity and shutter speed are increased to prevent blurring for indoor photographing.
	CREATIVE	This mode allows the user to adjust the picture's shutter speed to allow for fast-moving objects to appear "frozen" in position for maximum sharpness or with some blurring for a more creative picture.

Table 4-7: The predefined scene modes available for the Sports Mode

Scenery Mode

Scenery Mode (figure 4-18) is used for a variety of landscape scenes, most outdoors and requiring a greater depth of field and capturing a variety of colors. This mode has the scenarios listed in table 4-8.

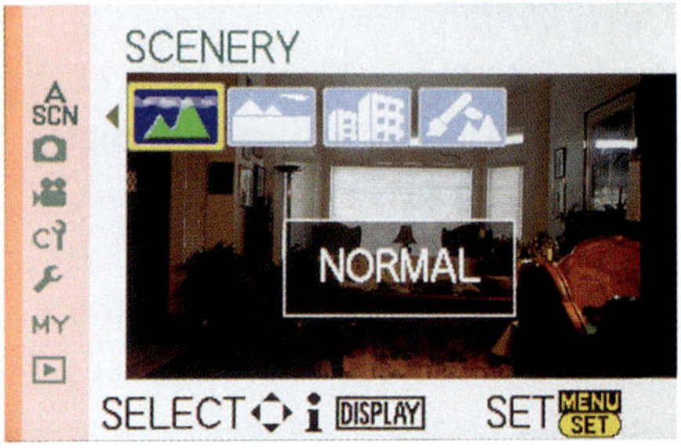

Figure 4-18: The Scenery Mode options with the NORMAL predefined scene mode selected

Screen Icon	Predefined Scene Mode	Description
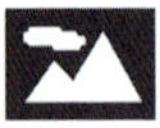	NORMAL	This mode's camera settings help to create a sufficient depth of field to capture the depth and vastness of a normal landscape scene.
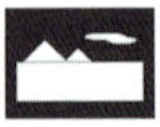	NATURE	This mode is the best setting for capturing natural scenery images. The focus is broad and covers the complete scene.
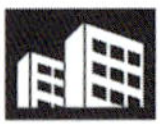	ARCHITECTURE	This mode displays the guidelines according to the MENU/SET>REC>CUSTOM>GUDIE LINE option setting. The displayed guidelines help the user to center and/or align the subject.
	CREATIVE	This mode allows the user to adjust the picture's shutter speed to allow for fast moving objects to be captured clearly or with some blurring for a more creative resulting picture.

Table 4-8: The predefined scene modes available for the Scenery Mode

Portrait Mode

Portrait Mode (table 4-9, figure 4-19) should be used when you are taking a picture or video containing at least one person. Face Detection is enabled for both pictures and videos, so the camera will find and set focus on the face. In addition, Face Recognition functionality is enabled when you're taking pictures. When a face has been detected, the camera's software will also search through its maximum six registered faces to see if there is a match. If so, the person's registered name and age will be displayed with the image and resulting picture.

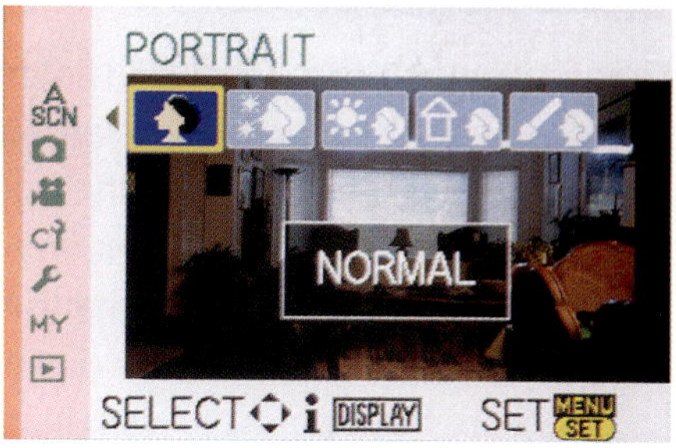

Figure 4-19: The Portrait Mode options with the the NORMAL predefined scene mode selected

Screen Icon	Predefined Scene Mode	Description
	NORMAL	This mode shades the background and adjusts the image to better capture the subject's skin tones.
	SOFT SKIN	This mode smoothes out the exposed skin much like airbrushing. Note: Part of the background will also be smoothed out if its coloring is close to the subject's skin color.
	OUTDOOR	This mode prevents the subject's image from appearing to be in shadows and too dark to recognize.
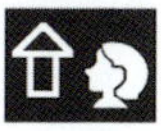	INDOOR	This mode sets the ISO sensitivity to ensure that the image is in focus with proper lighting.
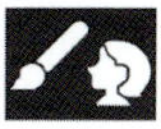	CREATIVE	This mode allows the user to set the camera's aperture to create background blurring for an artistic resulting picture.

Table 4-9: The predefined scene modes available for the Portrait Mode

Quick Menu

Going through the extensive list of menu commands using the MENU/SET button to change your image's settings can be cumbersome. The task is simplified and quickened by using the Quick Menu option. It simplifies command selection by listing only the most important commands and their values and enabling you to make setting changes. The Quick Menu is available in Intelligent Auto and all of the mode dial options except My Color.

There are three points to keep in mind when using Quick Menu. First, the Quick Menu option can be activated in two ways. You can press the Q.MENU button on the upper-right side on the back of camera (figure 4-20a) or you can touch the Q.MENU icon on the LCD screen (figure 4-20b). Both will display the Quick Menu data on the LCD screen.

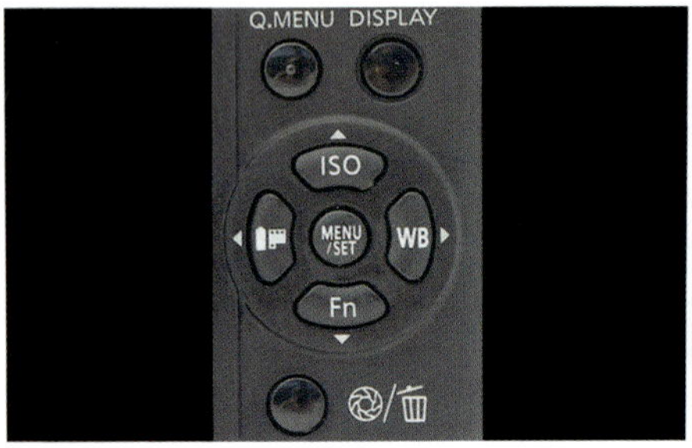

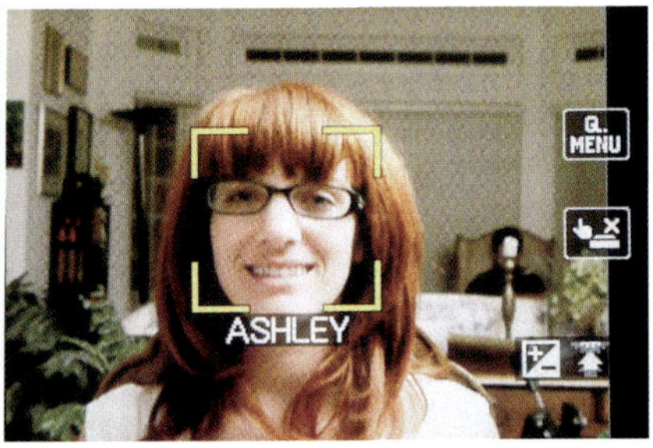

Figure 4-20a: Q.MENU button on the back of the camera;
Figure 4-20b: Q.MENU icon located on the LCD screen

To display the touch Q.MENU icon on the LCD screen, ensure the following command is set:

MENU/SET>CUSTOM>(pg 6) TOUCH Q.MENU>[ON]

Second, as covered in chapter 3, how you navigate through the Quick Menu data will depend on how you entered Quick Menu, the value chosen for the LCD DISP.STYLE command, and your chosen data display screen format. If you used the Q.MENU button on the back of the camera, you can use either the directional arrow buttons or the touch screen. If you initiate the Quick Menu mode using the touch Q.MENU icon on the LCD screen, you must use the touch screen method to navigate through the Quick Menu data.

The LCD screen's display style (MENU/SET>CUSTOM>(pg 4) LCD DISP. STYLE) dictates some of the navigation rules. The LCD Monitor style displays the Quick Menu options with the selected option's available values in a drop-down list. The Viewfinder style displays only the Quick Menu options. To see the selected option's values, you will need to push the MENU/SET button or push in the rear dial. To navigate through the available options, use the up and down directional arrow buttons or rotate the rear dial. As always, experiment with the different styles and determine what works best for you.

Regardless of which data display screen format you had selected for displaying your image's command criteria, you will be presented with only two Quick Menu screen formats: (1) Quick Menu data along with the image's settings displayed across the top of the display screen and (2) the LCD Info Display format.

The third point covers what Quick Menu displays. What you see on the LCD screen will be based on the selected mode dial option. If a command option is not available for editing for the selected mode, it will not be displayed on the Quick Menu.

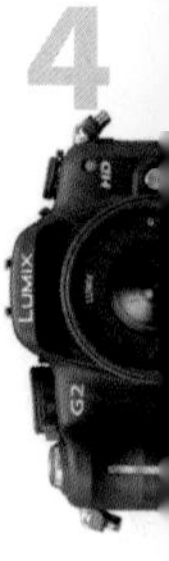

Recommendations

It is not always obvious what is going on within the camera's software when in Intelligent Auto Mode or one of the predefined scene modes. We recommend that you review your work and evaluate your photographs to determine if the results satisfy your needs. Check out the camera command setting nuances for a specific predefined scene mode. You can always view the image's camera settings through the selected data display screen format as described in chapter 3. You can also review the camera settings after the fact through the Playback Review button. Keep in mind that the camera's software is doing a best guess and implementing decisions based on what is considered to be a "typical picture." Just because the Intelligent Auto or predefined scene modes determine your camera's settings, it doesn't mean you can't make some adjustments of your own.

We recommend that you review the image's histogram display to determine whether the exposure appears optimum. You can always activate the Exposure Compensation scale and make exposure adjustments while taking pictures. Again, play with this tool and see what changes it makes to your resulting pictures. Experiment with your options. You can view the available camera commands through the Quick Menu or through the menu controls using the MENU/SET button. Play with them and become familiar with how they will change your picture-taking experience.

If the results are satisfactory, you may decide that there is no need to learn more about the camera or photography. However, we believe you will grow out of using these scene modes and will wish to explore using the camera semi-automatically or manually. Your picture and video camera settings become the building blocks to the semi-automatic and manual processes covered in chapters 5 and 6. Panasonic has done an excellent job at making sure what you learn when you first start using the camera is useful later on as you explore more of the camera's capabilities and your picture and video recording creativity.

Taking Partial Control of the Camera

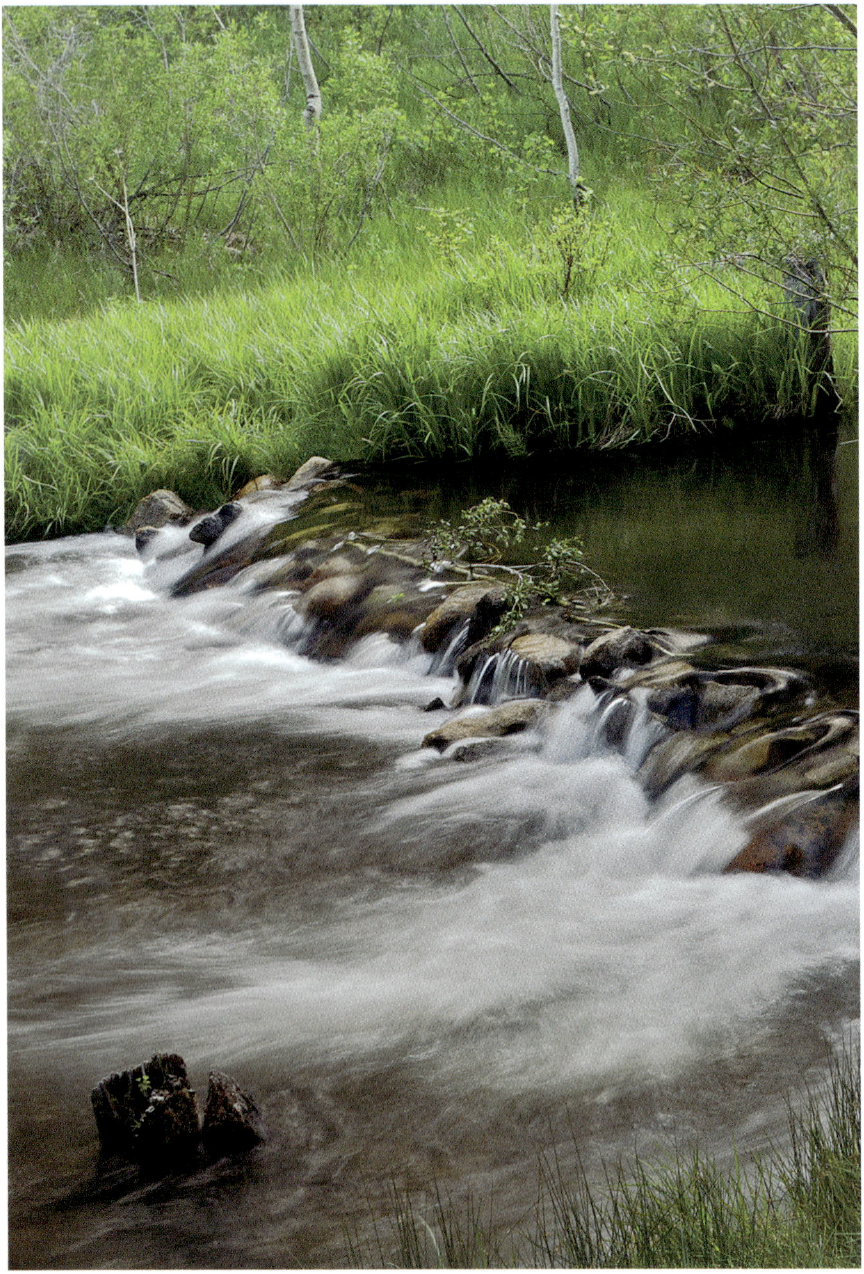

5

Introduction: Taking Partial Control

This chapter is about starting to take over the operation of the camera and using your own settings. You will still use some automatic operations but you will be conscious of how automation will affect your image. The major advantage of operating the camera this way is that you will always be aware of what settings are being used to take the picture. When you're using the Intelligent Auto Mode or predefined scene modes, many of the selected camera settings are hidden. For example, the majority of these commands set the camera's ISO automatically. The camera will increase the sensor's sensitivity to ensure that a fast enough shutter speed is selected to prevent camera motion from blurring the image. When using the camera semi automatically, this safety net will not be in operation. Experience rather than reliance on the camera's software will dictate camera settings.

This chapter involves shifting the mode dial on the top of the camera off the automated predefined scene modes and selecting one of the following: S, A, P, or M (figure 5-1). We will discuss the S, A, and P Modes in this chapter and the M Mode in chapter 6. Panasonic uses the letters AE as an abbreviation for automatic exposure and it cites them as Shutter-Priority AE Mode, Aperture-Priority AE Mode and Program AE Mode. We will refer to them simply as Shutter-Priority (S), Aperture-Priority (A) and Program (P) Mode, respectively.

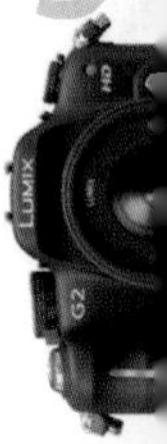

Three Semi-automatic AE Modes: Shutter-Priority (S), Aperture-Priority (A), Program (P)

Using the S, A, and P Modes gives you greater control over the camera. Unlike with the predefined scene modes or Intelligent Auto Mode, you can select the shutter speed, aperture, WB, or ISO. This will allow you greater artistic control in creating the image; however, there is an increased risk in selecting a setting that will detract from the image quality.

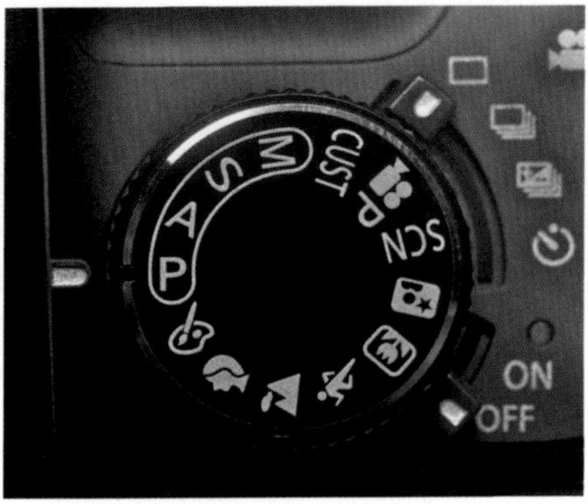

Figure 5-1: The mode dial is the largest knob on the top of the camera. Note: the P Mode is selected

Shutter-Priority (S) Mode

When you turn the mode dial to S, you have selected the Shutter-Priority Mode. In this mode, you set the shutter speed while the camera selects the aperture for a proper exposure. Photographers who shoot action sequences and worry that a slow shutter speed may blur the image of a moving object prefer this mode. When S Mode is selected, the letter S appears in the lower-left corner of the display screen with the shutter speed number glowing yellow (figure 5-2a). If you turn the rear dial, this number changes. The yellow number 5 in figure 5-2a refers to the camera set at 1/5 second exposure and under your control when turning the rear dial. Pressing the shutter-release button halfway reveals the aperture number that the camera has selected for the photograph (figure 5-2b). If the exposure is incorrect, you can easily see and correct this. The view on the display screen will be either too bright or too dark, with the histogram indicating either over- or underexposure. To correct this, press in the rear dial to activate the Exposure Compensation tool, changing the Exposure Compensation scale's color to yellow.

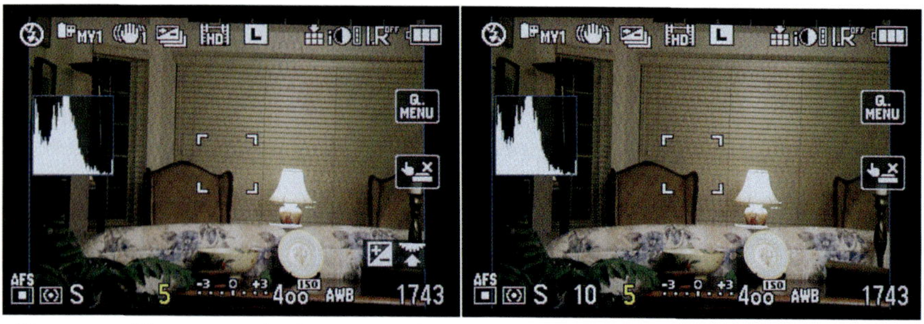

Figure 5-2a: The camera display screen when set to Shutter-Priority (S) Mode. Note the S on the lower-left corner; Figure 5-2b: The display screen showing the camera is set for f/10 (the number 10 displayed in white)

When you are changing the exposure with Exposure Compensation, your shutter speed stays fixed, but the lens aperture opens or closes. As you rotate the rear dial, you will see tick marks extend beneath the Exposure Compensation scale as you lighten or darken the displayed image (figure 5-3a). The histogram's color will change from white to yellow, and its position and shape in its box will change. Unfortunately, if you exceed the lens minimum or maximum aperture, this changing data will be incorrect. Suppose you are at f/16, the minimum aperture of the lens, and you apply underexposure requiring the lens to be set to f/22. All of the previously mentioned indications for underexposure will appear—the darkening of the screen, the extension of the tick marks under the Exposure Compensation scale, and the shifting of the histogram to the left. This makes it seem as if you had exceeded the lens minimum aperture. You will not notice until you press the shutter-release button fully to fire the camera. At this point, the camera will not fire and the shutter speed and aperture numbers turn red and start blinking.

As mentioned in chapter 3, the Exposure Meter (EXPO.METER command) will show valid shutter speed and aperture settings for the image (figure 5-3b). It displays the limits of your shutter speed and lens aperture and you can see when you exceed the lens's or camera's capabilities making the EXPO. METER command very useful.

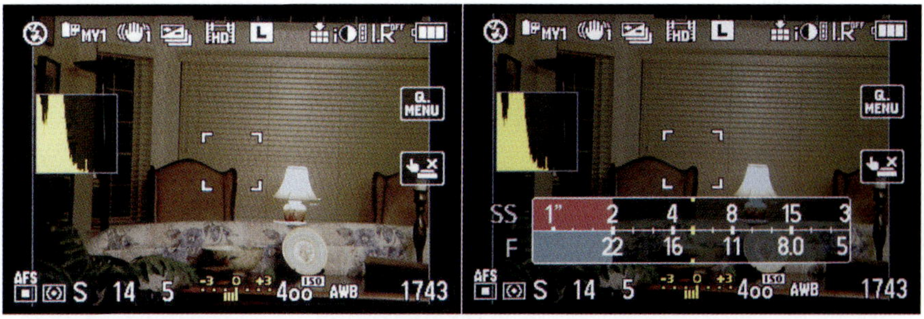

Figure 5-3a: The Exposure Compensation scale turns yellow when activated. Here it is set for -1 f-stop or underexposure; Figure 5-3b: When Exposure Meter is activated, a dual row of numbers indicating the allowable aperture and shutter speed combinations displays

Shutter speed awareness is important for two reasons. The most obvious reason is in action photography when you freeze the motion of a rapidly moving event. A fast shutter speed of 1/500 of a second or faster is desirable when "freezing" a rapidly moving athlete. Conversely, using a slow shutter speed, for example, will blur the details of a rapidly moving object. With experience, you can attempt to combine the two effects by choosing a shutter speed that causes only parts of the image to be blurred (figure 5-4a, figure 5-4b). As an example, a stream can be rendered with rapidly moving water appearing as a blur while slower moving eddies appear more defined with the stationary rocks and grass razor sharp.

The second reason is the need to have a fast shutter speed to overcome the inherent jittering that occurs when you handhold a camera to take a picture. Under these conditions, a shutter speed slower than 1/30 of a second may capture your normal body movements, blurring the subject's fine detail. The camera has a "jitter" icon warning you that the shutter speed is too slow for reliable handholding of the camera when shooting. When this icon appears, you should increase the light or raise the ISO so you can use a faster shutter speed. Another option is to stabilize the camera by mounting it on a tripod.

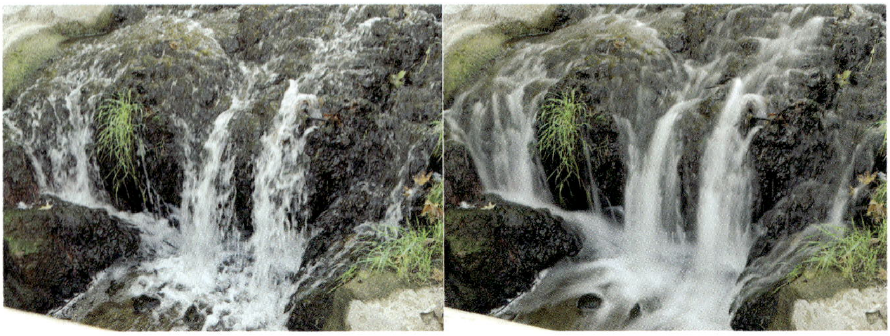

Figure 5-4a: A small stream recorded with a shutter speed of 1/80 of a second; Figure 5-4b: The impression of movement is enhanced when using a longer shutter speed (0.5 second)

Anomalous Behavior of Exposure Compensation and False Information

Hopefully, by the time this book goes to press, the description of the anomalous behavior of the Exposure Compensation control will be corrected by a firmware update for the Panasonic G2. We expected that, as you exceed the limit of the lens aperture setting, you wouldn't be able to turn the rear dial and see a change in the Exposure Compensation scale, the position and shape of the histogram display, and the continuing change in brightness of the display. This behavior is unexpected, and we hope that it will be corrected in future models of the Panasonic G2 or in a BIOS update.

Aperture-Priority (A) Mode

Aperture-Priority (A) Mode is the converse of S Mode. You select the aperture and the camera selects the shutter speed. This mode is used when controlling the depth of field is critical for image composition. For example, in close-up photography, depth of field is narrow, and if the lens aperture is opened, the decreased depth of field can blur parts of the image. This is better managed by using A Mode. Turning the rear dial changes the lens aperture. To activate Exposure Compensation, press in the rear dial. Unlike with S Mode, the aperture value is maintained but the shutter speed changes as you apply over- or underexposure to the camera's recommendation.

As before, you know which function is active by studying the display. In figure 5-5a, you will see the letter A in the lower-left corner of the display indicating you are using A Mode. The yellow colored 6.3 indicates the aperture you have set and that is under the control of the rear dial. Pressing the shutter-release button halfway reveals the number 25 in white, indicating the shutter speed. When you're controlling the aperture, its number is highlighted in yellow. When you're controlling Exposure Compensation, its scale is colored yellow.

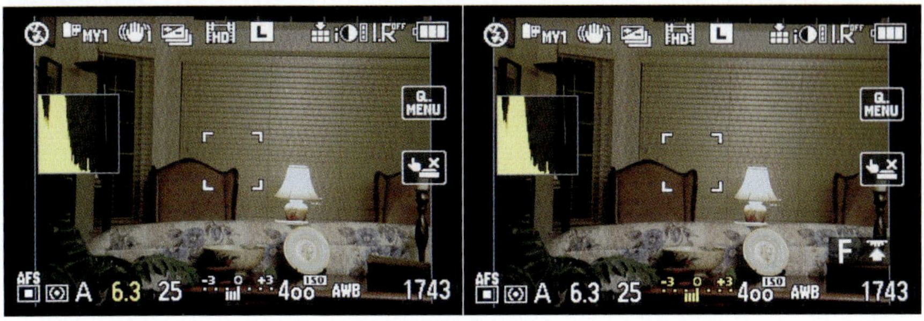

Figure 5-5a: A Mode is selected. The camera's aperture is f/6.3 with a shutter speed 25 (1/25 second); Figure 5-5b: Exposure Compensation is active and set to provide 1 f-stop underexposure

A Mode is most valuable when using an older lens lacking an electronic coupling to the camera body. This includes manual focus lenses where focusing requires turning a ring connected to a helical gearing system to move the lens as well as an aperture ring that opens and closes an iris diaphragm. Even though they are regarded as a sophisticated lens design, such optics are regarded as obsolete.

Most modern digital cameras are not designed to work with these types of lenses. Judging focus with the optical viewfinder of modern cameras is almost impossible because of the low magnification of the view and the granularity of the focusing screen. The latter obscures fine details, and this defect increases as one stops down a lens of older design. In contrast, the Panasonic viewfinder provides a high magnification bright view, making it easier to focus such lenses.

When using the A Mode, the Panasonic G2 provides automatic exposure when used with microscopes and telescopes. Under these conditions you cannot control the lens aperture from the camera body with the rear dial. Varying the shutter speed makes the A Mode the tool to use to control exposure when using these nonstandard devices.

Program (P) Mode

Program (P) Mode is similar to Intelligent Auto Mode and the other automatic modes because it sets both shutter speed and aperture, but there is an important difference. You are in complete control of both. You will have to make the decision whether a fast or slow shutter speed is preferred or if the aperture should be opened or closed. There is a function, Program Shift, which allows you to shift both aperture and shutter speed without varying the exposure.

Remember, to maintain exposure, there is a commensurate change between shutter speed and aperture. If you change one control, the other must change to maintain constant exposure. Program Shift allows you to vary the shutter speed with a commensurate change of the aperture, or vice versa, while maintaining exposure. An icon consisting of a double-arrowed diagonal line is displayed with the P on the display screen when you are using Program Shift.

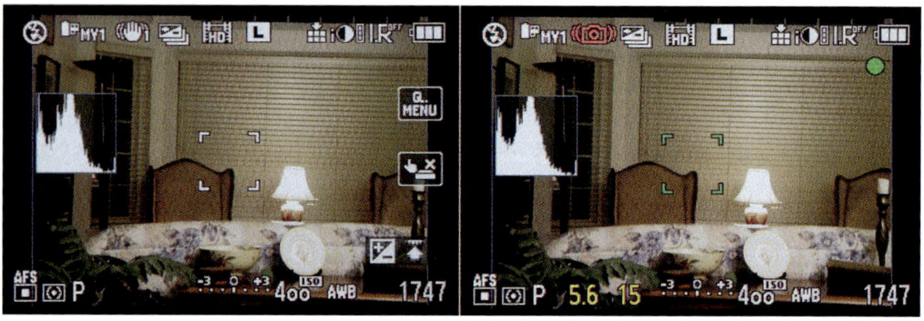

Figure 5-6a: When P Mode selected, shutter speed and aperture are not initially display on the screen; Figure 5-6b: After you press the shutter-release button halfway, the aperture (f/5.6) and the shutter speed (1/15 second), become visible

The letter P in the lower-left corner of the display screen reminds you that you are in P Mode (figure 5-6a); however, you do not know what aperture or shutter speed has been set until you press the shutter-release button halfway. Then two sets of numbers appear in yellow (figure 5-6b). If you rotate the rear dial, the Program Shift icon (double-arrowed diagonal line) appears next to the P, and the numbers change in value. Exposure is not affected since a change to shutter speed is balanced by a commensurate change to the aperture.

Exposure Compensation is also available within the P Mode, but with an interesting aspect. As you apply increasing or decreasing compensation, the camera alternates between changing its aperture and changing its shutter speed. This alteration ceases only when the aperture limit for the lens is reached, then the camera changes only its shutter speed. This is consistent with the reasoning that neither the aperture nor the shutter speed has higher priority.

Recommendations

Of the three modes, S, A, and P, which should you use? Generally, for day-to-day photography we select the P Mode. This sets both the aperture and shutter speed and it provides us with the greatest flexibility in using the camera. In this mode, the camera tries to select a fast enough shutter speed suitable for taking sharp pictures when handholding the camera.

When we work with subjects where the depth of field is critical, we prefer using the A Mode. Thus, in close-up work where we want enough depth of field to maintain sharpness around the subject, we like to be in control of the aperture. In this case we often work with f/16 and do not care to open the aperture wider than this. We also use A Mode in portrait work with a different goal. We want to narrow the depth of field and ensure that only the model's face lies within it. The rationale is to blur foreground and background structures to concentrate the viewer's attention on the subject's face. In addition, we use the camera with several nonstandard lenses and optical devices. A Mode provides automatic exposure by varying the shutter speed when using these devices.

We work in S Mode when we need to control the appearance of motion. In action photography, we will use a fast shutter speed to freeze motion. Also, when we feel creative and wish to blur the subject's outline to suggest rapid motion, we will adjust the shutter speed down a bit to give the subject some blurring.

There are a lot of creative choices you can make when using these three modes that are unavailable when using Intelligent Auto Mode or any of the predefined scene modes. The following sections will give you more options and help you understand how to take over more control of the camera and tailor your shots more to your liking.

ISO

Earlier, we referred to ISO as the gain control for the sensor. Functionally, an increase in ISO increases the sensor's sensitivity to light so that for a given shutter speed or aperture, it can record a dimmer scene. This increases your photographic options. Obviously, it will extend your capability by allowing you to take pictures at lower light levels. When photographing sports, raising the ISO increases the camera's sensitivity to light, so for a given f-stop, you can use a higher shutter speed. This enables you to capture a sharp image of a rapidly moving subject. Contrariwise, it allows you to maintain the highest-quality work by setting the ISO to 100. At this sensitivity, the camera renders the best images, and many scenic photographers insist on working at this gain level to obtain the sharpest images.

The ISO screen (figure 5-7a) is conveniently displayed by pressing the ISO button which doubles as the up directional arrow button. Once displayed, using either the left and right directional arrow buttons, or the rear dial changes the ISO value.

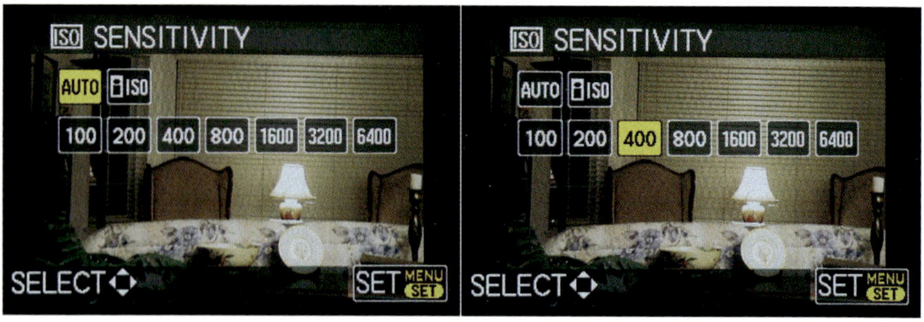

Figure 5-7a: The ISO screen shows the active value, AUTO, highlighted in yellow; Figure 5-7b: The ISO value can be quickly selected. Here it is set to ISO 400

ISO INCREMENTS

There are several ways to control ISO. It all starts by pressing the button labeled ISO on the back of the camera. Doing this brings up the ISO menu on the display screen. A series of numbers (ISO values) are displayed. Generally, there are two formats for displaying this data. One is to display in full f-stop increments so that you will see the numbers 100-200-400-800-1600-3200-6400. The other option is to display ISO values in 1/3 f-stop increments, expanding the number of choices to include two intermediate values between each of the previous values. So using just the range 100 to 400; you will see 100, 125, 160, 200, 250, 320, and 400.

The displayed ISO values are controlled by the following command:

MENU/SET>REC>(pg 3) ISO INCREMENTS>[1/3 EV], [1 EV]

where EV stands for Exposure Value.

Which value to use? We tend to use the 1 EV value setting—with fewer numbers displayed. It is faster to set the camera's ISO to the desired value and the difference in image quality between 1/3 EV steps, such as 100 to 125, while measurable, is for us practically negligible.

Letting the Camera Set the ISO

AUTO ISO

Along with selecting a specific ISO from the displayed ISO values, there are two additional settings: AUTO ISO and iISO (Intelligent ISO). AUTO ISO, as the name implies, adjusts the camera sensitivity automatically. Essentially, when ambient light levels are low, the camera raises its ISO so you can use a higher shutter speed. A higher shutter speed increases your chances of getting a sharp photograph when handholding the camera. If the setting is too dim to speed up the shutter to faster than 1/30 second, you are going to have to mount the camera on a tripod or accept some blurring on the resulting picture. If the camera thinks you are using too slow of a shutter speed, the camera jitter icon will appear, which is your signal to switch to a flash or a tripod.

You can set a ceiling on how high AUTO ISO increases the camera's sensitivity. Remember, as ISO increases, image quality degrades and setting an upper ISO limit is your safety net to keep you from getting an unsatisfactory image. If you feel image quality is unacceptable at ISO 1600, you can set the limit to 800 and be assured the camera will not use a setting that provides unacceptable results. Remember that many users claim image degradation is barely discernible at ISO 400 and starts being discernible at ISO 800. Thus, the most demanding photographer will set the limit to 400 while another photographer, willing to accept some image quality loss, will set it to 800 or even higher. To limit how high AUTO can set the ISO, use the following command:

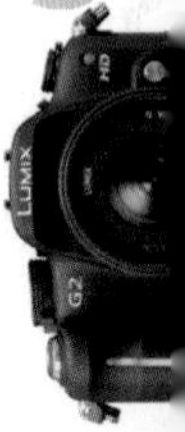

MENU/SET>REC>(pg 3) ISO LIMIT SET>[OFF], [200], [400], [800], [1600]

A legitimate question is, how high should the limit be set? Unfortunately, there is no definitive answer. The upper limit can be established only by personal use and experience. We had recommended 400 and 800 as a starting point with the assumption that most people will find 1600 unacceptable. But these guidelines are conservative, and they assume that you will be enlarging the image to make 8″ x 10″ prints. If you are using the camera for sending email attachments and the picture appears as a 3″ x 4″ image on the recipient's monitor, you may be very pleased by the camera's performance at ISO 800, or even higher.

iISO

Another selection that you see appear on the display screen after pressing the ISO button is Panasonic's Intelligent ISO (iISO). This is similar to AUTO ISO in that it will raise the camera's ISO in response to lower light situations, but it differs in that it also raises the shutter speed to prevent subject movement from blurring the image. This option, unique to Panasonic cameras, assumes you want to capture moving objects with maximum sharpness. You cannot use this option if you set the camera to S Mode, which locks the shutter speed to the value you set using the rear dial.

> **ISO and Image Degradation: Our Recommendation**
>
> The most obvious defect introduced by raising the ISO is noise—this is the granular appearance of blotches of color within regions that should have a smooth tone. Many reviews on the Internet, as well as messages from photographers on online forums, have commented that the Four Thirds and Micro Four Thirds cameras have higher levels of noise than APS or full-frame cameras. Admittedly, the Panasonic G2 has more noise at ISO 1600 or higher than the DSLRs made by Nikon and Canon.
>
> Rather than avoid shooting at these higher ISOs, experiment and find out for yourself the performance limits of your camera. If your goal is to make images strictly for Web use, you might be pleasantly surprised that the quality of your Panasonic G2 camera at ISO 1600 is acceptable for this work. We have been using an upper limit of ISO 1600 and have been pleased with the results. For critical work, we make sure we shoot in RAW and use third-party software (Noise Ninja) to help reduce the effects of noise. In comparison to images from our Nikon D300, the Panasonic G2 image is noisier, but its quality is good and it is by no means unusable.

Intelligent Exposure: Taming Extremes in Brightness

An unusual command is I.EXPOSURE (Intelligent Exposure Adjustment). You will not find it when you press the ISO button; rather you activate it by going into the REC menu (see the command at end of this paragraph). This setting adjusts both ISO and contrast. Its role is to take an image with a wide range of intensities and render it so details are retained in both the shadows and highlights. However, this command is capricious. Even though it is enabled in the menu, that does not guarantee that it will work on every image. In fact, there are reports on the Internet and in review articles that users cannot see its effects. These observations are due to its failure to be activated by the scene. Its effects are seen only when it detects large areas within an image that are very bright and large areas that are very dark, and it decides that these extremes are sufficient to justify a reduction in contrast.

Typically, we have not seen it work when the subject is illuminated from a light source behind the camera. Instead, we have seen it work when we are facing the light source and portions of it are included in the scene along with the deep shadows it generates from the subject—for example, shooting an interior with sunlight coming through a window. When these conditions are met, the command is executed and the photographer will see the I.EXPOSURE icon on the display screen change color from white to yellow after pressing the shutter-release button halfway.

The reduction in contrast is graded. If the command is set too low, the reduction in contrast is the least, while setting the command to high provides the greatest reduction. This command works on RAW and JPEG files. However, much of its effect on JPEG files appears to be due to image processing prior to saving the file. When you're viewing the RAW file, its effects are modest and its benefit arises from raising the ISO so details buried in the shadows become apparent. Thus, when you're reviewing the saved files on a computer, the greatest effect will be in the JPEG saved files. Do not be surprised if this command seems dormant—for most subjects, you will not see the results of its effects. The I.EXPOSURE command is as follows:

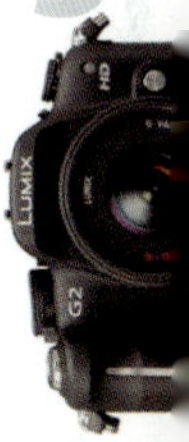

MENU/SET>REC>(pg 3) I.EXPOSURE>[OFF], [LOW], [STANDARD], [HIGH]

This command is unavailable in the Intelligent Auto and predefined scene modes.

To Use or Not to Use Intelligent Exposure Adjustment

When taking still photographs, we do not use Intelligent Exposure Adjustment. We work with RAW files and obtain equivalent effects with software. Indeed, because the files can be leisurely studied on a large monitor, we believe our results are just as good and, in some cases, superior to what we would get if we had allowed the camera to do the reduction in contrast. For our work, we found the Intelligent Exposure Adjustment command more useful for video recording.

	A Mode	S Mode	P Mode	M Mode	Intelligent Auto Mode
Manual ISO	X	X	X	X	
Auto ISO	X	X	X	X	
Intelligent ISO	X		X	X	X
Intelligent Exposure	X	X	X	X	

Table 5-1: Chart showing the relation between ISO settings and exposure modes

Commands That Affect Sensitivity

There is no single ISO setting that operates in all the camera's exposure modes (table 5-1). For example, Intelligent ISO will operate in most modes except in S Mode. Intelligent Exposure will work in most modes but not in Intelligent Auto Mode.

Recommendations

When we are out in the field and using the camera to capture spontaneous outdoor shots, we generally use the P Mode and AUTO ISO. It provides many of the conveniences of using Intelligent Auto Mode but allows us to retain control of many of the important camera functions. For example, we retain control of the automatic focusing mode. We usually set the camera to 1-area-focusing (chapter 2).

When photographing an outdoor scene, we set the camera's ISO to a specific value depending on the quality that we desire in the photograph. For daylight scenes, ranging from early morning to late sunset, we typically use ISO 100, and when the light levels drop, we will either mount the camera on the tripod or use the electronic flash.

For low-light work while handholding the camera, we will raise the ISO to 1600—for example, when photographing students in a high school stage production. Although there is degradation in image quality and noticeable noise, we feel the sacrifice in quality is acceptable. To minimize the loss of quality, we will save the images in RAW format and post-process the results using advanced noise reduction software, such as Noise Ninja, to reduce the effects of noise in our pictures.

We have not found iISO useful for our style of picture taking—we prefer to be aware of subject movement and select a shutter speed to provide a specific effect. We frequently will use a fast shutter speed of 1/500 of a second or faster to freeze motion and generate a sharp image of the subject. Other times, we will set the shutter speed to 1/60 of a second to create a blurring effect.

For example, at a track event, we pan the camera, keeping a runner in the center of the frame, and fire at this slow shutter speed so the background becomes blurred. This blurring of the background and the runner's feet gives an impression of speed and motion to the viewer. When photographing streams, we will sometimes use a slow shutter speed (several seconds) to generate an ethereal effect on the moving water.

Such effects require using a tripod and remote release to prevent camera movement. In addition, we have not been using I.EXPOSURE either. Because of the menu command's unpredictable nature, we have preferred to control the camera's operation to generate a specific image output rather than have the camera take control of the final image's appearance.

White Balance

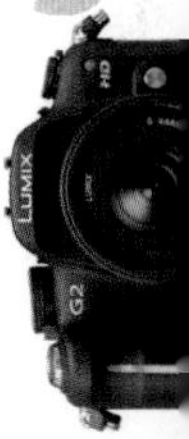

In chapter 2, we mentioned that the human eye and brain combined are remarkably capable in accurately identifying colors illuminated by different light sources. That is to say, a green leaf appears the same whether it is outdoors, illuminated by direct sunlight, lying in the shade cast by the side of the building, or indoors and illuminated by a desk lamp.

Each of these scenarios has a unique illuminant whose ratio of red to blue light differs—the light in the shaded side of the building having the highest percentage of blue, sunlight has a lower percentage, and indoor incandescent light has the lowest. A digital camera records accurately the differing tints from a leaf reflecting the light from these different sources and records it in different colors. These variations in appearance are aesthetically disturbing even if they are an accurate representation.

To record colors as we perceive them, the camera has to be calibrated to the light source and, in effect, be told what the light source is. You can dial in the light source manually; however, this is inconvenient and, if you dial in the wrong light source, can result in an image with horrible colors. This was especially true with DSLRs relying on optical viewfinders. The photographer would fail to notice his mistake until he studied the saved image. To get around this problem, camera designers have cleverly created a means for the camera to calibrate itself to the light. It essentially analyzes all the colors it receives and, by determining what the average color should be, makes a "best guess estimate" on the identity of the light source. This is what occurs when the camera is set for Automatic White Balance (AWB) (figure 5-8a). For the most part, it does a good job and the majority of scenes are recorded with pleasing colors. For most of the camera's operation, the user sets it for AWB. But like all sampling and statistical techniques, it can be fooled and the Panasonic G2 provides you with tools to override this automatic function.

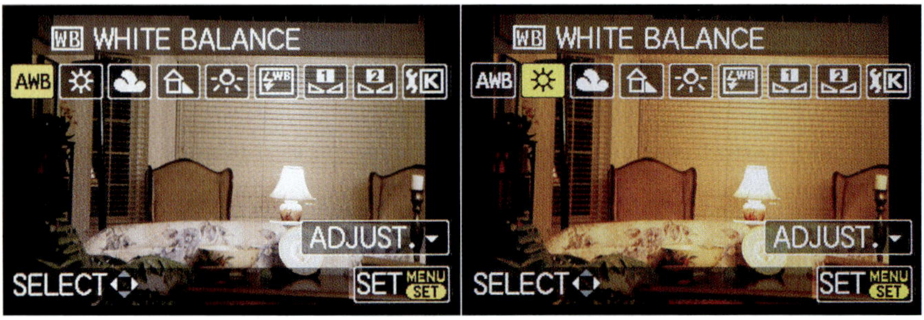

5

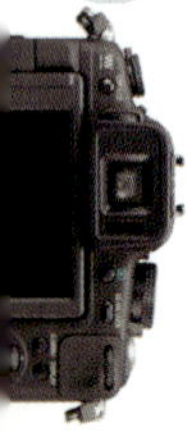

Figure 5-8a: The display screen after pressing the WB (right directional arrow) button. Note AWB is selected. Figure 5-8b: White balance for a preselected setting. Note daylight is selected

When you start using the camera manually, you turn off AWB by presetting it to the light source. By pressing the right directional arrow button labeled WB on the right side of the back of the camera, you will see on the display screen icons representing different light sources. Use the left and right directional arrow buttons to move the yellow box to different icons. In figure 5-8b, the selection box is shifted to the icon representing daylight. Table 5-2 provides the Preset White Balance icons and the type of lighting that they should be used with.

Open Sunlight	Overcast Skies	Shade	Indoor Light	Electronic Flash
		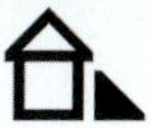		

Table 5-2: The Preset White Balance icons and the light source they represent

To use an image's lighting icon, follow these steps:

1. Press the WB button on the back of the camera (right directional arrow button).
2. Select the icon representing the image's light source: Either touch the icon or highlight it using the directional arrow buttons or turning the rear dial.
3. To accept the changed setting, touch the SET icon on the display screen, press the shutter-release button halfway, or press the MENU/ SET button.

The icons in table 5-2 provide a mnemonic for the possible light sources, making them easy to remember. However, they only serve as a rough guide of the illuminant's color. For example, the Indoor Light icon assumes that all such lights are a specific bulb type that emits a specific color. In fact, indoor bulbs can have a color temperature of up to several hundred K (kelvin). Depending on the voltage applied, a bulb can burn with a ruddy red light or a more brilliant white light. In the case of overcast skies, the light color is dependent on the extent and type of cloud cover. For those who need to be precise in setting these values, you need to use the color temperature scale.

5

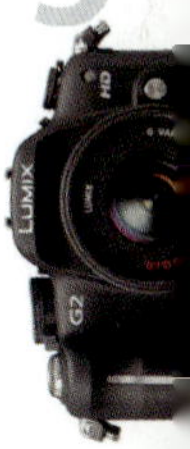

Color Temperature Scale	Calibrating to a White Source: Select Icon 1 or Icon 2	
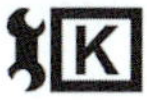		

Table 5-3: Icons for quantitatively setting color temperature

In the WB screen the letter K is on the icon for the color temperature scale (table 5-3). Chemists and physicists know this stands for kelvin and provides a quantitative way of specifying color temperature. Rather than discuss the scientific and physical basis of the scale, it is sufficient to say it is a means of quantitatively measuring the color tint provided by the light source.

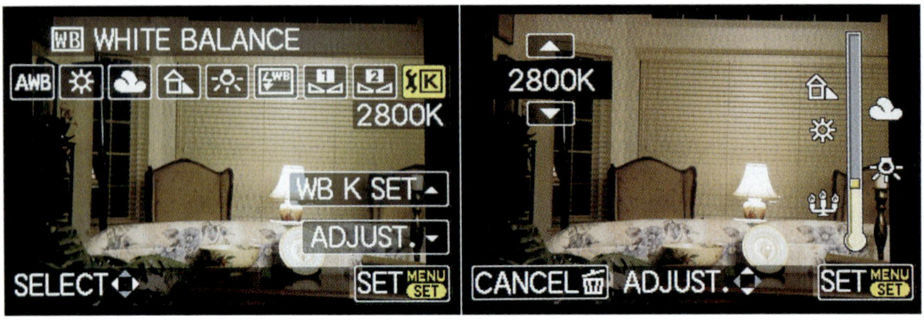

Figure 5-9a: Selecting the K icon for setting the color temperature to a numerical value; Figure 5-9b: The color temperature scale set to 2800 K

Follow these steps to use the color temperature scale:

1. Press the WB button on the back of the camera (right directional arrow button). Then highlight the icon for the color temperature scale (figure 5-9a). This can be accomplished by touching the icon with your finger or by using the directional arrow buttons or turning the rear dial. Select the icon by pressing the MENU/SET button or the up directional arrow button on the camera body. This results in a screen displaying a vertical line on the right side and a number sandwiched between an up and down arrow key (figure 5-9b).
2. Select the color temperature either by using the up or down directional arrow buttons or by touching the bar on the thermometer with your finger and raising or lowering the "temperature." The numbers on the left side of the screen will change according to height of the yellow "temperature" bar. The number will range from 2500 K to 10000 K.
3. When the number reaches the value you want, touch the SET icon on the display screen or press the MENU/SET button on the camera body.

Knowing the color temperature of the light source is necessary for using the color temperature scale. You must either measure this value with a color light meter—an expensive and relatively rare tool—or rely on the data provided by the manufacturer of the light source. Unfortunately many light sources are not so rated, and what can be frustrating is that incandescent bulbs do not maintain a constant light temperature. These bulbs age and the light become bluish. Also their color temperature is dependent on their operating current and the light becomes reddish with a drop in voltage. We used the color temperature scale most commonly in a science laboratory and a photography studio, where the color temperature of a light source is known and its value inputted accurately. For example, the tungsten illuminator on microscopes is rated at 3200 K, a value provided by the lamp manufacturer, and this is dialed into the camera's white balance scale. For those who need the utmost rigor in recording their data, this scale is invaluable. However, for the majority of us, it is of limited use, especially considering that there is, practically, an even better device for setting color temperature.

Our favorite method of setting color temperature calibrates the camera directly against the light source. You do not need to know the color temperature of your light source in K. All you need is a blank white sheet of paper. To set the camera's white balance, follow these steps:

1. Press the WB button on the back of the camera (right directional arrow button).
2. Highlight the icon for Calibrating to a White Source by using the touch screen, the rear dial or the right and left directional arrow buttons. There are two icons, one with the number 1 (figure 5-10a) and the other with the number 2. Each of the two icons will remember a calibration setting, so you will be able to store two settings.
3. Once the number 1 or 2 is highlighted, press the up directional arrow button to proceed to the next step.
4. The screen changes. The periphery is grayed out and a targeting rectangle with a yellow border becomes visible (figure 5-10b).
5. Aim the camera at the white sheet of paper, making sure the paper fills the targeting rectangle.
6. Touch the SET icon on the screen or press the MENU/SET button.

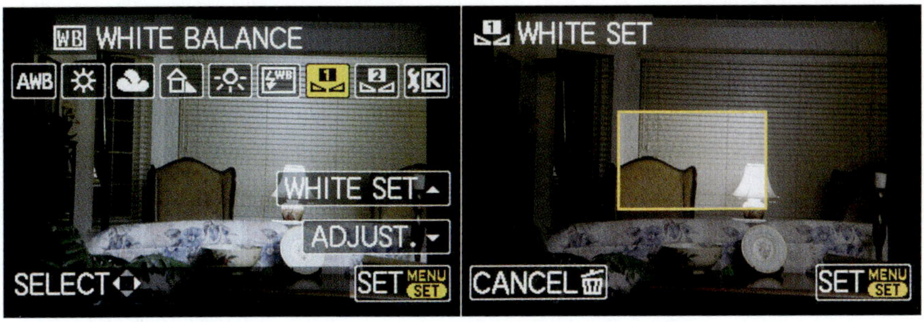

Figure 5-10a: White balance set to a previously calibrated value stored in Icon 1;
Figure 5-10b: Display screen to set calibration value

White balance is now set for the icon selected. It is also saved in the camera's memory and can be recalled when you next select Calibrating to a White Source 1 or 2 icon.

This operation calibrates the camera to the light source and stores this value in the selected Calibrating to a White Source memory icon. When you select these icons, the camera will use this calibration value for white balance. We found this procedure to be very reliable, and it has become our preferred method of manually adjusting the camera to the light source when it matters to be exact. When working with a microscope, we would remove the specimen from the field of view and calibrate against a clear region. The camera would then be calibrated to the light. We found it to be a more accurate adjustment; colored specimens were rendered better than when the camera was calibrated selecting the Kelvin setting. We presume this was due to an incorrect printed value for color temperature of the light source.

When available, color temperature values are for new bulbs. As a bulb ages, its glass envelope blackens, shifting its color to a blue tint. Manually setting the color temperature with the light source's original Kelvin setting does not take into account the progressive deterioration of the light source. Calibrating WB through the camera with the white paper process takes into account changes caused by the light source going bad. Using the calibration to a white source will eliminate bulb aging as a source of color temperature error.

Fine-Tuning WB

On occasion, the previous procedures may be imperfect for setting white balance. This can be true when using fluorescent lights or other light sources that do not provide a full spectrum of light. Under these conditions, there is a command for touching up white balance to your satisfaction. This operation, as well as color bracketing, will be covered in chapter 6.

RAW and JPEG

Earlier we recommended saving your files as both RAW and JPEG rather than selecting just one format. Each file format has its advantages. A major benefit in saving in RAW format is the ease with which white balance errors can be corrected outside of the camera. The Silkypix Developer Studio software included with your Panasonic G2 camera opens the RAW files. On the side screen, you will see a slider and a color temperature scale for fine-tuning the white balance (figure 5-11). The slider allows you to rapidly evaluate the different color temperature settings, simplifying this task if you had captured the subject with the wrong setting. Additionally, there is a pull-down menu

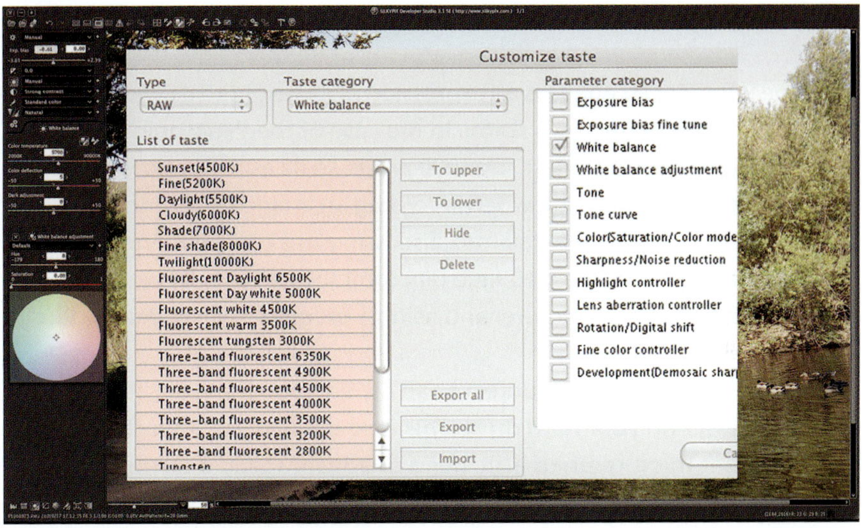

Figure 5-11: From Silkypix Developer Studio showing the controls for adjusting a RAW image file's color temperature

listing a variety of light sources, enabling you to find your illumination type. There are, for example, a dozen settings for a variety of fluorescent light bulbs. This illustrates the precision post processing software provides in adjusting color balance. If you open a JPEG file, this menu will be unavailable.

Recommendations

The majority of our photographs are taken with the AWB setting. The camera does a satisfactory job in rendering pleasing colors from subjects illuminated with different lighting styles. We have noted, however, that indoor lightning with incandescent lamps can throw off AWB. Under these conditions, our images have an orange-red hue. To obtain more neutral colors, we will use the WB setting for indoor lighting. For very difficult lighting conditions, where there are several different light sources—for example a mix of incandescent and fluorescent bulbs—we calibrate the white balance against a white sheet of paper.

Rarely do we preset the color temperature with the aid of the color temperature scale. At first, we used this method for studio work, close-up work with indoor lighting, or for microscope work. However, we abandoned this procedure and started using the Calibrating to a White Source setting.

Again, this is where we recommend saving the files in RAW format. Virtually all programs that read RAW files have a straightforward command for readjusting white balance when it is set incorrectly in the camera

Revisiting Format and Pixels

The aspect ratio of an image is an expression of its height to its width with the two numbers separated by a colon. In the case of the Panasonic G2 camera, its nominal image array is 4000 by 3000 pixels, so its aspect ratio is expressed as 4:3. You can alter this ratio when recording an image by setting the aspect ratio to 3:2, 16:9, or 1:1. We deferred discussing this topic until now because creating pictures with a desired ratio is accomplished easily by working on an image transferred to a computer and using a program such as Adobe Photoshop or GIMP software.

Basically, you crop your subject to an aspect ratio that suits its composition and save it on your hard drive. This is so easily done after the image is recorded that there seemed little need or advantage in describing how to do this in the camera. However, it is time to review this topic because you can, by specifying the aspect ratio beforehand, compose your image to fit within the frame. By doing this, you are excluding parts of the sensor from contributing to forming an image, thereby reducing the number of pixels saved. For example, when you use a 3:2 or a 16:9 format, you are not using portions of the top and bottom of the 4000 by 3000 pixel array sensor. The pixel arrays in these formats are respectively 4000 by 2672 pixels and 4000 by 2248 pixels. This reduces the number of pixels that are saved within the file. The aspect ratio is set with the following command:

MENU/SET>REC>ASPECT RATIO>[4:3], [16:9], [3:2], [1:1]

This option can shrink both your JPEG and RAW file size by using fewer pixels. Another means of shrinking the file is by using even fewer pixels by saving the JPEG files as medium or small. The reduction in pixels used for JPEG files can be seen in table 5-4. The decision to save an image at less than a 4000 by 3000 pixel array is efficient if your goal is to view the file on the computer or send it as an email attachment. For example, our laptop computer has a 17-inch display of 1920 by 1200 pixels. An image saved as 4000 by 3000 pixels cannot be displayed on our computer in its entirety—we can see only a fraction its area and much of the image, 2080 by 1800 pixels worth, will extend beyond the borders of the computer screen.

However, if you chose the option of saving a JPEG file at its smallest pixel array, you will have an image made up of 2048 by 1536 pixels. The resultant image is still too large to fit on the computer's screen, but it is a much better fit. So if a 4000 by 3000 pixels image file is used as an email attachment, half will not be displayed on the recipient's computer screen (assuming they are using the same size computer screen as you). But if the email attachment is made with the smallest JPEG file size, then almost all of it will be visible. The situation improves even more if you use a different aspect ratio—say 16:9—and save the file as S. This image will be 1920 by 1080 and it can be viewed in its entirety on the recipient's laptop screen only if the recipient screen size is greater than 1919 horizontal.

Another benefit of downsizing the pixel arrays is that the reduced file size facilitates sending picture files on the Internet. Smaller files can be sent and received faster.

Aspect Ratio 4:3		Aspect Ratio 3:2		Aspect Ratio 16:9		Aspect Ratio 1:1	
Size	**Pixel Array**	**Size**	**Pixel Array**	**Size**	**Pixel Array**	**Size**	**Pixel Array**
L 12M	4000 X 3000	L 10.5M	4000 X 2672	L 9M	4000 X 2248	L 9M	2992 X 2992
M 6M	2816 X 2112	M 5M	2816 X 1880	M 4.5M	2816 X 1584	M 4.5M	2112 X 2112
S 3M	2048 X 1536	S 2.5M	2048 X 1360	S 2M	1920 X 1080	S 2M	1504 X 1504

Table 5-4: Number of pixels (size) and the pixel array by aspect ratio. L, M, S refers to the file size controlled by the PICTURE SIZE command; M = megapixels when following a number

Another option for controlling JPEG file size is to compress it to varying degrees using MENU/SET>REC>QUALITY. When shooting JPEG, you have the option of saving it as Fine or Standard. Fine provides the highest image quality and larger file size, while Standard sacrifices image quality by reducing the file size in half.

So what are the benefits in being able to change the overall number of pixels or shrinking the JPEG file size by half. The first advantage is you can store more images on your memory card with the smaller files. This is obvious, but an even more important advantage in keeping the file size small is the increased efficiency when the camera is rapidly fired. When you're firing in Burst Mode of 3.2 images per second (BURST RATE = [H]), the images are stored in a fast but small memory buffer that can rapidly take in images. Once it is filled, offloading images is determined by how rapidly they can be cleared from this fast memory to the memory card, which takes in image files at a slower rate.

With large files, it may take only 7 to 8 images before the firing rate is reduced. To clear this memory buffer, the files have to be offloaded to your memory card, and since this is a slower process it becomes a bottleneck for capturing many images rapidly. Once the fast memory buffer is full, the camera will not fire until an image is written to the memory card.

The fast memory buffer can hold more images if their file size is small, so if you need to fire long bursts of shots at 3.2 frames per second, you would minimize the file size by either shrinking their overall size or compressing them more or by using both strategies. For rapid sequence photography, you may decide not to save the files in RAW format since this is the largest file size. To reduce the JPEG file size, you use this command:

MENU/SET>REC>PICTURE SIZE>[L], [M], [S]

Recommendations

As mentioned earlier, we always recommend storing both JPEG and RAW files. However, you can see that there are a couple of situations in which saving the files in JPEG alone is desirable. If you are firing many photographs rapidly, you can fire more shots and download them to your memory card without interruption if you save the files as JPEGs and you compress them to a [M] or [S] size.

Another advantage to saving files in JPEG as a smaller pixel array is being able to use the EX. OPT. ZOOM (Extended Optical Zoom) function to obtain more magnification on your camera. While it is of limited value in still photography, it is advantageous in video recording mode. It will, when applied to video work, provide you with a "longer" reach with your lens, allowing you to double or triple the lens magnification with no loss of quality when shooting video. Extended Optical Zoom will be covered in chapter 6 when we discuss videos in depth.

Customizing Automatic Focusing

We often take automatic focusing for granted; however, it can be customized to operate as you would like. This ranges from total automatic to fully manual, and as a consequence, we discuss focusing commands in two chapters, here and chapter 6.

On the top of the camera you will find the auto focus mode dial. It moves through 1-area-focusing, 23-area-focusing, AF Tracking, and Face Detection. These settings can be customized for adjusting the region of the display screen to be used for focusing and the size of the area to be selected for focusing.

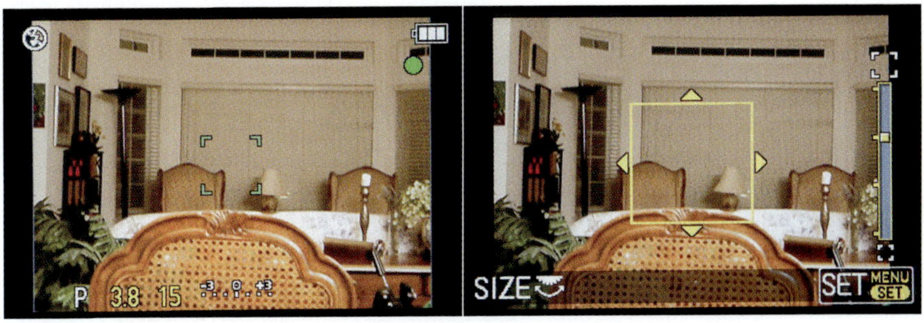

Figure 5-12a: The green target indicates the area used for focusing;
Figure 5-12b: The target can be enlarged to one size larger

1-area-focusing

1-area-focusing focuses on only one defined area in the screen, demarcated by green brackets (figure 5-12a). The size (figure 5-12b) and position of this rectangle can be changed. This can be accomplished by using the directional arrow buttons or by the touch screen. Here are the steps for doing so:

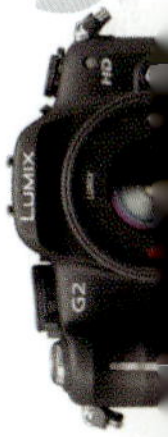

1. Turn auto focus mode dial to the 1-area-focusing icon.
2. Press the Q.MENU button for several seconds.
3. Wait until the AF target (yellow border) and side bar appears (figure 5-13b). Adjust the size of the AF target by either rotating the rear dial or touching the slider displayed on the side and moving it up and down to increase or decrease the size of the targeting square.
4. Position the AF target by using the directional arrow buttons or by touching the AF target and moving it to the desired position. (Note that this will not change the size and shape of the metering spot.) To return the target to the center of the screen press the Trash Can button
5. To complete the operation, execute one of the following: touch the SET icon, press the MENU/SET button, or press the shutter-release button halfway.

Enlarging the AF target is useful for helping the camera to focus under difficult lighting conditions. Use a larger target size to facilitate focusing. A smaller target focuses on a limited area within the display. When used, it responds like the larger target in that when focus is achieved, the target turns green and a green circle appears in the upper right corner of the screen (figure 5-13b).

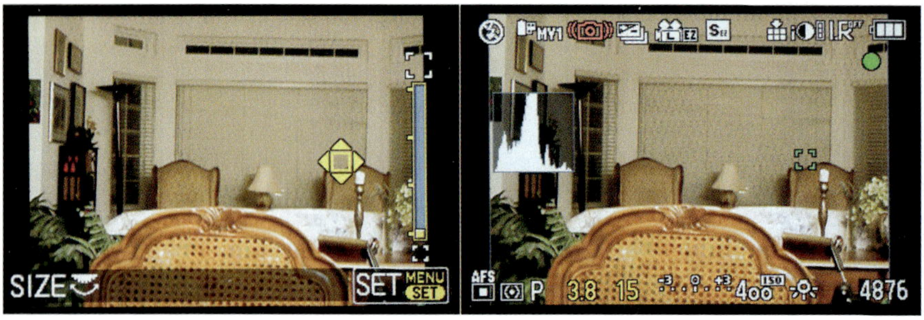

Figure 5-13a: This is the focusing target reduced to its smallest size;
Figure 5-13b: Depicts the target being used for focusing

23-area-focusing

As mentioned in chapter 2, multiple areas (up to 23) are distributed throughout the viewing screen, so any portion of the screen can be used for focusing. However, it is possible to divide the screen into nine sectors and restrict focusing to specific sectors (figure 5-14a).

By setting the camera to 23-area-focusing and pressing the Q.MENU button for a few seconds you will see the central sector is active with its associated five rectangles (figure 5-14a). These rectangles are the actual focusing areas the camera will use.

By turning the rear dial or touching one of the white crosses one can select another sector. Pressing the MENU/SET button activates the selected sector as the focusing area. You can cancel this selection with a second press of the MENU/SET button as shown in figure 5-14c.

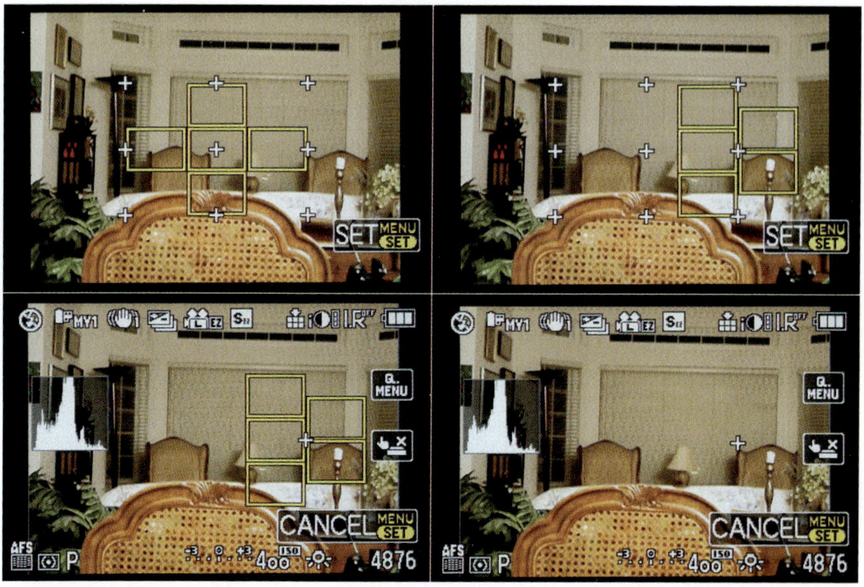

Figure 5-14a: This screen appears when the camera is set to 23-area-focusing and Q.MENU button pressed for a few seconds; Figure 5-14b: Focusing will be restricted to the right side of the screen; Figure 5-14c: The screen after pressing the MENU/SET button or icon; Figure 5-14d: The active screen when limiting the area to be used for focusing

You can restrict focusing to one of the nine sectors following these steps:

1. Turn auto focus mode dial to the 23-area-focusing icon.
2. Press the Q.MENU button for several seconds.
3. Wait until AF areas are displayed—yellow border rectangles with white cross (figure 5-14a). The central cross with the surrounding five rectangles represents the sector to be used for focusing. The other eight crosses mark the center of the eight additional sectors that will not be used for focusing.
4. Select the area to be used for focusing by using the directional arrow buttons or by rotating the rear dial. In figure 5-14b, the right cross had been selected and the focusing area is now the five rectangles on the right side of the screen.
5. Press the shutter-release button halfway to acknowledge you wish to use this area for focusing. The yellow-bordered rectangles showing the areas to be used for focusing will remain briefly (figure 5-14c). The rectangles will disappear, leaving only the white cross to remind you focusing will be restricted to the right sector of the screen (figure 5-14d).

You will probably not want to retain a restricted region for focusing permanently. To cancel settings, press the MENU/SET button.

It may be simpler to use the touch screen commands for selecting a limited region for focusing. After selecting 23-area-focusing, do the following:

1. Touch the screen at the area you wish to use for focusing. A set of five yellow outlined rectangles will appear that mark the focusing areas. Within the center of the set of rectangles is a white cross.
2. Remove your finger. The rectangles will disappear and a white cross will mark the center point of the focusing area.

Again, you will probably not want to retain a restricted region for focusing permanently. To cancel, press MENU/SET.

Recommendations

When shooting the camera handheld, we seldom use the touch screen to modify the focusing targets. It is awkward to raise the camera with one hand and use the other to position the focusing target over the subject. It is faster to simply aim the camera and place the focusing target over the subject and lock focusing by pressing and holding the shutter-release button halfway.

Once focus is locked, the camera can be moved, the image composed, and the picture taken with a full press of the shutter-release button. Modifying the Auto Focus targets is more conveniently done with the camera aimed for the best composition and locked into position on the tripod. Then the Auto Focus target can be positioned over the precise region to be used for focusing.

Automatic Focusing: Speeding Up Focusing at the Expense of Battery Power

The Panasonic G2 camera's auto focus feature does not focus as rapidly as many DSLRs. To conserve battery power, focusing is not started until the user raises the camera and starts pressing the shutter-release button. To capture a sharply focused image, the camera does not fire until focus is established. To speed up the firing of the camera, there are commands for overriding these operations.

These commands involve some sacrifice and risk. Basically, one command uses more battery power by starting the focusing motor prior to pressing the shutter-release button halfway. The other command allows the camera to be fired even if focus is unconfirmed, increasing the chance of collecting a fuzzy, unfocused image.

To allow for focusing earlier in the picture-taking process, use the following command:

MENU/SET>CUSTOM>(pg 2) PRE AF>[OFF], [Q-AF], [C-AF]

Q-AF

The Q-AF setting starts the focusing motor when the camera is held steady. When you are carrying the camera, it is under continuous movement and its focusing motor is off. But once you aim it at your subject in preparation for taking a picture, the camera becomes motionless because it is being aimed. This stability initiates the automatic focus motor. This can use up the battery unnecessarily when you are sitting with the camera stationary and it is constantly refocusing.

C-AF

The second setting, C-AF, is even more wasteful of battery power. It keeps the motor on continuously, even when the camera is moving, so the camera is always attempting to find focus. Eventually, the time will come when you aim the camera at a subject you wish to photograph. The continuous activity of the focusing motor will ensure that you are near focus, even before you start pressing the shutter-release button.

Setting the PRE AF command to [Q-AF] or [C-AF] is fine, but please remember to turn your camera off when you are not using it. This will conserve your battery while also obtaining focus quickly when you want to take a picture.

FOCUS PRIORITY

The following command turns off a camera's safety device for ensuring sharply focused pictures. By turning the FOCUS PRIORITY command to [OFF], you will have set the camera to fire whether or not focus is achieved. Pressing the shutter-release button fully will fire the camera.

MENU/SET>CUSTOM>(pg 2) FOCUS PRIORITY>[OFF], [ON]

Recommendations

We have worked with these commands and have not adopted either for our photography. From our experience, the major delay in camera firing is the time the lens motor drives it from slightly out of focus to in focus.

Presumably, there is a little hesitation as the camera compares contrast between the in-focus and out-of-focus setting. While we don't doubt that firing the camera is faster by using FOCUS PRIORITY command set to [OFF] or setting the PRE AF command to [Q-AF] or [C-AF], it is not dramatically faster.

For still photography, we recommend turning the PRE AF command to [OFF] and keeping the FOCUS PRIORITY command set to [ON]. When we need the camera to fire immediately after pressing the shutter-release button, we set the camera's Focus Mode lever to Manual and forego the convenience of automatic focusing.

Automatic Focus in Dim Light

The automatic focus system in the camera needs light to operate. In dim surroundings when ambient lighting is too low for automatic focusing, the camera will provide more light by projecting a red beam to illuminate the subject. Normally, this provides enough light to achieve automatic focus. However, the beam can be annoying. Obviously when shooting a stage production in a dimly lit theater, you do not want the red beam to intrude on the production. For nature photography, the chance of having it come on can ruin a wildlife shot. Panasonic provides a command to disable the red beam so it does not come on:

MENU/SET>CUSTOM>(pg 3) AF ASSIST LAMP>[OFF], [ON]

Set the command to [OFF] to disable the red beam.

Locking Focusing with AF/AE

AF/AE LOCK

At the rear of the camera is a button labeled AF/AE LOCK, and as its name implies, it can be used to lock in exposure or focus or both. The button's action is controlled by a menu command:

MENU/SET>CUSTOM>(pg 2) AF/AE LOCK>[AE], [AF], [AF/AE]

Select one of the options to determine how the AF/AE LOCK button will operate: AE (Automatic Exposure), AF (Automatic Focus), and AF/AE (both Automatic Focus and Automatic Exposure). Once the AF/AE LOCK command is set, aim the camera at an area you wish to focus on or to use to set exposure.

Press the AF/AE LOCK button to set and lock focus, exposure, or both according to the AF/AE LOCK command's setting. As long as you continue to hold down the AF/AE LOCK button, you can move the camera while retaining these settings until the picture has been taken.

AF/AE LOCK HOLD

If you like using AF/AE LOCK button, you may be interested in its additional command, AF/AE LOCK HOLD. This allows you to press the AF/AE LOCK button once and retain the locked focus, exposure, or both until you press the button a second time. Also, the command is canceled when you take the picture. Here's how to turn this command [OFF] or [ON]:

MENU/SET>CUSTOM>(pg 2) AF/AE LOCK HOLD>[OFF], [ON]

Turning off the command forces you to keep the AF/AE LOCK button depressed to keep the camera's focus, exposure or both set. Releasing the button loses the setting.

Recommendations

We do not use this button very much. Instead, we press the shutter-release button halfway to lock focus, and if we are unhappy with the exposure, we use the rear dial and Exposure Compensation.

Manual Focus: Overriding Automatic Focusing

Our discussion about using manual focus will span this chapter and chapter 6. Here we will discuss overriding automatic focus with the lens-focusing ring. In chapter 6 we describe using manual focus as the sole means of focusing.

When using a Micro Four Thirds lens for this camera, you can readjust the automatic focus by turning the lens-focusing ring. To permit this action, use the following command:

MENU/SET>CUSTOM>(pg 3) AF+MF>[OFF], [ON]

Once this command is set to [ON], you first start automatic focus by pressing the shutter-release button halfway. After focus is locked, you can turn the focusing ring and alter the focus point. Frequently in nature work or macro photography, the automatic focus will lock onto an object in front of or behind the subject of interest. If this occurs, this command provides a convenient means of fixing the error. This command only works with Auto Focus Single (AFS) and after the camera has locked in focus. It does nothing when using Auto Focus Continuous (AFC).

To obtain more precise focusing, it may be desirable to have a more magnified image of the subject within the display screen. You can raise the magnification with this command:

MENU/SET>CUSTOM>(pg 3) MF ASSIST>[OFF], [ON]

This command, when coupled with AF+MF, will increase the magnification in the display screen. There will be a decrease in the field of view—that is, only the central portion of the screen is magnified. But this can be very useful in macro photography when you need to have precise control of your focus. If you need even more magnification, you can turn the rear dial one click and the image will be enlarged further.

To return to the lower magnification to see the full field of view, fully depress the shutter-release button. The field will drop down immediately in magnification. Note that this function will not work if you have **MENU/SET>REC>(pg 4) EX. OPT. ZOOM** and **MENU/SET>REC>(pg 4) DIGITAL ZOOM** both set to **[ON]**.

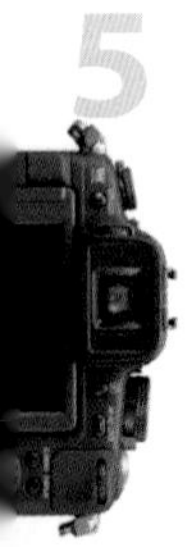

Turning Off Automatic Focus

The auto focus mode dial can set the camera to manual focus, MF, where the automatic focus is disabled and you directly control focusing with the lens-focusing ring. Since the MF setting turns off automatic focusing, there is no delay in firing your camera when pressing down the shutter-release button. Subjectively, this can make the camera feel more responsive in your hand.

Depressing the shutter-release button fully results in a more rapid capture of the image. This can be used advantageously in photographing rapidly changing events—and you should not avoid using Manual Exposure Mode because automatic focus is disabled. Remember, many excellent action photographs were taken with manual focus lenses prior to the development of automatic focus. The percentage of in-focus shots may be less, but it should not dissuade you from using the camera to capture rapid events.

Recommendations

When using the supplied Micro Four Thirds lens, we always turn on AF+MF so that we can touch up focus. This does not interfere with the normal operation of the camera, and having this capability is worthwhile.

When shooting rapidly changing events, we frequently disable the automatic focus by setting the focus mode dial to MF so the camera will fire more quickly. The increased speed in the camera's operation obviates the disadvantage of losing automatic focus.

When used for fast capturing of the subjects, we do not use the MF ASSIST command. The reduction of the field of view with this command interferes with action photography.

Manual Operation of the Camera

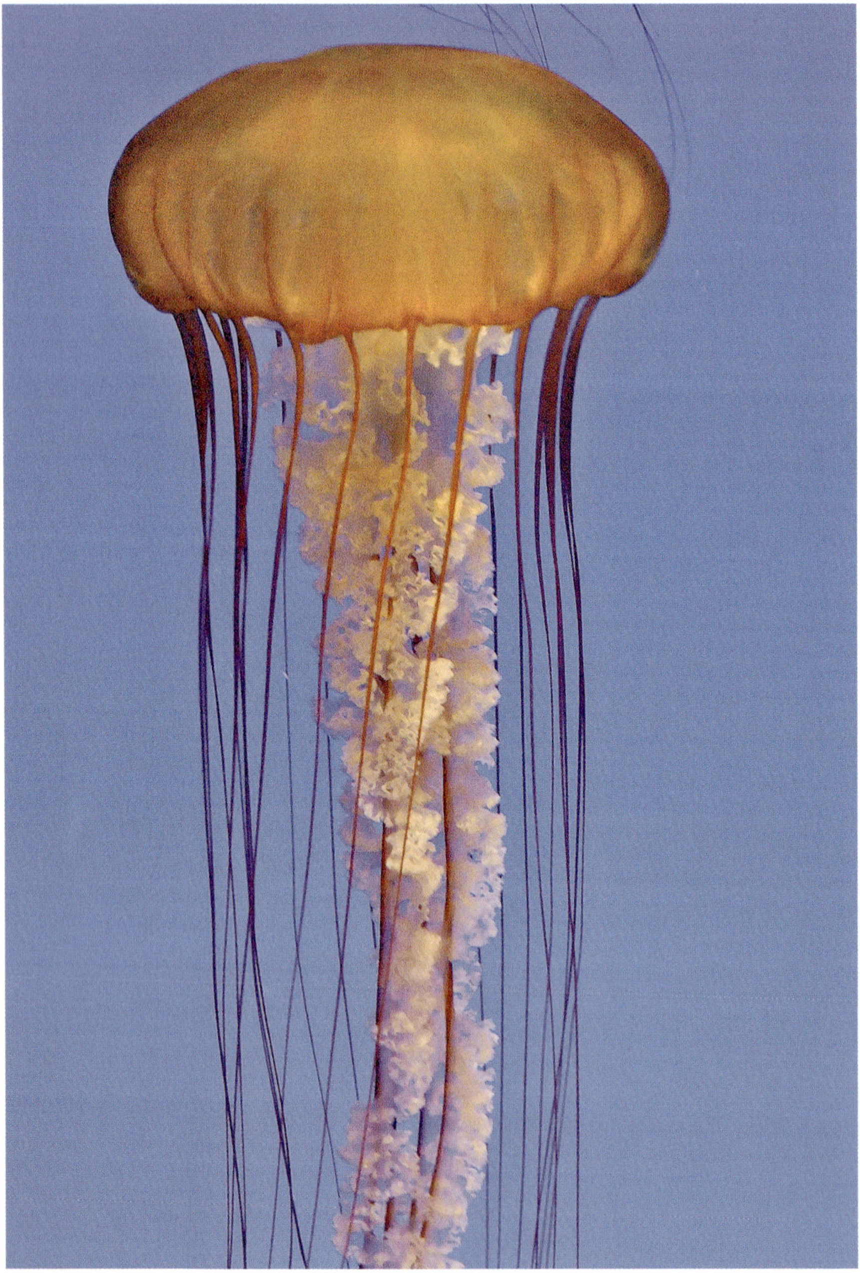

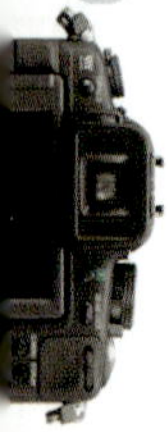

Introduction: Manual Operation

Where chapter 4 dealt with an automated camera setting its own aperture, shutter speed, or focus, this chapter is about taking control of the camera and using it in the traditional manner by setting its controls yourself. This provides the perfect tool for learning how to creatively use aperture and shutter speed. By working with these controls and keeping notes of their effects on your photographs, you can teach yourself to provide the effects you wish to impart to your image. If you wish to go beyond the normal use of the camera, such as using it on a telescope or microscope to record astronomical events or scientific experiments, this knowledge is essential. Finally, if you simply wish to be able to use the camera consistently and reliably under all lighting conditions, learning how to operate your camera manually is indispensable.

In addition, we will cover some advanced automated features that can be utilized when you're operating the camera in a manual mode. These features will provide you with a greater range of controls for the image. For example, you can instruct the camera to set a command value incrementally for each picture in a series. This creates a series of images (bracket) in which each is slightly different in some discrete fashion, and you can then select and use the best for your final purpose. You can also set the camera to take a series of shots and vary the exposure slightly. Simplistically, you might think of this as a "shotgun" approach of hitting the right exposure. But it can be a valuable working tool when coupled with image processing.

For example, a scene may have so much variation in light values that a single photograph cannot capture the details in both the shadows and the highlights. To record all the variations in brightness, it requires taking a series of pictures at different exposures. For example, three photographs can record the entire intensity range, one recording the brightest areas, the second recording mid-intensity areas, and the final one recording low-intensity areas. These three images can be combined to provide a composite image, and by using third-party software, you can generate a picture displaying all these intensity variations. This technique is known as high dynamic range (HDR) photography, and it illustrates how taking control of your camera can expand its capabilities.

Manual Exposure Mode Controls

Turning the mode dial to M sets the camera to the M Mode and displays M in the display screen's lower-left corner. The aperture and then shutter speed numbers are displayed to the right of the M.

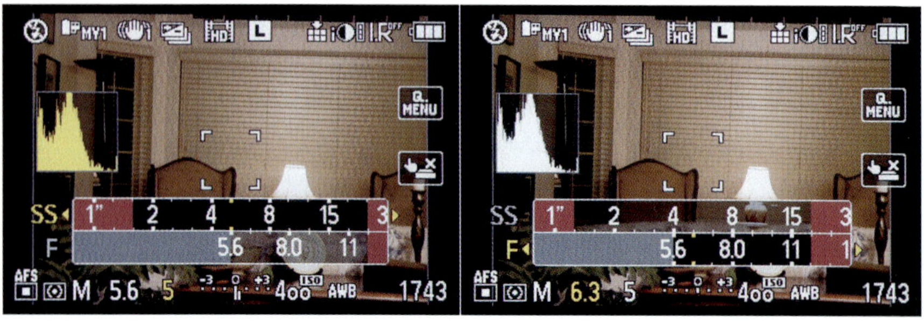

Figure 6-1a: Shutter speed (5) under user's control where the aperture (5.6) is not;
Figure 6-1b: Aperture (6.3) under user's control where the shutter speed (5) is not

Both the aperture and shutter speed numbers will be visible at all times, unlike in either A or S Mode, where you have to press the shutter-release button halfway to display both (figure 6-1a). In M Mode, either the aperture or the shutter speed will be displayed in yellow, indicating which is under your control when you rotate the rear dial. Pressing in the rear dial toggles the control between the two settings, alternating which number will glow yellow (figure 6-1b).

You use Exposure Compensation and the rear dial to adjust the aperture and the shutter speed for exposure. When the camera has too much or too little light for a correct exposure, there is a series of tick marks under the Exposure Compensation icon. The number of tick marks displayed indicates how far off exposure you are. Each mark is 1/3 f-stop, and you have a plus or minus 3 f-stop range. To adjust for proper exposure, you change the aperture or shutter speed to minimize the number of marks until they disappear.

6

Extremely Long Exposure "B"ulb Shutter Speed

When you shoot in P, S, or A Mode, the Panasonic G2 camera is capable of up to a 60 second exposure. However, M Mode will allow you to use an even longer shutter speed (up to 4 minutes). When in M Mode, turn the rear dial until the shutter speed numbers switch from a numerical value to the letter B. This will occur once you go beyond a 60-second exposure. At this setting, the shutter will open when the shutter-release button is fully pressed and will remain open as long as you continue to hold the button down. The B shutter speed is unavailable in any of the semi-automatic P, S, and A Modes, Intelligent Auto, and the predefined scene modes.

The term Bulb, or abbreviated as B, has been around from the early days of film photography, and the origins of the word are uncertain. There are a couple of explanations of how this nondigital term arose. One states it comes from the time when the shutters were opened pneumatically by squeezing an air bulb attached to the camera's shutter. The photographer would manually squeeze the air bulb to open the shutter and release the air bulb to close the shutter when they deemed the film had been sufficiently exposed. Another possible name origin comes from the early days when photography used external flashbulbs. The photographer would manually open the camera's shutter, set off the flashbulb allowing the image to be exposed on the film and then close the camera's shutter to stop the exposure. Regardless of how the term Bulb for shutter speed came about, it represents a shutter opened for an indeterminate amount of time and whose closure is controlled by the photographer releasing the shutter-release button.

Knowing When You Are beyond a Shutter Speed of a Second

Normally, the Panasonic G2 camera shutter speed displays in fractions of a second. So when you see the number 4, it is actually ¼ second. You know when the shutter will be for a second or longer when you see the symbol ″ following the shutter speed number–for example 1″ represents 1 second. When this symbol is present, your shutter speed is now a second or longer.

Noise Reduction with Long Exposure

Images generated from long exposures may suffer from fixed pattern noise—such as pixels glowing a bright color. This image defect is corrected by a procedure known as dark frame subtraction. This is accomplished by using the LONG SHTR NR command (figure 6-2a, figure 6-2b). This command is as follows:

MENU/SET>REC>(pg 3) LONG SHTR NR>[OFF], [ON]

The command has three behind-the-scenes steps.

1. First, the camera takes an image with the shutter open for the designated time. This will record the image plus the fixed pattern noise.
2. The camera then takes another exposure but does not record an image. This is the "dark frame" and creates a reference map recording the position of the glowing pixels.

3. The final step is to subtract the "dark frame" contents from the first image, thus removing the bright pixels. The image subtraction erases the glowing pixels and generates an accurate picture of the subject.

This command doubles the time it takes to record an image. For example, if you take a photograph with a 10-second exposure, the camera will, at the completion of the exposure, automatically run a second exposure of equal time to create the dark frame. For exposures that run over several seconds, this can create a tedious wait so some people will turn this command off.

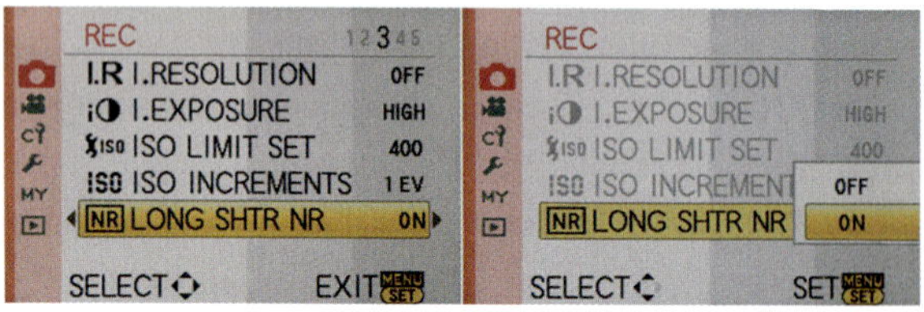

Figure 6-2a: Long Shutter Noise Reduction is ON;
Figure 6-2b: Option to turn OFF Noise Reduction

MENU/SET>REC>(pg 3) LONG SHTR NR>[OFF], [ON]

Normally, this command is [ON], and we recommend that you keep this setting to obtain the best possible picture.

Metering Modes

When using the camera in M Mode, it is important to know the method being used to measure light. There are three methods used by the camera's built-in meter: [*Multiple*], [*Center Weighted*], and [*Spot*] (table 6-1). The default and most commonly used method is [*Multiple*]. The camera uses the entire area within the display screen to measure light and from this calculates the exposure. This measurement is more than a simple averaging of the entire scene—there is an algorithm that balances the exposure, helping to prevent overexposure of the highlights and underexposure of the shadows.

Historically, various digital camera manufacturers have developed and refined these algorithms, and while they do an excellent job in generating a pleasing exposure, the strategy employed is complex and not explained to the photographer. You simply use this type of metering and trust it will do a good job. For the most part, it is very reliable.

The second method is [*Center Weighted*], which uses an easily understood algorithm for measuring light. Based on the assumption that the most important subject will be in the center of the display screen, this metering pattern prioritizes exposure so that the center of the display screen is well exposed. The peripheral areas are still evaluated for adjusting the overall exposure, but they are given less priority. Historically, this has been a popular pattern for measuring light in an SLR camera. While this older technology has the virtue of simplicity, it is not as consistent as [Multiple] area metering and it results in more "missed" exposures.

[(•)]	[( )]	[•]
Multiple	Center Weighted	Spot
Meters whole area Complex algorithm	Meters whole area Simple algorithm	Meters one spot Simple algorithm

Table 6-1: METERING MODE command icons

The most direct algorithm for metering is [*Spot*]. When it's selected, you see a small cross displayed on the screen. The light meter measures the light on this region of the display screen and the remainder is ignored in evaluating exposure. You know precisely how much light is coming off from a single area—it is not being influenced by the light from other areas of the scene. The area being metered does not have to occupy the center of the screen. If you set the camera to 1-area-focusing, the cross initially occupies the center of the focusing target. Use the directional arrow buttons to position the cross to a different location on the display screen. The camera will meter the light at the new location and determine the exposure for that spot.

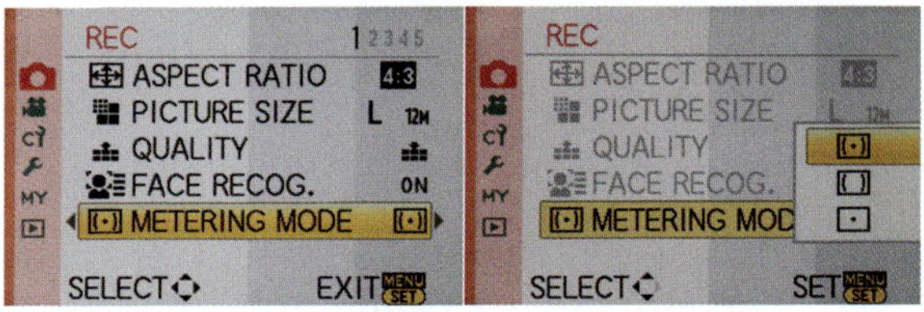

Figure 6-3a: METERING MODE command [Multiple] option selected; Figure 6-3b: Commands for different metering modes revealed

The metering method is selected with the following command (figure 6-3a, figure 6-3b):

MENU/SET>REC>METERING MODE>[*Multiple*], [*Center Weighted*], [*Spot*]

Recommendation

To have full control within the M Mode, you need to know where and how much light the subject reflects. In this respect, spot metering is the superior metering method since you know exactly where the meter is reading.

Its disadvantage is its specificity. Because it measures such a restricted region, a single measurement may not give an accurate exposure estimate for a complex scene that has deep shadows and bright highlights. Such a scene requires several measurements over different regions, and an experienced photographer uses these measurements to determine the optimum exposure for the entire scene. In a sense, this is what multiple metering is supposed to do—it calculates the varying light intensity over the entire scene and gives an estimate of what it believes to be the correct exposure for the overall picture.

With the spot metering option, you have to carefully measure individual regions, a process that takes time and is best done with an immobile subject. It also requires experience in knowing how a sensor collects light of differing intensities. But, its advantage is that an experienced photographer will be able to predict the results of a given exposure.

For example, we use spot metering for technical photography. When doing copy work of line drawings, we will take a spot measurement of the area on the paper that has no marking. Experience has taught us that overexposing that region by 1 2/3 f-stops best records our line copy work: Black lines are recorded as being jet black and the white paper is recorded as a

Micro Four Thirds and the Four Thirds System

Manufacturers of DSLRs prefer their customers to buy a lens made by them rather than a competitor, and to ensure buyer loyalty, they have a proprietary lens mount usable only on their camera bodies. The Micro Four Thirds system is unusual in that two companies follow its guidelines so that you can use a lens from Olympus as well as Panasonic. If other companies subscribe to this standard, then their lenses will also be compatible with your Panasonic camera body.

The Micro Four Thirds lens was derived from an earlier system called the Four Thirds Lens system, developed by Olympus. This was the first system designed specifically for digital cameras, and its lens line was designed to give superior performance when mated to digital sensors. These lenses share many of the characteristics of the Micro Four Thirds system; however, they require the purchase of a special adapter so that they can be mounted on the Panasonic G2 camera body. With the adapter, the lens will communicate with the camera body, and you have automatic exposure and control of the lens diaphragm from the camera body's rear dial. Some of these lenses are extremely good optically and can be used advantageously on the Panasonic G2 camera.

brilliant white. For work with other subjects, we rely on multiple metering and carefully study the resultant histogram. We then adjust the exposure on the basis of the histogram display. We hardly use center-weighted metering.

Manual Focusing Micro Four Thirds Lenses

We described in chapter 5 how to focus a Micro Four Thirds lens by turning the ring surrounding the lens. Normally the lens-focusing ring is inoperable when the focus mode lever is set to AFS or AFC. There are times when the camera's auto focus is not enough and you will want to be able to fine tune the focus using the lens-focusing ring. The following command will activate the ring when the camera is set to an auto focus mode:

MENU/SET>CUSTOM>(pg 3) AF+MF>[OFF], [ON]

We recommended that this be set to [ON] since it does not disturb the normal operation of the automatic focusing. However, you may wish to turn off automatic focus entirely and focus manually. This is accomplished by turning the focus mode lever to MF, enabling the lens-focus ring automatically. Since the AF+MF command only pertains when the camera is in an auto focus mode, its setting has no affect on the camera when the focus mode lever is set to MF. To improve the focus accuracy of an immobile subject, you can use the following command:

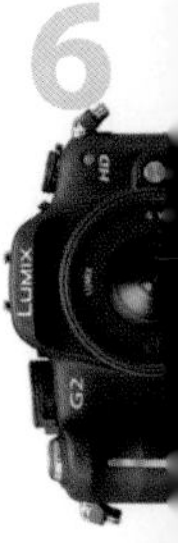

MENU/SET>CUSTOM>(pg 3) MF ASSIST>[OFF], [ON]

When this command is set to [ON], turning the lens-focusing ring will magnify the image on the display screen. With this high magnification view, fine subject details can be seen easily, thus facilitating focusing. When you wish to see the entire field of view, pressing the shutter-release button halfway will reduce the magnification.

Manual Focusing Four Thirds Lenses

To use the older-style Four Thirds lens, you will need a special adapter, model number DMW-MA1, sold by Panasonic. The Four Thirds lenses, especially the telephoto zoom lenses, provide a longer focal length and faster aperture than your current lens. We have used the Olympus Zuiko 70-300 mm zoom, 50 mm macro, 12-60 mm Zoom, and 50-200 mm zoom with our Panasonic G2 camera. All these lenses were used in the MF Mode and operated smoothly with the DMW-MA1 adapter.

All of the commands related to manual focus described earlier work with the Four Thirds lenses. However, automatic focusing is so slow that we do not recommend using it with the Four Thirds lenses, and as a consequence we do not recommend using the AF + MF command with these lenses. With this command, manually turning the lens-focusing ring will not be possible until the camera first finds focus. This takes so long, it is simpler and faster to simply set the focus mode lever to MF and focus the lens manually.

Manual Focusing Any Lens

The Panasonic G2 camera is the most versatile camera body for mounting lenses. You can make it work on telescopes, microscopes, and camera lenses from almost any manufacturer. We will discuss this in more detail in the next chapter, but we should point out in this section a little used command, SHOOT W/O LENS:

MENU/SET>CUSTOM>(pg 7) SHOOT W/O LENS>[OFF], [ON]

This command controls the camera's shutter firing if there is no lens attached to the camera body (figure 6-4). The default command value is [OFF], meaning the camera will not fire unless it detects there is a Four Thirds or Micro Four Thirds lens attached to the camera body. We set the command to [ON] for the camera to be used on microscopes, telescopes, or virtually with any lens that can be mounted on the camera body. In essence, the camera can be used to take pictures with any optic that can project an image onto its sensor. Having this command active does not interfere with any of the camera's regular function, so we leave it on.

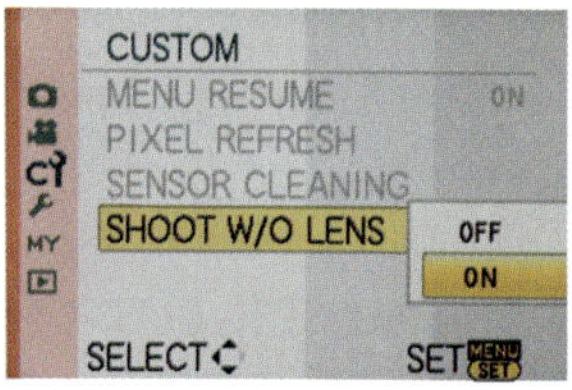

Figure 6-4: SHOOT W/O LENS command options

Touch Screen

The Panasonic G2 camera is the first interchangeable lens camera with a touch screen on a movable rear LCD display screen. At first, we thought the touch screen feature provided a minor convenience when using the camera. After all, the difference in effort between setting menu commands from a touch screen versus pressing buttons on the camera's back is minimal. But as we gained more experience with the camera, we came to the conclusion that this feature was a major advantage.

Focusing

Our change in attitude was a result of using the camera on the tripod where it was fixed in position and we needed to find focus for different areas on the screen. Remember, with 1-area-focusing, a target is placed on the subject to be focused. You can position a focusing target anywhere on the display screen with the directional arrow buttons. When a camera is locked in position on a tripod, this is surprisingly inconvenient. You have to either use multiple button presses or apply continuous pressure to move the focusing target along a horizontal or vertical line. Usually, it is necessary to alternate between pressing the left and right directional arrow buttons and then up and down directional arrow buttons to position the focusing target precisely. In contrast, a simple touch with one's finger on the LCD screen in the desired location instantly moves the focusing target to the point of interest.

The steps for using the touch screen to focus are as follows:

1. With the camera mounted on a tripod, set the focus mode lever to AFS and the auto focus mode dial to 1-area-focusing.
2. Next, find the point where you want to focus on the display screen and touch it with your finger. A yellow-bordered square appears.
3. If this is overlying the region you want to focus on, press the shutter-release button halfway and the camera will focus. Focus confirmation is signaled with a green circle and the target turning green.
4. Fully depress the shutter-release button and the picture is taken.

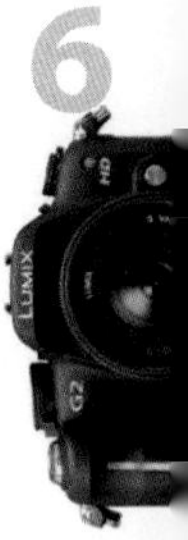

Another valuable feature allows you to identify the area you wish to focus on, touch that area of the screen, and the camera will then focus on that point and fire immediately upon acquiring focus. Accomplishing this task is described below.

Activate Shutter

The touch screen shutter icons are controlled by the TOUCH SHUTTER command:

MENU/SET>CUSTOM>(pg 6) TOUCH SHUTTER>[OFF], [ON]

When this command is set to [ON], the ability to fire the camera by touching the LCD screen is enabled. This is shown by the presence of one of two touch screen shutter icons. To use target shooting as an analogy, an icon with an X indicates that the function is enabled but the firing safety is on, so you cannot fire the camera by touching the screen (figure 6-5a). When you touch this icon, the safety is released and you will see the icon turn yellow and the X disappear. The safety is switched off, so now the camera can be fired whenever you touch the LCD screen (figure 6-5b).

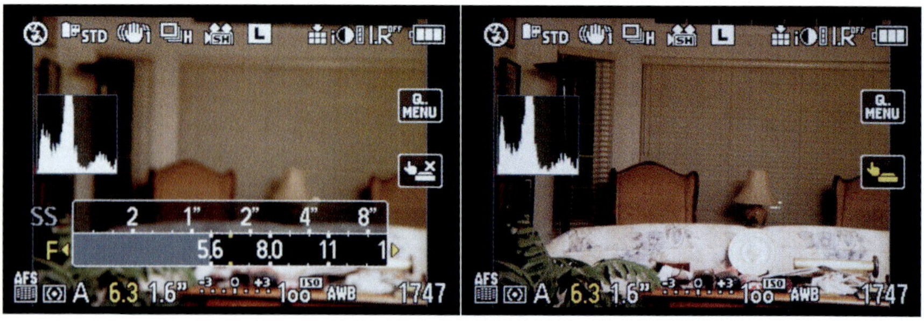

Figure 6-5a: Touch screen shutter icon indicates camera will not fire if screen is touched;
Figure 6-5b: Touch screen shutter icon indicates camera will fire if screen is touched

Image Magnification

The touch screen facilitates manual focusing, making it easy to provide increased magnification at a given region of the screen. Essentially it is a one-touch instant zoom command providing a higher magnification image on any place you touch the screen. If the camera's focus mode lever is set to MF and the MF ASSIST command is set to [ON], all you need to do is touch the screen and the image will be magnified at the point of contact. This magnification of the subject facilitates focusing. To reduce the magnification to see the whole field of view, press the shutter-release button halfway.

Other Touch Screen Operations

There are several other functions where you may find using the LCD touch screen capability advantageous. You can use the LCD touch screen to identify the subject you wish to have tracked when the auto focus mode dial is set to AF Tracking. You can reposition the Histogram and the cross-hair guidelines using the touch screen. You can also display the Quick Menu, play back your pictures by sweeping your finger across the screen or tapping to zoom in to better view the picture's detail. As with many things, experiment using the LCD touch screen. We are sure there will be many functions you will decide are easier to do using this option.

My Color

The mode dial's My Color Mode provides an optional set of color schemes for displaying the camera's images in either still or video photography. These colors are seen in still photographs when the camera saves the file as a JPEG. If you create dual JPEG and RAW files, you will not see the alternate color renderings in the RAW file format. This is most evident when you select the [MONOCHROME] option—the JPEG file will show the image with its colors muted so it almost appears as a black-and-white image. In contrast, the RAW file will show a full color image.

There are eight different color schemes that provide a different ambience to the photograph:

[EXPRESSIVE], [RETRO], [PURE], [ELEGANT], [MONOCHROME], [DYNAMIC ART], [SILHOUETTE], and [CUSTOM]

The effects of these settings are best evaluated on the LCD screen. To do so, set the camera's mode dial to My Color Mode. You will see the last viewed color scheme displayed (figure 6-6a). Use the right or left directional arrow buttons to cycle through the different color schemes (figure 6-6b). When you find a pleasing color scheme, select it by pressing the MENU/SET button or by pressing the shutter-release button halfway.

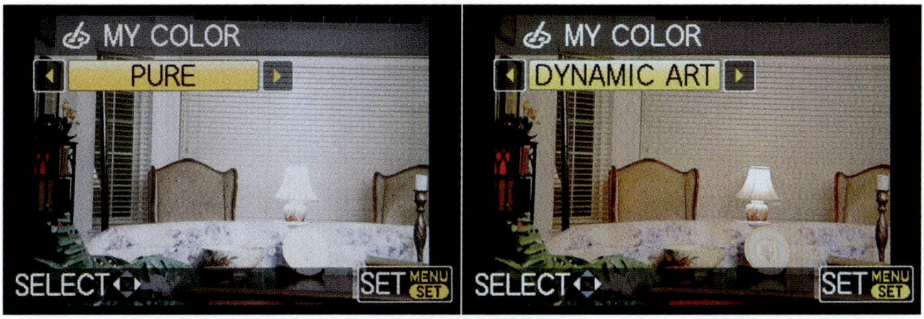

Figure 6-6a: My Color Mode's [PURE] color scheme selected;
Figure 6-6b: Continue to scroll through My Color Mode's options. Here [DYNAMIC ART] is selected.

My Color Mode's [CUSTOM] selection allows you to customize your settings by shifting colors from light blue to red and adjusting their brightness and saturation (figure 6-7a). This is done by pressing the down directional arrow button and going through the various options. Adjust these to your taste following the prompts on the screen (figure 6-7b). In the event you need to start your customization over, there is a reset option to return the settings to the camera's default.

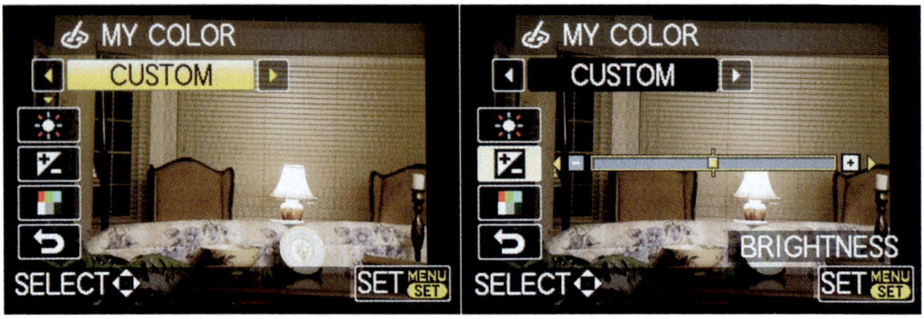

Figure 6-7a: My Color Mode's [CUSTOM] color scheme;
Figure 6-7b: Brightness control has been selected

At first, My Color Mode seems to be a duplication of Film Mode, which also provides a customized color-processing step to the final image. This is not the case. Aside from the fact that the color repertoire is different, My Color Mode does not transfer its color values when you shift the mode dial to any other operation. That is to say, if you go to a semi-automatic, manual, or predefined scene mode, the color interpretation provided My Color Mode is lost. This is not the case for Film Mode, discussed next.

Film Mode

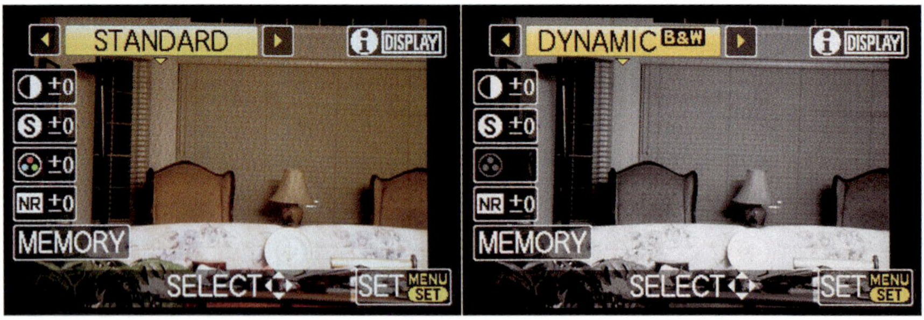

Figure 6-8a: Press the Film Mode (left directional arrow button) and the last viewed color scheme is displayed; Figure 6-8b: Color scheme [DYNAMIC B&W] is displayed. Note: The display screen shows the image as it will be captured.

The Film Mode provides you the opportunity to build a customized color setting that can be applied to videos or picture files. Film Mode provides greater control than My Color Mode in that it provides sharpening filters for enhancing details as well as noise filters for removing the noise when high

ISO settings are used. Functionally, Film Mode is the image processor for those who do not care to do image processing on their computers.

The Film Mode is initiated by pressing the left directional arrow button on the back of the camera when in live view mode. You will see a color scheme option displayed, and if you repeatedly press the left or right directional arrow button, you will see a sequential appearance of the various color schemes:

> **[STANDARD COLOR], [DYNAMIC COLOR], [SMOOTH COLOR], [NATURE COLOR], [NOSTALGIC COLOR], [VIBRANT COLOR], [STANDARD B&W], [DYNAMIC B&W], and [SMOOTH B&W])**

Pressing the right or left directional arrow button brings up the name of the next color scheme (figure 6-8a). The color scheme's colors are applied to the subject displayed on the LCD screen, allowing you to see the effects on the image (figure 6-8b). This way, you will be able to judge if the setting will give you the effect you are looking for in your picture or video. The camera remembers the last color scheme you selected so it will be retained until you go into Film Mode and change it.

Once in the Film Mode, continue to press the horizontal directional arrow buttons until you eventually find two settings that do not have a descriptive color or black-and-white label: [MY FILM 1] and [MY FILM 2]. These are customized color schemes that you make. If you keep pressing the horizontal directional arrow buttons, you will also find the option [MULTI FILM]. This is an entry command that allows you to choose up to three My Film options and fire a burst of shots with each shot recording one of your selected My Film options. Again, this will be discussed later.

Once you have selected a color scheme, you can customize it by pressing the down directional arrow button and selecting a color scheme control.

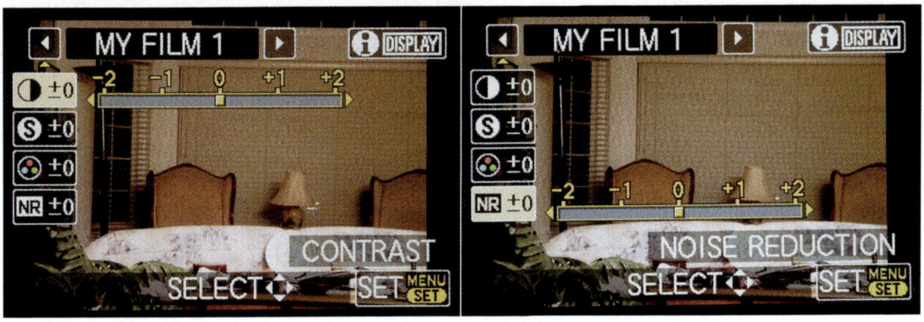

Figure 6-9a: Column of controls that indicate the available adjustments;
Figure 6-9b: Controls from top to bottom, contrast, sharpness, color saturation, and noise level. Noise Reduction (NR) is selected.

You can adjust contrast, sharpness, color saturation, and noise level. When you find the control you wish to adjust, press the left and right directional arrow buttons. Alternatively, you can touch the horizontal bar to alter the setting. In figure 6-9a the [Contrast] option has been selected, and by pressing the right and left directional arrow buttons, you can adjust its setting. The change in contrast can be seen on the display screen with its value shown on the slider bar. In figure 6-9b, NR, representing Noise Reduction, has been selected.

You will note in these two figures that the [MEMORY] control is missing—contrast this to figure 6-8a where it is present. The [MEMORY] option is available only if you are altering one of the following standard color schemes provided by Panasonic:

[STANDARD COLOR], [DYNAMIC COLOR], [SMOOTH COLOR], [NATURE COLOR], [NOSTALGIC COLOR], [VIBRANT COLOR], [STANDARD B&W], [DYNAMIC B&W], and [SMOOTH B&W]

When you select [MEMORY], all the changes you entered in the above commands will be saved and given a label for later recall. These can be customized and saved as either [MY FILM 1] or [MY FILM 2]. Once saved, these settings will be available when you call up the Film Mode. When you press the left directional arrow button, you can recall these settings by selecting [MY FILM 1] or [MY FILM 2]. Your alterations to [MY FILM 1] or [MY FILM 2] are automatically saved when you press the MENU/SET button, so it is unnecessary to use [MEMORY].

The final option in Film Mode to be discussed is [MULTI FILM]. This option allows you to select three Film Mode color schemes and then fire a burst of shots, one for each of the selected color schemes. Scroll through Film Mode's color schemes to find [MULTI FILM] (figure 6-10). The [MULTI FILM] color scheme has three options, labeled [MULTI FILM1], [MULTI FILM2], and [MULTI FILM3]. Press the down directional arrow button once to be positioned on the [MULTI FILM1] row. Once there, you can cycle through the selections using the left and right

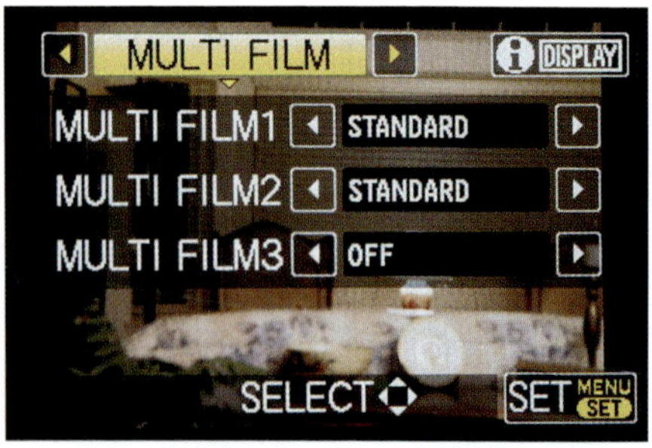

Figure 6-10: [MULTI FILM] command with [MULTI FILM1] and [MULTI FILM2] both assigned the [STANDARD] color scheme

directional arrow buttons and select one of the Film Mode color schemes for [MULTI FILM1]. When you find one you like, press the down directional arrow button to select the option and go down to [MULTI FILM2]. Again, cycle through the color schemes, selecting one by pressing the down directional arrow button to position on [MULTI FILM3].

Repeat the process to select a color scheme for [MULTI FILM3]. If you wish, you can select [OFF] and stop with only two colors schemes selected, as was done in Figure 6-10. Press the MENU/SET button to save and exit the [MULTI FILM] color scheme. When you fire the camera, it will take up to three pictures with each picture using one of the selected color schemes. One word of warning, when you fire the camera, make sure it is set to fire in Burst Mode. Otherwise, you will have to press the shutter-release button three times to collect the different color schemes. In Burst Mode, a single depression of the shutter-release button will take all three pictures, automatically.

Recommendation

The Film Mode and My Color Mode provide interesting color effects with some limitations. For still photographs, these effects are apparent only when you use JPEG for saving your images. The altered colors are not used by RAW—this format saves the initial data from the camera's sensor with minimal processing. So if you select black-and-white, as an example, for Film Mode, your JPEG file will appear as a black-and-white image, but your program for viewing and working with RAW files will display the subject's color. You can render these colors from the RAW file to duplicate the effects seen in your JPEG file—but it seems easier and simpler to save the images directly in JPEG. Perhaps the best solution is to save the image as both JPEG and RAW; one shows the effects of Film or My Color Mode and one (the RAW file) is amenable for image processing.

A perfectionist would argue that a higher-quality picture can be generated from the RAW file, and while theoretically correct, the difference in quality is not that great—especially if the photographer takes care to ensure that exposure and white balance is correctly set. For our black-and-white work, we use the Film Mode to provide a black-and-white image and save in both JPEG and RAW. When we are viewing our images on our Apple computers (depending on the viewing program used) they may display as black-and-white and other times in color.

Table 6-2 lists how they are displayed depending on the viewing program. This is another reason to save the image files as both RAW and JPEG. By doing so, you will have the benefit of having the customized color work you

Apple Program	RAW	JPEG
Finder	black-and-white	black-and-white
Preview	color	black-and-white
iPhoto '11	color	black-and-white

Table 6-2: List of Apple viewing programs and how the saved RAW and JPEG color scheme images display

developed as well as the unaltered picture from the camera. When working with videos, you will not have the dual-file approach for saving the images and therefore My Color and Film Mode colors will be recorded on the video.

Fine-Tuning White Balance

In chapter 5, we described how to use standard settings for white balance and how to calibrate your camera to a light source using a white sheet of paper. For most of us, this is sufficient. However, the Panasonic G2 camera provides even greater control by allowing you to fine-tune the settings by eye. It requires first applying the standard white balance strategies and, if you don't get the desired results,, providing additional tinting.

This adjustment is used when the standard white balance presets are inadequate for adjusting color balance. This can be a result of very unusual lighting conditions, such as when several different light sources provide illumination. You may have an interior scene, for example, whose subject is illuminated by daylight streaming through the window, an incandescent light on the table, and fluorescent lights on the ceiling.

These extreme conditions can fool the white balance calibration—especially when fluorescent lights are involved because they may not emit a full spectrum of light. To compensate for these unusual lighting regimes, the Panasonic G2 provides a means of adding tints to the image. These slight additions of hue will be recorded in both JPEG and RAW files. The command is Finely Adjusting White Balance. It is a continuation of using the commands available when you press the right directional arrow button and initiate white balance adjustment (Figure 6-11a). When you first press the WB button and select a white balance preset, there is a prompt to press the down directional arrow button, or to touch the screen at the white-bordered rectangle containing ADJUST. This brings up a screen (figure 6-11b) showing the controls for tinting the color. Press either the vertical directional arrow buttons to control the magenta/green tint or the horizontal directional arrow buttons to control the amber/blue tints. Apply these controls until you neutralize the colorcast. The degree of tinting is shown by the displacement of a yellow mark within a large white-bordered square. As seen in figure 6-12a, pressing the up directional arrow button applies a green tint and the yellow mark moves up the vertical line. To apply magenta, the down directional arrow button is pressed and this will move the yellow mark down the vertical line (figure 6-11b). If you wish to return to the neutral position, press the appropriate directional arrow buttons to return the yellow mark to the center of the vertical line.

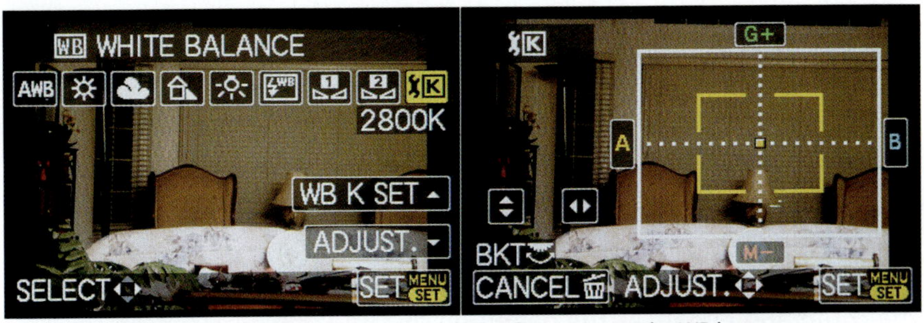

Figure 6-11a: The LCD display screen after pressing the WB button; Figure 6-11b: This screen shot shows the fine adjustments controls for tweaking color balance by eye

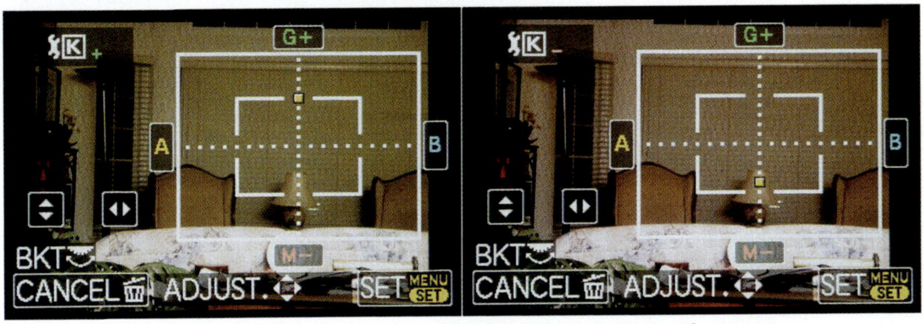

Figure 6-12a: The display when applying a green tint to the image; Figure 6-12b: The display when applying magenta to the image

If you desire, you can do a white balance bracket and take three shots in which the white balance is varied. This is accomplished by using additional commands in this screen. In figures 6-12a and 6-12b, the letters BKT, representing bracket, appear in the lower-left corner of the display screen next to the rear dial icon. When you turn the rear dial, two yellow marks that serve as limit indicators appear in the display. They will indicate the range of your bracket from either green to magenta (turn rear dial to the right) or amber to blue (turn the rear dial to the left). Press the MENU/SET button to select the bracket series. Press the shutter-release button to execute the white balance bracket series.

Intelligent Resolution

The Panasonic G2 has a menu command, I.RESOLUTION (Intelligent Resolution) that increases edge definition, enhancing the visibility of fine detail and the reduction of noise in areas lacking fine details. We have applied I.RESOLUTION and seen its effects on JPEG files. It does provide a sharpening effect and improves the rendition of fine details in these files. We also apply this command on our videos.

MENU/SET>REC>(pg 3) I.RESOLUTION>[OFF], [LOW], [STANDARD], [HIGH]

The command provides four options (figure 6-13). Its greatest effects are exerted when using [HIGH] and its effects are least when using [LOW]. The command can be turned to [OFF]. The command enhances the definition of fine details while at the same time providing noise reduction in regions that have an even tonality. We use this command on files saved as JPEGs and feel that it does a good job in displaying fine details.

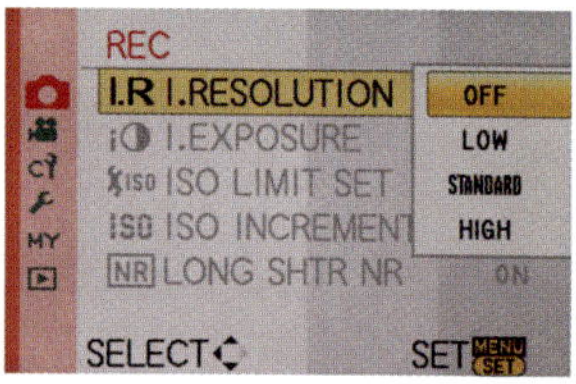

Figure 6-13: I.Resolution command with its four options

Getting More Magnification from the Lens

Extended Optical Zoom

Another rationale for using the JPEG file format is to extend the magnification of your lens. According to Panasonic, you can make your lens provide 2x more magnification with no loss of quality. This claim seems too good to be true—and in a way, it is. However, studying the camera specifications and analyzing what is going on reveals the truth in Panasonic's claim.

First, Extended Optical Zoom for still photographs only works if you save in JPEG and if you save the file so that its picture size is less than [L]. We will use the 4:3 aspect ratio of 4000 by 3000 pixels for this explanation, but keep in mind that it works with other aspect ratios.

It is critical for still photographs to make sure that you specify saving the file in JPEG and using [M] or [S] for Picture Size. Using this as an example, the native sensor size is 4000 by 3000 pixels and you save the image with this pixel array when you save the PICTURE SIZE command as [L]. But suppose you decide to save the file as [S]. When you save the image in JPEG with this setting, the image file is only 2048 by 1536 pixels, or basically 3 megapixels—not the original 12 megapixels. If you look at the LCD screen or the viewfinder, you will see the same size image that you see if you saved in [L]—in other words, Panasonic engineers had figured out how to take the original 4000 by3000 pixel image and compress it so it can be displayed with only 2048 pixels by 1536 pixels.

Now what happens when you set the Panasonic to Extended Optical Zoom? Well, the camera will show you the center of the 4000 by 3000 pixel sensor. Rather than use the procedure of downsizing the pixel display of the whole sensor, it uses all the original pixels that occupy its center, i.e., it cropped down the image to show and save only the central 2048 pixels by 1536 pixels.

Normally, most photographers would not find this optical zoom to be advantageous for their still photography. You can get the same effect by simply saving the 4000 by 3000 pixels, and then cropping down to the central 2048 by 1536 pixels with an imaging program, such as Photoshop. But when you do this trick in the camera, you get one benefit. The view on the display screen doubles in size. It is as if your lens is now twice as powerful as it was earlier. Thus, for viewing through the camera, it is as if you had a 2x telephoto. Since, to get this effect, you had to "downsize" the sensor to 2048 by 1536 pixels, the resultant extended zoom does not show any degradation in quality from this setting. For still photography, this seems a minor advantage.

Where Extended Optical Zoom has a unique value is when you shoot video. When you use the video recording mode AVCHD Lite, you are recording only 1280 by 720 pixels. This situation is analogous to the example in the preceding paragraph. Normally, you would be using the whole sensor and its output will be adjusted to 1280 by 720. But, if you select Extended Optical Zoom, the image will be taken with the central 1280 by 720 pixels of the 4000 by 3000 pixel sensor. This will mean your lens will gain 3.1x more magnification than what you would normally expect. The magnification is slightly higher for the video mode because we are recording in the 16:9 aspect ratio. It provides you with an extended telephotographic lens, and when you use the camera in this fashion, the video will appear to be as good as the one collected without activating this command.

The Extended Optical Zoom command is as follows:

MENU/SET>REC>(pg 4) EX. OPT. ZOOM>[OFF], [ON]

Normally the command is set to [OFF], so to activate the command, set it to [ON]. The EX. OPT. ZOOM command is not enabled when MENU/SET>REC>PICTURE SIZE = [L] and when MENU/SET>REC>QUALITY = any of the RAW file formats. If you want to still use this command in the video mode and save RAW files on your memory card, you will have to set the mode dial to Motion Picture P Mode. Then, you will see be able to set the command.

MENU/SET>MOTION PICTURE>(pg 2) EX. OPT. ZOOM>[ON], [OFF]

The default setting for this command is [OFF], and you will need to turn it to [ON] to use it.

DIGITAL ZOOM

The DIGITAL ZOOM command differs from EX. OPT. ZOOM in that there will be a noticeable degradation of the image. When describing how the EX. OPT. ZOOM command worked, we pointed out that it was working directly with the pixel from the sensor. That is to say, there was a one-to-one correspondence between the sensor pixel and the pixel that was outputted for the saved file.

However, the DIGITAL ZOOM command does not follow this guideline. It takes the single pixel of the sensor and then remaps it so that it now occupies the space of 2 or 4 pixels in the final image. As a result, the image appears blocky—or as Panasonic describes it, there is image deterioration. The command for this is as follows:

MENU/SET>MOTION PICTURE>(pg 2) DIGITAL ZOOM>[OFF], [2X], [4X]

Normally the command is set to [OFF]. To activate the command, set it to either [2X] or [4X]. The DIGITAL ZOOM command is enabled using the same rules you use with the EX. OPT. ZOOM command. The DIGITAL ZOOM command is not enabled when MENU/SET>REC>PICTURE SIZE = [L] or when MENU/SET>REC>QUALITY = any of the RAW file formats.

If you want to still use this command in the video mode and save RAW files on your memory card, you will have to set the mode dial to Motion Picture P Mode. Then you will see be able to set the command. The [2X] setting doubles the magnification, while [4X] doubles it again.

Choosing File Formats: JPEG

A few photographers feel that choosing the file format in which to save their images boils down to image quality. If you want the highest-quality image, you use RAW and work with software outside of the camera to translate the file and generate high-quality images. Instructing the camera to save files in JPEG will reduce image quality and should not be done. Although technically correct, you should use a balanced approach in choosing file formats. If the situation warrants, images should be saved as JPEGs if it improves the camera's performance.

One reason for choosing JPEG over RAW is the need to store images on the memory card. A RAW file is almost twice the size of the equivalent JPEG (highest quality saved), and you can save almost twice as many pictures on your card by using JPEG. And by choosing the highest JPEG compression, you can shrink the file size even more.

In addition, many image processing commands are available when you save your files using JPEG. As mentioned earlier, Film Mode has noise reduction controls to reduce the effects of shooting at high ISO. There are also the various color schemes on Film Mode and My Color Mode that will be retained only if you save the files as JPEG. Using our experience in recording black-and-white images, we enjoy the convenience of the images having this appearance without the need to use the RAW processor to remove the color and convert the images to monochrome. What makes black-and-white especially convenient is the electronic viewfinder. It provides a preview of the subject as a monochrome image, and this facilitates composition. When you are using an optical viewfinder on a DSLR, the eyepiece will show a color image, and this can detract from framing a powerful back-and-white image.

Finally, judicious use of JPEG gives you an additional option when shooting videos outside of the Motion Picture P Mode. You can use the EX. OPT. ZOOM to get some additional reach if you do not have an extreme telephoto lens. This can provide a 2x to 3x increase in zoom factor.

Saving images as JPEGs can provide advantages in creating a digital image. You should experiment with the options available when using this file format.

Optical Image Stabilizer (O.I.S.)

The Optical Image Stabilizer (O.I.S.) counteracts the minute tremors and movements that occur when handholding a camera and ensure taking sharp photographs. Generally, a fast shutter speed setting helps hide these tiny movements at the time of exposure. But as the shutter speed becomes longer, the chance of movement occurring while the shutter is open increases and the image appears smeared. Panasonic's O.I.S. helps prevent image blurring resulting from this "jiggling." You know the command is active by the stabilizer icon (table 6-3) on the display screen (figure 6-14a, figure 6-14b). If the shutter speed becomes so slow that there is a danger of obtaining a blurred image, the stabilizer icon is transformed into the red jitter icon. To avoid taking a blurred image, you should mount the camera on a tripod and make sure it is held rigidly. Or, you can increase the ISO and/or ambient light to allow for a faster shutter speed. The STABILIZER command has four settings:

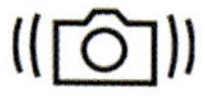	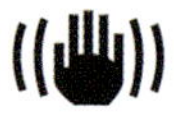
Jitter warning Use tripod or faster shutter speed	Stabilizer status May be followed by 1, 2, 3, or OFF

Table 6-3: Stabilizer and jitter icons and descriptions

MENU/SET>REC>(pg 2) STABILIZER>[OFF], [MODE1], [MODE2], [MODE3]

Set the command to [OFF] when the camera is mounted on a tripod. If the STABILIZER command is active when the camera is held absolutely steady, it can generate a blurred image.

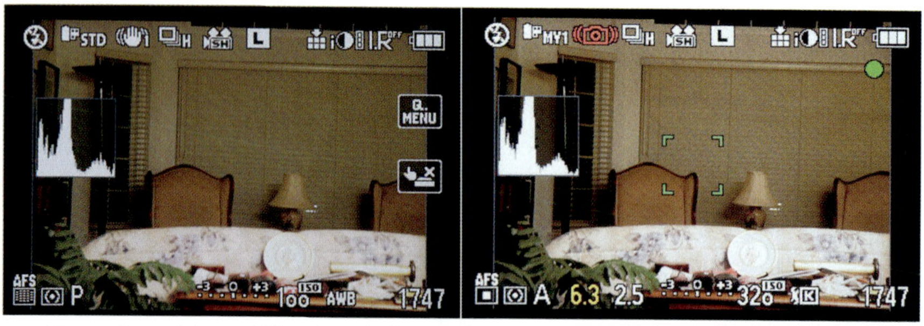

Figure 6-14a: The stabilizer icon indicates the exposure has not been evaluated yet; Figure 6-14b: The jitter icon has replaced the stabilizer icon, and the use of a tripod is recommended.

Selecting [Mode1] makes the stabilizer function active at all times, and so its effects will be visible on the LCD screen while you are holding the camera (figure 6-15). With older Panasonic lenses, there is a Stabilizer On/Off switch, and you could do a direct comparison of the effectiveness of the stabilizer by holding the camera and turning the switch to On or Off. The lens provided with the Panasonic G2 camera lacks this feature. Using the menu command described earlier is the only way it can be turned off. [MODE2] turns on the stabilization process, but it only works at the moment the shutter-release button is pressed. [MODE3] is for shooting an action event when you are panning the camera along a horizontal axis. The stabilizer works in the vertical plane, and is inactivate on the horizontal plane.

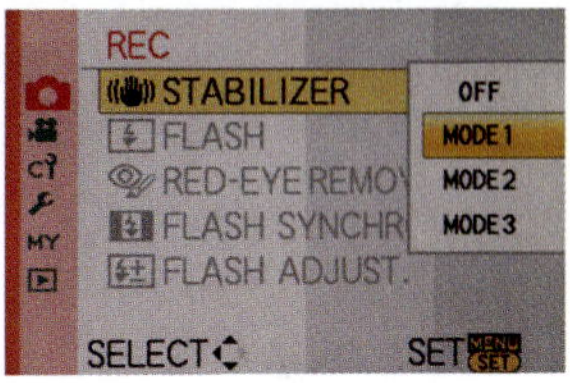

Figure 6-15: STABILIZER command in [MODE1]

O.I.S. Variation Among Micro Four Thirds Lenses

The Optical Image Stabilizer (O.I.S.) mechanism is located in some Panasonic lenses. Many of the telephoto zoom lenses have an on/off switch on their barrel for this mechanism; however, some of the newest lenses lack this switch—its function has been incorporated as a software command. Consequently, the STABILIZER command varies when you attach different lenses. In the case of our 14-140 mm lens, which has the on/off switch, the STABILIZER command exists but there is no [OFF] option in the menu. In contrast, the lens supplied with the Panasonic G2 camera lacks this on/off switch on its barrel and you can only turn it off in software.

If you use a lens made by Olympus, designed for the Micro Four Thirds system, you will not have any O.I.S. capability. That camera manufacturer has built the stabilization mechanism into the camera body, so none of its lenses have this feature. In addition, some of the petite "pancake" lenses from Panasonic will not be equipped with the O.I.S. mechanism.

AUTO BRACKET

Although the AUTO BRACKET command can be used in the predefined scenes modes, we have found it more useful in the P, A, S, and M Modes.

This command will automatically take a series of shots, each at different exposure settings. At first glance, one might think this is unnecessary; the camera's built-in meter does an accurate job of indicating exposure and slight errors in measurement can be corrected by using Exposure Compensation. However, The AUTO BRACKET command's value is important in providing a range of exposures for high dynamic range (HDR) photography.

HDR combines several shots taken with different exposures to generate a file with an expanded dynamic range. When this file is rendered with tone mapping software, it is possible to display all these intensities in a single image. This is a technique you can use to overcome the limitations of your camera by using image processing. You use this when you cannot record all the intensity values in the scene with a single exposure; objects in the shade will be hidden in the darkness and the brightest areas will be overexposed because the sensor is overwhelmed by too much light. Typically, by using a single exposure, only the mid tones will be recorded. Figures 6-16a-c displays three of a series of 7 exposure bracketed photos. The exposure is varied by a total of + and – 2 f-stops using 2/3 f-stop intervals (three on each side of the optimum exposure). Figure 6-16d is the combined image using HDR software.

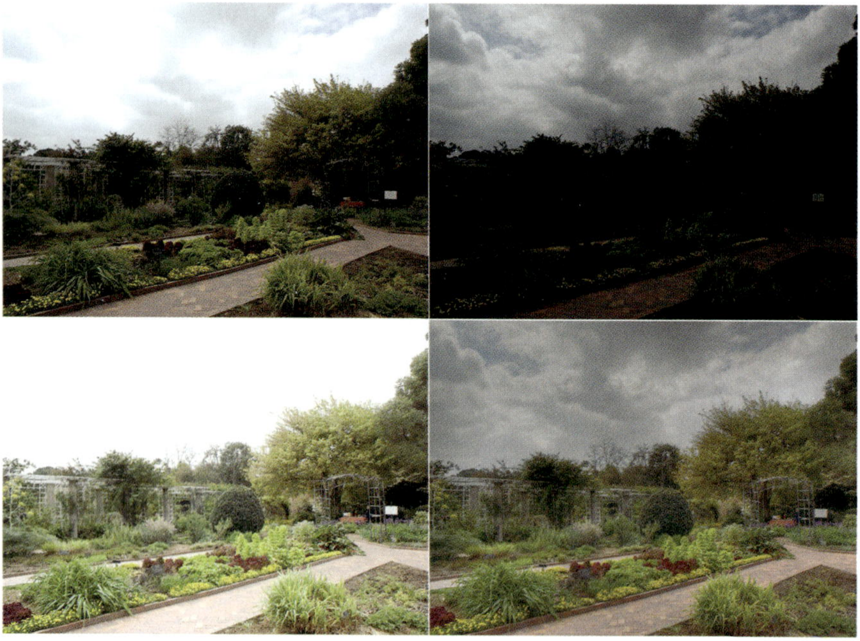

Figure 6-16a: Single recommended exposure;
Figure 6-16b: 2 f-stop under exposure;
Figure 6-16c: 2 f-stop over exposure;
Figure 6-16d: HDR image

To record all these intensity variations, several different exposures need to be shot. Specifically, you will take one shot for recording the highlights (figure 6-16b), another to expose the mid–tones (figure 6-16a), and finally, a third shot to record the shadows (figure 6-16c). Individually, the photographs will be unsatisfactory, but by using the right software (tone mapping), you can merge them into a single image that will have all the information in highlights, mid-tones, and shadows (figure 6-16d).

To accomplish this requires collecting a set of varying exposures. As a starting point, we would need to tell the camera how many exposures to take and how much variation there need be between exposures. Here is the command to do this:

MENU/SET>REC>(pg 4) AUTO BRACKET>STEP>[3 1/3], [3 2/3], [5 1/3], [5 2/3], [7 1/3], [7 2/3]

Each of the options describes the number of shots and their variation, so 3 1/3 means three shots, taken at 1/3 f-stop intervals. Or at the other extreme, you can use 7 2/3, taking seven shots at 2/3 f-stop intervals where the resulting 7 shots will span + and – 2 f-stops from the optimum exposure. Then you need determine the order in which you take the photographs:

MENU/SET>REC>(pg 4) AUTO BRACKET>SEQUENCE>-[0/-/+], [-/0/+]

The option [0/-/+] starts the exposure sequence at the exposure recommended by the camera meter and then proceeds from underexposed to overexposed images. The second option, [-/0/+], starts the exposure on the underexposure side, proceeds to the recommended exposure, and then goes to the overexposure side. The bar on the bottom of the screen will show how and when the burst will be fired.

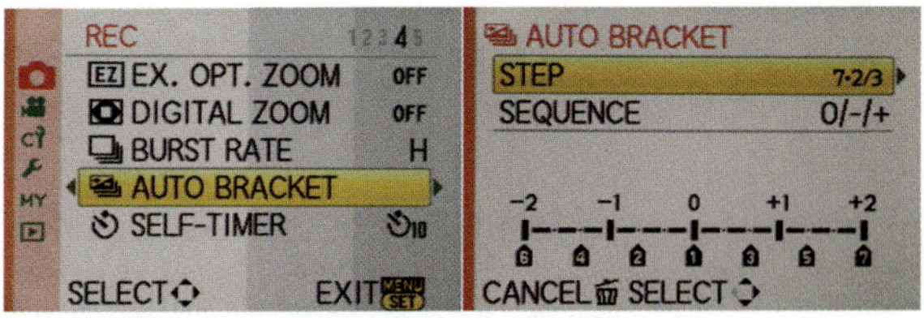

Figure 6-17a: AUTO BRACKET command highlighted; Figure 6-17b: AUTO BRACKET command's two options: [STEP] and [SEQUENCE]

Executing Auto Bracketing

Once the AUTO BRACKET command values have been selected, you are ready to fire your shots. We do not use the AUTO BRACKET command as a shotgun approach to find a shot with the best exposure. Rather, we use it to explore HDR photography. We tend to select the maximum [7 2/3] for seven shots at 2/3 f-stops increments. This way, we have the most data to work with and the best chance of getting a picture we want to keep.

If you are interested in pursuing HDR photography, we have a couple of more recommendations. First, use the camera in A Mode. This will force the camera to maintain a constant aperture and then it will vary the shutter speed for over- and underexposing the shots. Second, maintaining a constant depth of field is essential for merging the pictures; otherwise, you will lose definition in those areas that drop out of the depth of field. Third, we recommend mounting the camera on a tripod.

Any shift in the camera position will blur the resultant picture when they are merged. Finally, use a remote release to release the shutter in order to prevent movement prior to or during exposure. If you do not set the camera to Burst Mode, you will be forced—at the settings we recommend—to press the shutter-release button for each exposure. This will force you to keep track of when you have completed the series. It is easier to use the Burst Mode and have all the shots fire with one press of the shutter-release button.

Setting the Function Button

The down directional arrow button doubles as a Function button and will initiate a saved command. The Function button's value is set by the Fn BUTTON SET command:

MENU/SET>CUSTOM>Fn BUTTON SET>

The Fn BUTTON SET command has 10 options from which to select:

[FOCUS AREA SET]
[ASPECT RATIO]
[QUALITY]
[METERING MODE]
[I.RESOLUTION]
[I.EXPOSURE]
[EX. OPT. ZOOM]
[GUIDE LINE]
[REC AREA]
[REMAINING DISP.]

To set the Fn BUTTON SET command:

1. Select MENU/SET>CUSTOM>Fn BUTTON SET.
2. Press the right directional arrow button once to display the list of options.
3. Using the up and down directional arrow buttons, scroll through the list of options. Highlight one and press the MENU/SET button to select. You will be returned to the CUSTOM menu with the selected option's associated icon display next to the Fn BUTTON SET command.

Cleaning the Sensor

Each time you turn on the camera, it will automatically clean the sensor. There may be times when you feel an extra cleaning is in order without turning the camera off and back on. You can use the following command to have the sensor cleaned:

MENU/SET>CUSTOM>SENSOR CLEANING

To set the SENSOR CLEANING command:

1. Select MENU/SET>CUSTOM>SENSOR CLEANING.
2. Press the right directional arrow button once. The following message is displayed:

   START PROCESSING? [YES], [NO]

   Select [YES] to start the sensor cleaning process. Two messages will display: first "SENSOR CLEAN" and then "PROCESS FINISHED."

   Select [NO] to stop the process.

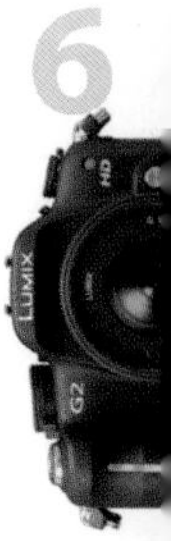

Note: Although the Panasonic G2 manual states the camera's sensor is cleaned by "blow(ing) off the debris and dust", we have also found while reviewing other Panasonic material that the sensor is cleaned by vibrating the sensor at 50,000 times per second. Regardless of how it actually occurs, use the SENSOR CLEANING command if you feel an additional cleaning is required.

Custom Mode

The setting and use of custom settings can be confusing. There are several commands used and multiple locations within the menu structure to look to accomplish setting and utilizing custom settings. The following briefly lists the basic components and terminology:

- Custom Mode refers to the CUST icon on the mode dial.
- The CUSTOM MODE menu option is the first option within the Custom Mode's menu structure. This menu option contains the three custom setting groups. Use this command to save a group of custom command settings for future use.
- The CUSTOM menu option displays in all of the main menu structures when the MENU/SET button has been pressed. The CUSTOM menu allows you to set values for many commands. It also contains the CUST. SET MEM. command, which you will use to select a custom setting group. Note the CUSTOM menu is available in all of the 13 modes on the mode dial–Custom Mode included.

The Custom Mode is accessed using the CUST icon on the mode dial. This mode allows you to save up to three sets of camera command settings to recall and use to take your pictures. The three custom settings groups are identified as: C1, C2, C3. They are all initially set to the P Mode command values.

Although the camera will save most of your command settings, only 10 are displayed on the Custom Mode's CUSTOM MODE command:

MENU/SET>CUSTOM MODE>[C1 SET1], [C2 SET2], [C3 SET3]>[*10 command settings – See list below*]

AF/AE LOCK
AF/AE LOCK HOLD
AF+MF
FOCUS PRIORITY
AF ASSIST LAMP
PRE AF
Fn BUTTON SET
AUTO REVIEW
LONG SHTR NR
SHOOT W/O LENS

Not all of the command values will be saved in the custom settings groups. The following lists commands which are not saved: [CLOCK SET], [TRAVEL DATE], [NO.RESET], [RESET], [LANGUAGE] and [SCENE MENU]. In addition,

[BABY1]/[BABY2] and [PET] birthday and name settings in Scene Mode are not saved along with the data registered with [FACE RECOG.]

Save Custom Settings

Although only 10 commands are displayed when you're viewing each custom settings group within the CUSTOM MODE command, each saved custom settings group contains all of the camera's command values at the time the group was saved minus the ones listed previously. If you wish to replace a saved custom settings group value, take the following action:

1. Go into the appropriate main menu option and change the command value.
2. Select CUST. SET MEM on the CUSTOM menu and press the right directional arrow button to display the list of of custom settings groups: [C1], [C2], or [C3]:

   MENU/SET>CUSTOM>CUST. SET MEM.>[C1], [C2], [C3]

3. Using the up and down directional arrow buttons, select the custom setting group you wish to replace with the new settings. Press the MENU/SET button.
4. You will be asked the following question:

   OVERWRITE CURRENT CAMERA STATUS AS CUSTOM SET n? [YES], [NO]

   Note: n will be the number 1, 2, or 3 associated with the selected custom settings group.

   Select [YES] to replace the selected custom settings group with the new settings. Select [NO] to stop the process and return to the display screen.

Whatever the camera command values were at the time the custom settings group was overwritten, are then saved in the selected custom settings group.

You do not have to be set to the mode dial's Custom Mode icon to set a custom settings group. You can select any of the 13 mode dial icons, but you must be on the mode dial's Custom Mode icon to see the saved settings.

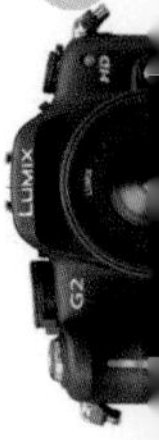

View Saved Custom Settings

As mentioned earlier you can only easily view 10 of the saved command settings through the Custom Mode. To do so, go through the following steps:

1. Move the mode dial to Custom Mode.
2. Press the MENU/SET button to display the CUSTOM MODE command containing the three custom settings groups: [C1 SET1], [C2 SET2], [C3 SET3].
3. Using the up and down directional arrow buttons, select one of the custom settings groups.
4. Once selected, press the right directional arrow button.
5. The saved custom settings display. To exit, press the Trash Can button.

Once you are viewing a custom settings group, if you decide to select the group, press the MENU/SET button. Otherwise use the Trash Can button to back out of the specific custom settings group's 10 commands value screen and continue to back out of the menu structure.

Utilize Saved Custom Settings

This is easy. To utilize a save custom settings group, execute the same steps as you would when viewing the saved 10 commands except in step 5 press the MENU/SET button to activate the saved command settings instead of the Trash Can button to exit.

As long as you are still set to the Custom Mode icon, you will be using the selected custom settings group. You are able to temporarily override any of the saved settings by selecting a command in the menu structure and changing the value. This does not change the saved custom settings group value, but the new command value will be in effect until you select a different custom settings group or exit the mode dial's Custom Mode.

Recommendation

Due to the way we use our camera, we have not found this to be a useful feature. There is no indicator on the display screen letting you know which of the custom setting groups you had selected. We rarely take pictures in the same location with the same settings, and when we have, there has been a significant amount of time between the situations that having preset custom command settings at our disposal has not been necessary. This is not to say it would not be useful for you. If you are taking pictures in a studio and will be using the same group of camera settings over and over again, this might be a very handy feature. The major drawback with this feature within the Panasonic G2 camera is that there is no easy way to know which custom setting group you selected. It is easy to be confused as to what group of settings you have selected and whether you had temporally overridden any of the command values. So if you are going to utilize this feature, keep tight controls on what you have set up and when you are going to use them.

The System Approach Expanding the Camera's Utility

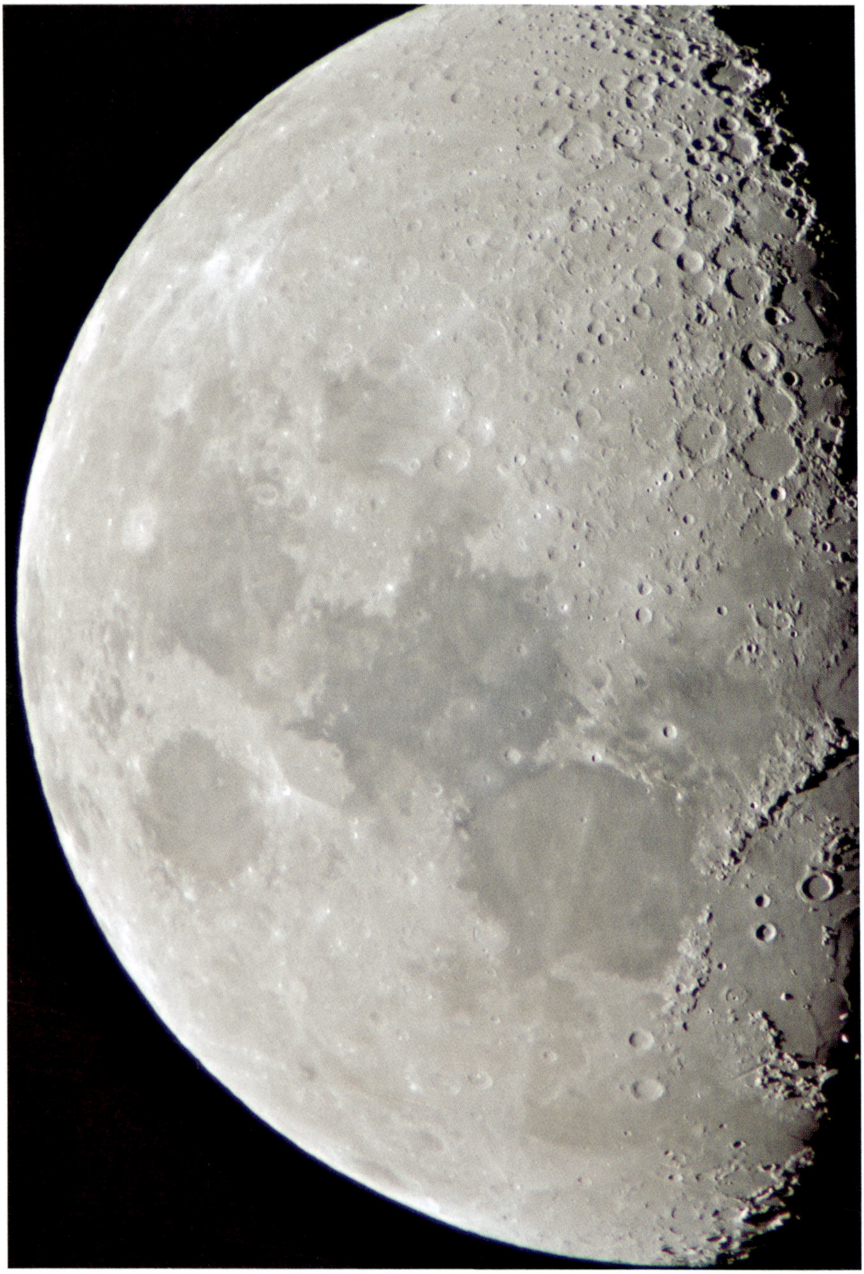

7

Introduction: Optical Accessories

If you have just bought a Panasonic G2 camera and the only camera you previously owned was a point-and-shoot compact camera, you will be in for a pleasant surprise. With the availability of accessory lenses and adapters, your camera will be able to record minute microorganisms or photograph the stars. If you already own an interchangeable lens camera, you will be pleased with how well your investment in lenses and accessories will integrate with your new Panasonic G2 camera.

For the neophyte just starting with photography, supplementary lenses can provide a new perspective on recording scenes. You can use a super wide-angle lens to encompass a greater area in an interior shot, or you can employ a telephoto lens for obtaining a close-up portrait of a wary animal. Additionally, you can play with perspective to generate a picture that emphasizes the expanse of a scene or use the extreme telephoto to "flatten" a scene so that objects appear to be juxtaposed. All of these tricks become possible once you mount different lenses to the camera body.

You may already have an extensive collection of lenses with your single-lens reflex (SLR) body. A Panasonic G2 camera can be a useful addition because it is smaller and lighter than most of its competitors. It becomes a handy camera to take out on spontaneous trips and informal family gatherings where a larger camera's weight and size can discourages its use. Also, the Panasonic G2 camera has the unusual and invaluable characteristic of working well with lenses made by virtually all other manufacturers. We have used Nikon lenses with the Panasonic G2 camera body for our technical work (a mix of close-up photography and photomicrography). For these tasks, the Panasonic's electronic viewfinder and its tilting rear LCD display screen is more usable than the Nikon body's optical viewfinder or its fixed rear LCD screen.

In addition to lenses, there are nonoptical accessories that will help your photography. Not the least of these is the tripod for holding the camera steady. Not only is this required for working with telescopes or telephoto lenses, it is invaluable for those who wish to get the maximum performance from their optics.

Optical Accessories: The Micro Four Thirds Lens

The Panasonic G2 camera is sold with a basic zoom lens with a focal length of 14 mm to 42 mm. By itself, it is a versatile photographic tool capable of handling most photographic assignments. However, you can expand these capabilities by purchasing additional lenses. The most convenient ones to use are those made by Panasonic and Olympus.

These lenses are designed as part of the Micro Four Thirds system. This system has a defined set of characteristics for how the lens and body communicate, the size of the sensor, and the mechanical connection between lens and body. Any lens will work on a Panasonic G2 camera body if its manufacturers follow the Micro Four Thirds standards. It is unusual when two manufacturers, Olympus and Panasonic, allow the user the flexibility to interchange each other's lenses on their camera bodies.

Such a strategy benefits the consumer by providing more choices for buying a lens. Typically a camera body and lens are restricted to a single manufacturer—Nikon lenses are used with Nikon camera bodies and Canon lenses are used with Canon camera bodies. If you buy a lens that is specified for the Micro Four Thirds system, you can be confident that it will work easily with your Panasonic G2 camera body (table 7-1). Generally, such a lens guarantees that the following will work: automatic exposure, automatic focus, and control of its aperture from the camera body. The only thing you lose when you buy a lens made by Olympus and use it on your Panasonic G2 camera body is Optical Image Stabilizer (O.I.S.), a feature for steadying the image and negating the effects of camera movement during exposure. This feature counters the movement of the camera, and in the case of the Panasonic, the mechanism is located within the lens. In the case of Olympus products, the stabilizer system works with the sensor in the camera body so their lenses will not have this feature.

Micro Four Thirds Lenses and Four Thirds Lenses

The Micro Four Thirds lenses evolved from the Four Thirds system, developed by Olympus. Originally, the lenses for this system were designed for DSLR cameras and the lens and camera bodies were to be more compact than its competitors'.

However, this advantage was soon lost as other manufacturers made smaller and lighter DSLRs. To regain its advantage in having a small interchangeable lens camera, Olympus designed the Micro Four Thirds system. This reduced the camera size by removing the optical viewfinder and replacing it with an electronic viewfinder using the output from the sensor. The lens can therefore be placed closer to the sensor, allowing for a reduction in both lens and camera body size.

Manufacturer	Description	Focal Length	35mm Equivalent	Stabilized?
Panasonic	Wide-angle zoom	7–14 mm f/4	14–28 mm	
Panasonic	Fisheye fixed focal length	8 mm f/3.5	16 mm	
Olympus	Wide-angle zoom	9–18 mm f/4.0–f/5.6	18–36 mm	
Panasonic	3D fixed	12.5 mm f/12	25 mm	
Panasonic	Wide-angle fixed	14 mm f/2.5	28 mm	
Panasonic	Normal zoom	14–42 mm f/3.5–f/5.6	28–84 mm	X
Olympus	Normal zoom	14–42 mm f/3.5–f/5.6	28–84 mm	
Panasonic	Normal zoom	14–45 mm f/3.5–f/5.6	28–90 mm	X
Panasonic	Normal zoom	14–140 mm f/4.0–f/5.8	28–280 mm	X
Olympus	Normal zoom	14–150 mm f/4.0–f/5.6	28–300 mm	
Olympus	Wide-angle fixed	17 mm f/2.8	34 mm	
Panasonic	Normal fixed	20 mm f/1.7	40 mm	
Cosina	Normal fixed	25 mm f/0.95	50 mm	
Olympus	Telephoto zoom	40–150 mm f/4.0–f/5.6	80–300 mm	
Leica DG	Macro fixed	45 mm f/2.8	90 mm	X
Olympus	Telephoto zoom	75–300 mm f/4.8–f/6.7	150–600 mm	
Panasonic	Telephoto zoom	100–300 mm f/4.0–f/5.6	200–600 mm	X

Table 7-1: List of Micro Four Thirds lenses that will work on the Panasonic G2 camera body

In comparison to other manufactures such as Nikon, Canon, Pentax, and Konica-Minolta (now Sony), Panasonic does not make an extensive range of lenses for its cameras. Keep in mind that these companies have been manufacturing lenses for their camera bodies for decades. Indeed, these companies got their start with film cameras, and consequently their higher number of lenses is a reflection of their longevity. The Micro Four Thirds system is new and has only been in production for a couple of years. However, it spans a range of 7 mm to 300 mm in focal length. For users familiar with 35mm film cameras, this would translate to a wide angle of 14 mm and a telephoto to 600 mm focal length.

It would be appropriate to briefly mention why we referred to 35mm film cameras and why we use the focal length of their lens as a reference. Long-time photographic enthusiasts started with 35mm film cameras and are familiar with how lens' focal length changes the field of view.

For these types of cameras, a 28 mm lens gives a wide-angel view and encompasses a field of view of about 75 degrees, a 50 mm lens provides a normal focal length and gives a field of view of 47 degrees, and a 100 mm telephoto provides a narrower angle of view of 23.5 degrees. The lens's focal length was equated with the angle of view.

This is unfortunate because it is incorrect—its association with the angle of view is dependent on the size of the sensor. Only if the sensor size is constant can focal length be related to the field of view. This was permissible with film because the predominant film was 35mm and it was about 36 mm by 24 mm in overall size.

Unfortunately, for the digital photographer, the overall size of their camera's sensor varies. Generally, the inexpensive sensors have a smaller overall size, while the larger sensors are more expensive. Only recently has the cost of sensors dropped, making a camera whose sensor matches the size of 35mm film much more affordable. Such cameras have what are called full frame sensors. In the case of the Four Thirds camera, its sensor is about half the size of a full frame sensor, making it 17 mm by 12 mm. This means the relationship between the field of view and focal length has changed dramatically. If you take a 50 mm lens and mount it on a Four Thirds camera, you will find that the sensor—because it is smaller—sees only half of the field of view a full frame sensor would see. If the full frame sensor sees a 47 degree field of view, then the Four Thirds sensor sees half that, resulting in 23.5 degree field of view. In other words, the field of view of a 50 mm lens on a Four Thirds provides the same field of view as a 100 mm lens on a full frame camera.

Because of this, digital photographers started referring to "crop" factor or full frame equivalents. In the case of the Four Thirds system, we started thinking in terms of 2. If you take a normal 50 mm lens of a film camera and want to see the same field of view on the Four Thirds camera, you would divide 50 by 2 and select a 25 mm focal length lens. By the same token, if you want to replicate the view of a film camera you would select a lens that would be half its focal length for your Panasonic G2. For example, if you've used a film camera and the view through its 300 mm is perfect, then the lens you would select for your Panasonic G2 would be a 150 mm focal length lens.

Recommendations

The Panasonic G2 camera comes with a basic lens that is an excellent and versatile photographic tool. We recommend that before you buy additional lenses, you spend some time mastering its capabilities. When you're taking pictures and videos, the appearance of the subject changes radically between using the 14 mm focal length and using the 42 mm focal length, and you should experiment with perspective changes when using this lens' wide-angle setting.

Fishermen are noted for using a wide-angle lens (14 mm focal length) to magnify the size of their catch. They proudly pose themselves holding the fish in front of them and have the photographer move in close, framing the fish so it appears double to triple its actual size. The results belie the truism that photographs cannot lie. If the photographer uses a 42 mm setting and photographs the fisherman holding the fish out in front, it will appear to have dramatically shrunk. This setting provides a more accurate perspective and shows the fish properly—much to the chagrin of a proud fisherman. Getting to know the strengths and limitations of your camera's lens will enable you to determine if you need any additional lenses.

The 14 to 140 mm Panasonic lens is very versatile, but this 10x zoom is more expensive and heavier than the supplied 14 to 42 mm lens. The 14 to 140 mm has special features such as a silent focusing motor that will not be heard when you're recording a video. The Olympus equivalent, 14 to 150 mm zoom, is not as well suited for video work, but it's a capable optical performer. Its lower cost and lighter weight may counterbalance the disadvantage of not having the image antivibration feature. For super wide-angle work, the Panasonic and Olympus each provide wide-angle zooms. Both will create dramatic perspective effects. The Panasonic lens provides a slightly wider field of view but at almost double the price. It has a constant aperture, but unlike the Olympus lens, it cannot take filters.

The Four Thirds System

The Micro Four Thirds system evolved from the earlier Four Thirds system design that was developed by Olympus and Kodak and was based on using a sensor with a 4:3 aspect ratio, hence its name. Associated with the sensor was a standardized lens mounting system. The small sensor size (half the dimensions of a 35mm negative) would enable the manufacturer to design smaller camera bodies and lenses.

In addition, a new bayonet-type mount with electrical contacts provided communication between lens and camera body so that the unit would be able to have automatic focusing and automatic exposure. By establishing and defining this standard, it was hoped other manufacturers would design camera bodies and lenses compatible with the system. The Four Thirds standard was designed at the onset to take advantage of digital imaging and represents a break from the design of film cameras. Its lenses are designed specifically to be used with a digital sensor so as not to vignette, and this was not the case when the lens was designed to be used on film.

The Four Thirds system is used by Olympus E series SLR cameras (figure 7-1a); however, it did not attain widespread popularity. The lenses were designed with a long back focus to allow movement for a swinging mirror and an optical viewfinder. Panasonic manufactured and sold cameras and lenses for this standard—and like the Olympus lenses, the Panasonic lenses were to be used on a DSLR camera. About two years ago, Olympus and Panasonic announced the development of a Micro Four Thirds system. This would maintain the same sensor size, but it was designed on a camera body that was not a SLR. Instead, the chamber containing the mirror and optical viewfinder was eliminated and an electronic viewfinder was developed (figure 7-1b). The design reduces the distance between the lens flange and digital sensor on the camera body, enabling the manufactures to design a smaller camera body and lens system. This has some important implications for the utility of the camera body on different types of lenses.

Because the Micro Four Thirds evolved from the original Four Thirds standard, there is a partial compatibility to the Panasonic G2 camera body. With the aid of an adapter (figure 7-2), these lenses can be fitted to the camera body, allowing you to control the lens aperture and maintain automatic exposure. Unfortunately, automatic focus is only partially implemented: Some lenses cannot automatically focus, and those that do don't focus with the speed and precision of a Micro Four Thirds system lens. However, these lenses can be used effectively by manually focusing them.

Keep this in mind if you buy Olympus Four Thirds system lenses with the intention of using them on your Panasonic G2 camera body. Also, you will lose the advantage of image stabilization.

Table 7-2 (on the following page) lists the lenses available from Olympus that will fit your Panasonic G2 camera with the aid of Panasonic's DMW-MA1 adapter. This adapter extends the lens from the body and provides electrical communication between the two. Many of these lenses are extremely good optically, and they tend to have a larger maximum aperture than the Micro Four Thirds system lenses. For example, the expensive 90-250 mm zoom lens has an aperture of f/2.8. As such, it makes a useful addition if you are interested in working with limited lighting situations. Some of these lenses, even if they are used only as manual focus optics, can be valuable for nature photography. Not all of these lenses are compatible with the Panasonic automatic focusing system; however, all lenses can be focused manually.

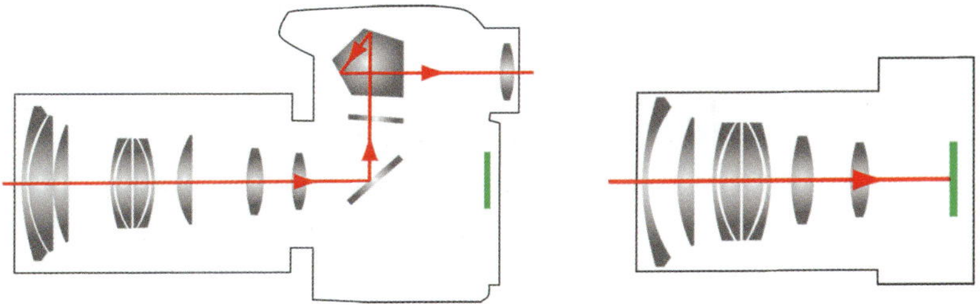

Figure 7-1a: The back focus of a DSLR lens has to be long enough to allow for the optical viewfinder and the movement of the mirror; Figure 7-1b: The Panasonic G2 Micro Four Thirds body and lens can be made smaller because the lens back focus is shorter

Manufacturer	Description	Focal Length	35mm Equivalent	Grade
Olympus	Wide-angle zoom	7–14 mm f/4	14–28 mm	SHG
Olympus	Fixed focal length	8 mm f/3.5	16 mm	HG
Olympus	Wide-angle zoom	9–18 mm f/4.0–f/5.6	18–36 mm	STD
Olympus	Wide-angle zoom	11–12 mm f/2.8–f/3.5	22–24 mm	HG
Olympus	Normal zoom	12–35 mm f/2.0	24–70 mm	SHG
Olympus	Normal zoom	12–60 mm f/2.8–f/4.0	24–120 mm	HG
Olympus	Normal zoom	14–54 mm f/2.8–f/3.5	28–108 mm	HG
Olympus	Normal zoom	14–42 mm f/3.5–f/5.6	28–84 mm	STD
Olympus	Normal zoom	18–180 mm f/3.5–f/6.3	36–360 mm	STD
Olympus	Fixed focal length	25 mm f/2.8	50 mm	STD
Olympus	Telephoto zoom	35–100 mm f/2.0	70–200 mm	SHG
Olympus	Telephoto zoom	35–90 mm f/3.5–f/5.6	70–180 mm	STD
Olympus	Macro fixed	35 mm f/3.5	70 mm	STD
Olympus	Telephoto zoom	40–150 mm f/4.0–f/5.6	80–300 mm	STD
Olympus	Macro fixed	50 mm f/2.0	100 mm	HG
Olympus	Telephoto zoom	50–200 mm f/2.8–f/3.5	100–400 mm	HG
Olympus	Telephoto zoom	70–300 mm f/4.0–f/5.6	140–600 mm	STD
Olympus	Telephoto zoom	90–250 mm f/2.8	180–500 mm	SHG
Olympus	Fixed focal length	150 mm f/2.8	300 mm	SHG
Olympus	Normal zoom	300 mm f/2.8	600 mm	SHG

Table 7-2: List of the Four Thirds system lenses that fit a Panasonic G2 camera using a DMW-MA1 adapter (SHG – Super High Grade; HG – High Grade; STD – Standard)

Focusing Four Thirds Lens

In the previous chapter, we discussed overriding automatic focus using the Panasonic and Olympus Micro Four Thirds lenses' focusing ring. This can also be done for the Four Third lenses, but there are some differences. First, the automatic focusing performance is slower and less precise with the Four Thirds lens than it is with a Micro Four Thirds. Indeed, we advise against using these models in AF Mode. If you set MENU/SET>CUSTOM>(pg 3) AF+MF to [ON], with the intention of overriding the slow automatic focus by turning the ring and achieving manual focus, you will be in for an unpleasant wait. The lens focusing ring is disengaged until the camera finds and locks focus.

So, if automatic focusing is slow, you will have to wait for the process to be completed before you can override manually. The necessity for waiting for the autofocus mechanism to find focus slows the camera operation by delaying your access for manual focus. As a result, we simply use the lens with M Mode. With this setting, the lens focus responds immediately to a slight turn. If you set MENU/SET>CUSTOM>(pg 3) MF ASSIST to [ON], there is an increase in magnification to facilitate focusing. You can see the finest subject details and focus precisely. Pressing the shutter-release button half-way drops the magnification so you can see the whole field of view.

Legacy Lenses, Discontinued Lenses

The Micro Four Thirds lenses have a shorter back focus than the Four Third lenses, and as a result, a short extension adapter is required to fit the latter on the camera body. Panasonic sells an adapter for Four Thirds lenses, and it can be seen in figure 7-2 on the left. Other SLR lenses can be used on the Panasonic G2 body and will also require an adapter. The adapter on the right is made by Voigtlander and attaches Nikon lenses to the Panasonic G2 camera body. The middle adapter is a C mount adapter.

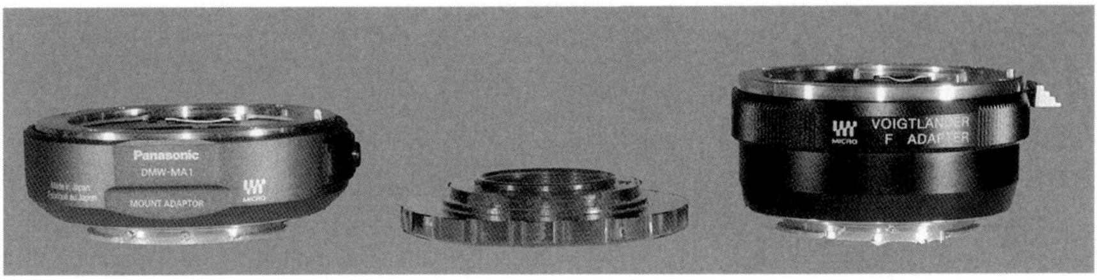

Figure 7-2: From left to right, Panasonic Four Thirds lens adaptor, C mount adapter; Voigtlander adapter for the Panasonic G2 camera body

A glance at an online auction site or a visit to a camera store reveals an abundance of used lenses. Many are orphans, abandoned when their owners replaced their film SLR with a digital camera. Optically excellent, these lenses are on sale because they lacked automatic focusing or their owners had switched to a camera brand incompatible with the lens. But for you, they may be a bargain—providing an excellent optical tool for your Panasonic G2 camera at a very reasonable price. Users of the Micro Four Thirds system cameras fondly refer to these older lenses as legacy lenses.

The Micro Four Thirds mirrorless design and the replacement of an optical with an electronic viewfinder gives this camera a short lens flange to sensor distance. If the distance is too great, a lens cannot focus to infinity, thereby limiting its capability to work at distances. If the distance is short, an adapter is easily fabricated to increase the distance between the lens and sensor. This is the situation with the Panasonic G2 camera body. Several manufacturers have built adapters that lengthen the Panasonic's dimension to accommodate other manufacturers' lenses. Lenses from Nikon, Canon, Pentax, Konica, Minolta, and Leica can be attached to and used on the Panasonic G2 camera body. In fact, the Panasonic G2 camera body is unique in that it is one of the few cameras that can mount and use Leica lenses.

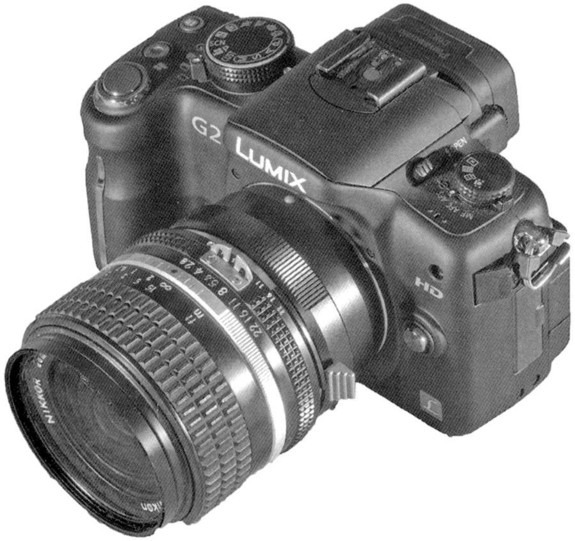

Figure 7-3: An old manual focus 28 mm Nikon lens with a Voigtlander adapter mounted on a Panasonic G2 camera body

Another feature of the Panasonic G2 camera body is its ability to work without being electrically coupled to a lens. Frequently the older, bargain lenses lack the mechanism for automatic focusing. Thus, when they are attached to a newer camera body, they must be focused manually by turning the focusing ring on the lens and determining if the image is sharp. With today's modern DSLRs, this apparently simple operation turns out to be a major obstacle.

Today's camera bodies are dependent on automatic focusing, and their viewfinders are ill suited as focusing aids. These viewfinders have too little magnification and are so dim that it is difficult to see fine subject details, making it almost impossible to focus visually. The dependence on automatic focus has deemphasized the need to have large, bright views of the subject. This weakness is not present in the Panasonic G2 camera. Their display screens are very bright, and they have an automatic gain control that intensifies the display if the subject moves into the shadows or a darkened area. Also, their displays have enough resolution that fine details can be seen readily—and for the most critical work, the magnification can be increased to evaluate the minutest details. In short, the view through this camera has enough magnification to judge focus. Achieving critical focus with high magnification is simple and precise.

The lack of electronic communication requires a camera to measure light intensity directly off the sensor. This is easily accomplished by measuring the diminution of light as one closes the lens aperture down. Unfortunately for the user of a camera with an optical viewfinder, the view gets progressively dimmer as the lens is stopped down. This can make an already dim view nearly useless. It does not help that as you do this, imperfections in the screen are made obvious and the subject is superimposed on an increasingly grainy screen. The Panasonic G2's electronic viewfinders do not suffer these defects. As mentioned in the previous paragraph, they compensate for decreasing light by brightening the display screen. The photographer, when closing the aperture down, does not notice any decrease in light, so he never loses track of his subject.

Adapters for Panasonic G2 Camera Body and Legacy Lenses

Several companies make adapters to attach older lenses to the Panasonic G2 camera body. Table 7-3 (on the following page) lists the various adapters and lenses available for this camera body. The price for the adapters range from a low of $20 for units purchased online to $200 or more for units produced by well-known manufacturers.

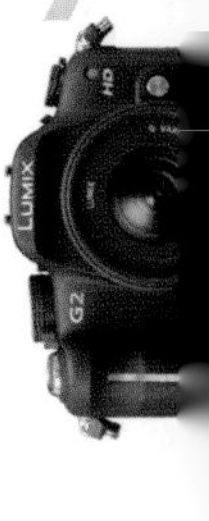

The more expensive adapters tend to be of higher quality. They are well built, and since we mount our camera on microscopes and telescopes, we accept their cost. However, we have tried some of the inexpensive adapters on several lenses. For casual use they work well, although there are some reports of mechanical problems with the mount. These are generally minor, such as a lens diaphragm ring facing upside down when mounted on the camera body. Whether you should purchase the economical versus the more expensive unit is a matter of personal preference.

Legacy Lens to Mount on Panasonic G2	Panasonic Adapter	Novoflex Adapter	Voightlander Adapter	Rayqual Adapter
Canon FD				X
Contax/ Yashica		X		X
Leica M	X	X	X	
Leica R	X	X		
M-42 Pentax/ Practica		X		
Minolta MD		X		
Nikon F		X	X	X
Olympus OM		X		X
Pentax K		X	X	
Sony Alpha/ Minolta AF		X		
T-2 Adaptall		X		

Table 7-3: Legacy lenses and the adapters that can be fitted to the Panasonic G2 camera body

We have purchased Nikon adapters made by Voigtlander from a company in California known as Cameraquest (figure 7-2, figure 7-3).

You can find the latest on the currently produced adapters at the following locations:

- Panasonic: **www.panasonic.net**
- Voigtlander: **www.voigtlaender.de/cms/voigtlaender/voigtlaender_cms.nsf/id/pa_home_e.html**
- Novoflex: **www.novoflex.com**
- Rayqual: **www.cameraquest.com**

Note that we could not find the home page for Rayqual. Cameraquest describes and sells Voigtlander products as well as Rayqual adapters on its website.

Exposure with Legacy Lenses

Legacy lenses will provide either automatic or manual exposure with the Panasonic G2 camera body; however, you need to select which mode dial option you wish to use. You have four choices: Manual Exposure (M), Aperture-Priority (A), Program (P), and Shutter-Priority (S) Modes as covered in chapters 5 and 6. For our work, we only use two of these: M or A Mode, the former providing manual exposure where we have to set the shutter speed and aperture, and the latter providing automatic exposure and an active Exposure Compensation tool. We do not use P Mode—it is really the equivalent of A Mode since it has no control of the aperture. Nor do we use S Mode since it does not provide a light meter for setting exposure. Remember, the camera does not control nor does it know the aperture that is set on the lens. So in the display, the aperture value will show 0.

Our favorite method of adjusting exposure with legacy lenses is to set the mode dial to A. When in this mode, pressing the shutter-release button halfway sets the shutter speed and a full press fires the camera and captures the image. It is the fastest method of finding exposure when using a legacy lens. If you wish to over- or underexpose the photograph, you do so by turning the rear dial since the Exposure Compensation tool is always on. The camera does not show the recommended shutter speed number when you first turn the mode dial to A. If you do not see a recommended shutter speed number, press the shutter-release button halfway.

To use this mode, we start with the lens wide open since this provides the narrowest depth of field and facilitates finding focus when turning the lens-focusing ring. After we find focus, we rotate the lens diaphragm ring to stop down the lens. You will see the shutter speed becomes longer as you turn the diaphragm ring. When you do this, the view on the display screen stays at a constant intensity even though you are reducing the light reaching the sensor.

Remember, the camera attempts to keep the display screen constant when light levels change. You see the display lighten and darken only when you turn the rear dial and change the Exposure Compensation value. The lightening shows the effects of overexposure while darkening shows the effects of underexposure. As described in earlier chapters, a series of tick marks will extend from the o mark. If more tick marks appear on the right, you are increasing overexposure. If they appear to the left, they indicate you are decreasing exposure. There is no display for the aperture—you will just see a o where the aperture value should be. Fortunately, many if not most legacy lenses have clicks marking at full or half aperture steps, so you can tell how many f-stops you have closed the lens down by the number of clicks you feel as you turn the diaphragm ring.

If you wish to control the shutter speed, set the camera's mode dial to M. Rotating the rear dial changes the shutter speed. The Exposure Compensation scale indicates how far exposure is off and when the correct exposure is achieved. If there is a line of tick marks to either the right or the left of 0, the exposure is not set correctly. You will turn either the rear dial or the lens's diaphragm ring to reduce its length. You will eventually reduce the number of tick marks so that none are displayed. If you change the aperture on the lens, you will have to correct by adjusting the shutter speed. We seldom use M Mode with our legacy lenses—using A Mode is much faster since it automatically adjusts the shutter speed when you change the aperture.

Focusing Legacy Lenses

We found a simple and invaluable feature on the Panasonic G2 camera body when working with legacy lenses. By pressing in the rear dial, we were able to raise the magnification of the image on the display screen. This is akin to using the MF ASSIST command described in the previous chapter. However, this feature did not require the command to be on. We did not see this feature described in the camera's manual, and it does not work when using either an Olympus Micro Four Thirds or a Four Thirds lens. It seems to be activated when using a legacy lens. This feature is absent on the Panasonic G1 or GH1.

You also have the option to zoom in on a portion of the image by touching the spot on the LCD screen. This will enable you to view parts of the image to help determine focus. We have found this useful when the camera is mounted on a tripod, microscope, or copy stand.

Useful Non-Panasonic Lenses

We have tested several non-Panasonic lenses with the Panasonic G2 camera body with excellent results. We used the following lenses and found them to be valuable adjuncts on the Panasonic G2:

Nikon Micro-Nikkor 55 mm f/2.8
Nikon Micro-Nikkor 105 mm f/2.8
Vivitar Series 1, 90–180 mm f/4.5 macro zoom
Nikon 180 mm f/2.8 AF
Nikon 300 mm f/2.8
Nikon 300 mm f/4 AF
Nikon 500 mm f/8

Recommendations

For the enthusiast, Panasonic and Olympus have a sufficiently wide range of lenses that can meet most of your photographic needs. They provide you with the most convenient solution for field photography. However, there is a paucity of specialized lenses such as perspective correction, a variety of fast lenses (wide maximum aperture), and super-long telephotos. The absence of these lenses can be partially solved by purchasing either Four Third lenses or legacy lenses. In both cases, there will be some loss in convenient field operation. Manual focus will have to be used.

Depending on the Four Third lens price, we do not recommend getting it unless you also buy an Olympus DSLR body. Some of these lenses are so expensive that if you purchase one, it makes more sense to simply buy an Olympus DSLR body to ensure that you work with a lens that provides rapid automatic focusing. The well-regarded 90-250 mm lens costs close to $5,000 and the Olympus's 50-200 mm lens costs close to $1,200. The former lens is so heavy and expensive, that it makes sense to buy a used Olympus E-420 body to guarantee fast automatic focus. There are less-expensive Four Thirds lenses, but for the most part, those overlap the current Micro Four Thirds lenses and you might as well stick within the Panasonic system. Of course, for the Olympus DSLR owner who already owns one of these lenses, the cost of the adapter is nominal. In this case, it makes sense to ensure that your Four Thirds lenses work on a Panasonic G2 camera body. But if you do not already own one, a more economical solution is to buy a legacy lens and the appropriate adapter.

We have used our older manual focus Nikon lenses to good effect. If you are interested in close-up work, manual focus macro lenses are excellent. In fact, we prefer using these lenses on our Panasonic G2 over the Four Thirds Olympus 50 mm f/2.0 Macro. Legacy lenses have superior controls for manual focusing. Four Thirds lenses lack this precision, and in a field such as macro photography where you primarily use manual focusing, legacy lenses are more convenient.

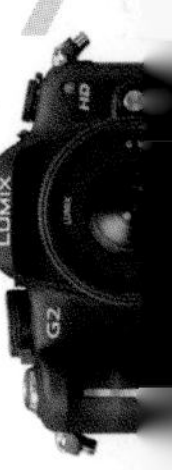

Research Microscopes

We discovered the Panasonic cameras when working in the laboratory and researching the utility of DSLRs on microscopes. It turns out the Panasonic G1 and GH1 were most suitable for photography through the microscope. This trend is continued with the Panasonic G2. So we now use this camera for our everyday picture and video photography.

This discussion will be limited to describing how the Panasonic can be mounted on a microscope. First, let's look at modern research microscopes. These instruments are very expensive and usually will be unavailable to the hobbyist, but if you are a working scientist or student, this section should prove helpful.

Many modern research microscopes have a trinocular head that has two eyepieces for visual work and a third vertically positioned eyepiece for mounting a camera (figure 7-4). Although this third tube will not be used visually, it is regarded as part of the tube system that carries eyepieces or oculars. Nikon, Leica, Olympus, and Zeiss make the most popular of the professional research microscopes, and in almost all cases their phototubes are not designed to mount large sensor cameras, such as DSLRs. In addition, many of these companies do not manufacture adapters for accomplishing this task.

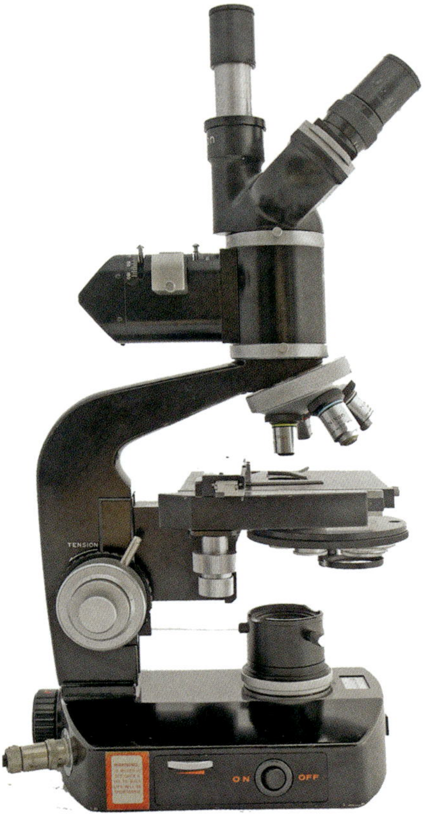

Figure 7-4: Nikon microscope with trinocular head. Only one of the binocular eyepiece tubes is visible. The third, vertical tube is for mounting a camera.

To directly mount a Panasonic G2 camera body, you would have to go to a third-party manufacturer. A popular source for this hardware is Qioptiq. Qioptiq (**www.qioptiq.com/optem-large-format-series.html**) makes a high-quality adapter, but the high price usually means it has to be purchased as part of a research grant rather than with personal funds. Its coupler is designed to mount a camera having a Nikon F mount.

So for a Panasonic G2 body, you will have to buy a Nikon adapter from Novoflex or Voigtlander to fit on your camera before you can attach it to the microscope adapter. Go to the company's website and download a PDF brochure describing its mounting system.

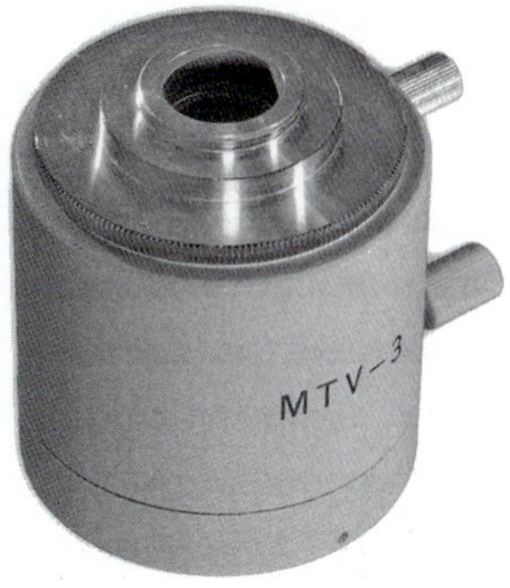

Figure 7-5: C mount from a microscope showing the mount's 25 mm diameter bore

An alternative and less-expensive solution is to take advantage of the fittings that are already on the microscope. Many photographic tubes are used with electronic cameras that have a C mount (figure 7-5). This is a threaded male adapter about 1 inch in diameter that screws onto a camera having a female thread. You can purchase a Micro Four Thirds adapter that provides this mount for less than $20 (figure 7-6). This can prove to be the most inexpensive method of joining your camera to a professional microscope. This strategy is not employed on DSLRs because their sensors are larger and tend to vignette when using a narrow bore adapter. Our work with an Olympus research microscope shows you can get even illumination with a Panasonic G2 with a C mount (figure 7-6) shows that the adapter does not cause vignetting.

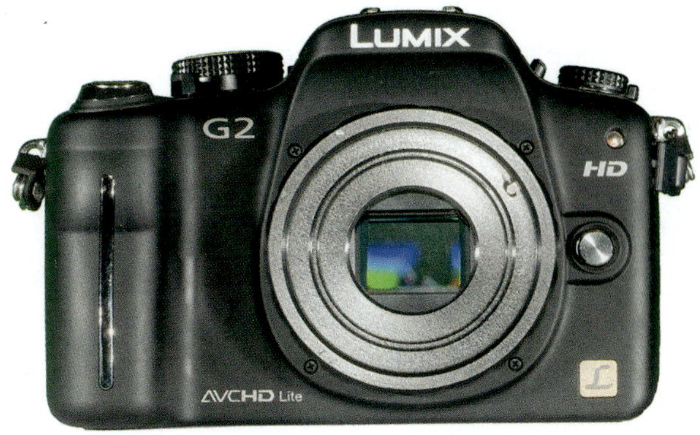

Figure 7-6: C mount adapter mounted on a Panasonic G2 camera. Note the small aperture that barely clears the camera's digital sensor

Laboratory, Teaching, Home Microscopes

These microscopes are less expensive and affordable to the hobbyist and amateur. Their cost can be reduced even more if purchased secondhand, but be careful. Purchasing used microscopes is not for the neophyte who is not able to determine the quality of the microscope lens. Make sure you either have an expert to help with the purchase or rely on a quality vendor who will support its product. This is not the time to rely on online auction sites.

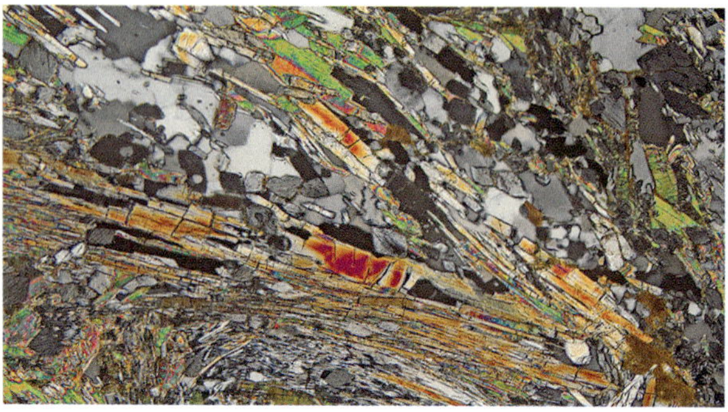

Figure 7-7: Photograph of a thin slice of granite. A set of polarizing filters was used to reveal the birefringent minerals

These used microscopes should be purchased with a trinocular head. The majority of these microscopes have a narrower photographic port than one found on a modern research microscope. For most microscopes, it is a narrow tube with a 25 mm outside diameter. The simplest adapter is a tube with a clamp on one end that fits outside the microscope tube. The other end is equipped with a bayonet mount for many common DSLR cameras. Although there is, as this book goes to press, none made specifically for the Micro Four Thirds system, this is a minor problem. Again, by using one of the adapters described in table 7-3, you can fit the Panasonic G2 camera on any microscope adapter.

For more background on attaching cameras to older microscopes, please check the online magazine *Miscape* at **www.microscopy-uk.org.uk/mag/indexmag.html**. Use the following steps when using the Panasonic G2 camera on a microscope:

1. Adjust the microscope with the slide, getting a good sharp image through the eyepiece.
2. Adjust the microscope's light source intensity so the view through the eyepieces is comfortable to the eyes. If the light is controlled with a voltmeter, run it at the voltage recommended by the manufacturer. If this is too bright, reduce the light intensity with neutral density filters.
3. Set the camera's focus mode lever to MF.
4. Set the camera's ISO to 100.
5. Turn the camera's mode dial to A Mode.
6. Use the following command: MENU/SET>CUSTOM>SHOOT W/O LENS>[ON].
7. Set the camera's WB to incandescent lights or set the Color Temperature Scale to 3200 kelvin. If this does not work, you can adjust the color temperature manually to obtain a white balance that will render the background to appear white.
8. Focus the image with the LCD screen.

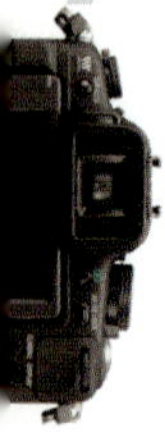

9. Fire the camera with a remote release, or if lacking that, set the camera's self-timer to a 2-second delay.
10. If the image appears to be blurred, try reducing the shutter speed to 1 second or less.

Remote Release

Panasonic sells a remote release accessory for its camera. It is expensive at $50, but for us, it is important to be able to take a picture without jarring or moving the camera, especially when we are taking pictures through a telescope or microscope. In addition, if you use the B setting on M Mode for exposures longer than 60 seconds, this accessory provides a convenient lock mechanism that will hold the shutter open. Keep in mind, exposures can run for a maximum length of 4 minutes.

Tripod

You may already own a tripod, but if not, this section is for you. This accessory is often overlooked when you first start taking pictures and videos.

A steady support for picture taking is essential for long exposures, extreme telephoto work, and obtaining maximally sharp images with the camera. Nonetheless, many photographers object to using one, arguing that it is bulky, that it reduces their mobility, and that it is a detriment for spontaneous photography. These arguments are all true, but consistently using a tripod will improve the quality of your work. In fact, its inconvenience may be its strongest benefit because it forces you to work at a more deliberate pace. Framing the subject can be done leisurely, the depth of field can be carefully evaluated, and time can be spent to ensure that the horizon is not canted in the picture. Composition can be carefully controlled, and this deliberate pace trains the photographer to visualize the image before snapping the shutter.

A good tripod can easily cost $300 with the more expensive units running over $1,000. Remember, a good tripod will outlast a typical camera and lens setup. One of our tripods is over 30 years old and still functional.

The more expensive tripods are made with carbon fibers and weigh only a few pounds. However, the less-costly heavier aluminum tripods are also suitable; their disadvantage is increased weight. This is not a good time to skimp on the cost of equipment. Inexpensive tripods are not only flimsy, they are slow to set up and they do not hold their settings.

Buying Tripods

We have acquired several tripods over the years. Our low-cost favorite is a Tiltall tripod purchased 30 years ago. The basic design of this older tripod is impeccable. Its only fault is its 7-pound weight. You can sometimes find them on online auction sites. Just beware of functional damage and wobbly legs. We typically use this tripod indoors, so we do not have to walk far or set it up quickly. At one time, Leitz sold this high-quality tripod. Now you can only buy these Leitz tripods used, online, for under $100. We have a carbon fiber tripod legs from Manfrotto and a tripod head from Acratech. Their combined weight is only 4 pounds. For faster setup, the head is equipped with a quick release mount. Without this accessory, we would have to turn and tighten a screw to fasten the camera onto the tripod. With the aid of the accessory clamp, we can quickly attach and detach the camera on the tripod.

That is to say, once you mount and position the camera, it may drift slowly out of position or, worse, topple over with your camera attached.

There are two parts to a typical tripod: the legs and the head upon which the camera is attached. The tripod head provides the mechanism for maneuvering the camera, allowing you to tilt it and aim it at your subject. This unit can be surprisingly expensive, especially if the intent is to use telephoto lenses. Any play in the mount or an inability to hold its setting can be aggravating, which will be exacerbated when working with the greater magnification of a long telephoto lens.

There are two types of tripod heads available: pan and tilt heads and ball heads. The pan and tilt heads are heavier, less-expensive units and will allow you to pan (horizontal movement) the scene and tilt (vertical movement) the camera. The ball head is lighter and more expensive. It allows you to move the camera on the tripod any way you want in a smooth motion.

Typically, to assemble the best tripod, you will purchase the legs and head separately, giving you an opportunity to customize your unit. The price range for these legs range from $300 to over $600, and the premium models are made of carbon fiber, making them lighter and very durable.

Gitzo makes some of the best legs, and they may cost over $500. The legs are built in sections, and to make them compact, each section telescopes into the other. Typically the legs can be collapsed for convenient transport. Some strength is sacrificed, and it will take more time to extend or collapse the legs.

We chose the less-expensive legs sold by Manfrotto at about $300 and combined them with an Acratech ball head.

A complete tripod with head and legs is less expensive, but if you work with telephotos with a focal length of 200 mm or greater, we expect you will upgrade and buy a more expensive unit.

Telescopes

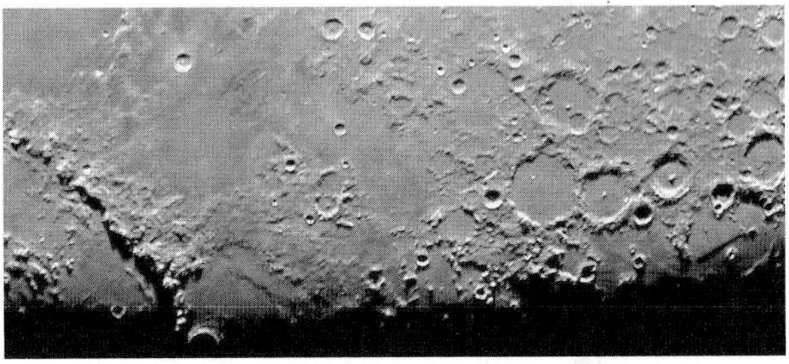

Figure 7-8: Moon shot taken with Panasonic G2 camera and Stellarvue telescope

Long-distance photography fascinates many photographers. The thought of photographing wildlife or obtaining a close-up of the moon makes the photographer long for a super telephoto lens. The longest telephoto lens made by Panasonic is a 100-300 mm zoom. This will provide impressive views, but suppose you want something even longer? Well one way to accomplish your goal is to attach your camera to a telescope. This can be accomplished easily if you have the right telescope and the right accessories. Mounting will be as simple as removing the lens, replacing it with an adapter, and inserting the camera and adapter into the eyepiece holder. An image of the subject is projected directly onto the camera's sensor—a method known as prime focus photography. Exposure is automated, and as with the microscope, it will be done with A Mode.

The first step is to find a telescope that can be used with your camera. Today, there are a tremendous number of telescopes. To keep the telescopes small enough for fieldwork with the camera, we will restrict our discussion to lenses having a front element ranging in diameter from 50 mm to 100 mm (2 to 4 inches). Any smaller than this and you are talking about an instrument whose performance can be equaled by using a telephoto lens. A telescope with an objective larger than 100 mm will be difficult to handle for fieldwork. An excellent telescope in the 50 to 100 mm range will be expensive; however, its optical performance will equal the best telephotos.

Tele Vue Optics, a company known for making some of the best lenses, makes a 76 mm telescope (480 mm f/6.3) that costs $1,500 new. Its optical performance rivals, if not exceeds, that of the finest telephoto lenses of Nikon or Canon, whose 500 mm optics cost $6,000 to $8,000. This is not to say that this telescope can serve as a replacement for a professional telephoto—but keep in mind that there is no lens this long in the Panasonic inventory. Also consider that you have the versatility of having an astronomical grade telescope as well as a superb long-distance lens, and the cost does not seem so formidable. Stellarvue is another company noted for making high-quality telescopes running around $1,000. The photograph of the moon at the beginning of this chapter was taken with its telescope and it had a 102 mm front objective. Stellarvue also sells a 80 mm telescope (model SV80 ED) telescope for $600.

We have tested the Panasonic G2 camera extensively on two telescopes: a Tele Vue-85 and a Stellarvue SV 102 ED. Both telescopes have a 2-inch eyepiece holder and were easily equipped with a 2-inch eyepiece adapter with the appropriate Nikon bayonet mount and a Panasonic Micro Four Thirds adapter for a Nikon mount. The camera was set on A Mode and manual focusing. For photographing the moon, we took advantage of the touch screen for providing an instant close-up of its surface. Focusing on the craters was easily accomplished (figure 7-8). Again, having higher magnification aided focusing, and this was accomplished by pressing the camera's rear dial. If we needed greater magnification than what the base telescope provided, we found that teleconverters provided 1.4x higher magnification.

You can also use the telescope to view terrestrial objects during the day. In this case, we use the viewfinder since the ambient daylight usually obscures the rear LCD screen.

A Caveat on Telescopes

Telescopes are expensive, and they do provide a far reach; however, while the Stellarvue and the Tele Vue telescopes are excellent astronomical instruments, the Panasonic G2 camera is sufficient for the primary target in the skies—the moon. This object is easy to find and is bright enough that you can set the ISO to 100 and shoot. Our shutter speed was 1/10 second when we took the shot in figure 7-8. To get higher magnification we used a teleconverter to provide a longer focal length. However, if you hope to shoot the planets or galaxies, you will have to invest in far more equipment. You will need to get an equatorial mount for planet photography and you will need to take much longer exposures. In this respect, the Panasonic camera is unsuitable for imaging faint objects requiring long exposures (minutes to hours shutter speed). Nonetheless, as a visual experience, telescopes of this size can provide a delightful view of the night skies and can open up a new hobby for the photographic enthusiast. As a terrestrial telescope, it can provide striking close-ups of animals.

Recommendations

We found the Panasonic G2 camera to be remarkably versatile and able to be applied to virtually any optical instrument. Its photographic capabilities are not limited to photographic lenses. Using specialized optical equipment such as telescopes and microscopes can expand its utility. Curiously, as your expertise increases and your desire to explore new areas expands, you may find that the accessories cost more than the camera. Even something as mundane as a tripod may prove to be surprisingly expensive; however, these accessories reveal the camera's full potential.

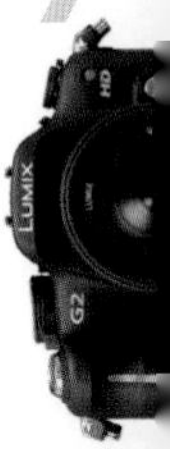

Flash Photography

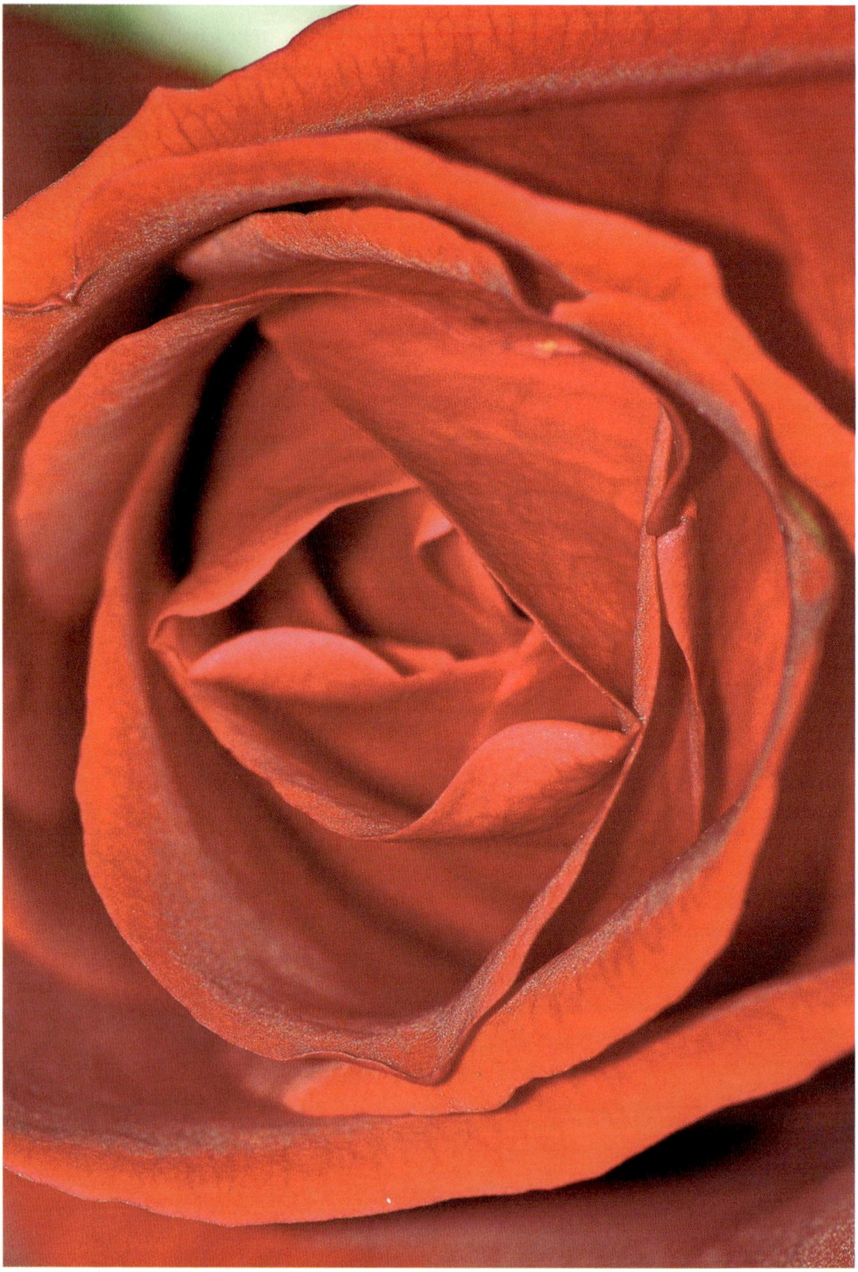

8

Introduction: Flash Photography

Frequently, there is not enough light to photograph a subject, forcing you to provide additional lighting to accomplish the goal. In the case of the Panasonic G2 camera, you have a built-in popup flash that can fire a brief burst of light to supplement ambient illumination. This is a handy feature, and under dim lighting, it will automatically adjust its output so you will get a well-exposed picture.

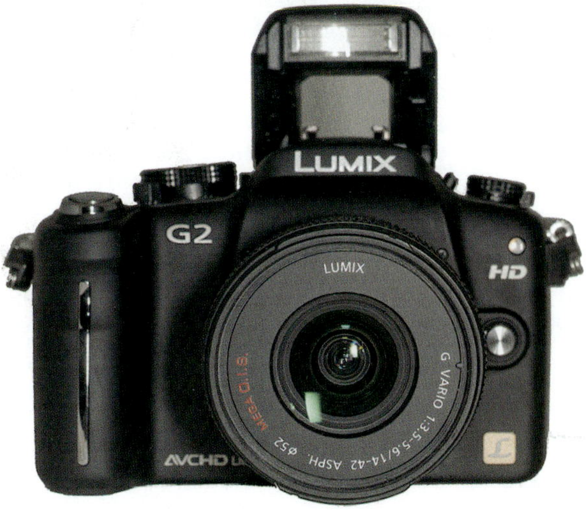

The use of the built-in flash is not limited to dim interiors. It can be used for outdoor scenes when your subject is back-lighted and their features are hidden by their own shadow. Under these conditions, the additional light from the camera's flash is used to lighten the darkened areas, filling them with supplementary light. Since you are adding light to the subject, this is described as a fill flash.

Unfortunately, the Panasonic G2's flash has one weakness: It is low-powered and cannot illuminate a large area. For this you need an accessory flash unit that slides into a receptacle on the top of your camera. Attachable flash units generate a much brighter burst of light. Also, the more advanced models provide the photographer with greater control by allowing indirect lighting. This is achieved with a swiveling and tilting flash head that aims its light toward a ceiling so that it reflects down onto the subject, providing softer lighting than that achieved by aiming the light directly at the subject. Indirect lighting, sometimes called bounce flash, diffuses the light, preventing the formation of harsh shadows. In the case of portraits, this will flatter a subject's skin by concealing fine wrinkles.

The camera has a wide range of settings to enable you to utilize the built-in flash effectively based on the subject. Once set, a corresponding icon is shown on the display screen to keep you informed of how the flash will operate when you fully press the shutter-release button. It is important to learn each of the flash settings and how best to utilize them to your advantage.

The Internal Flash

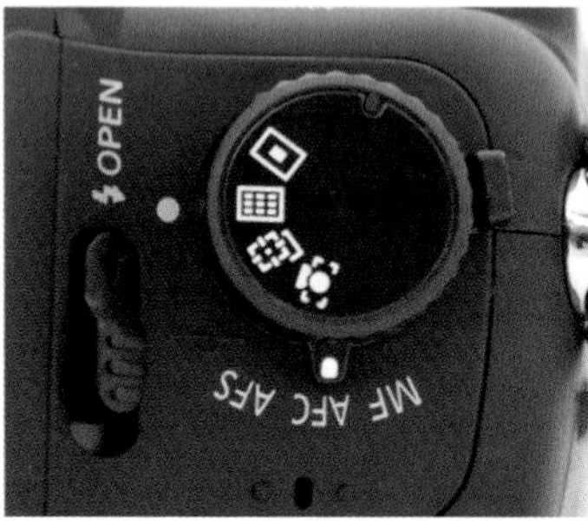

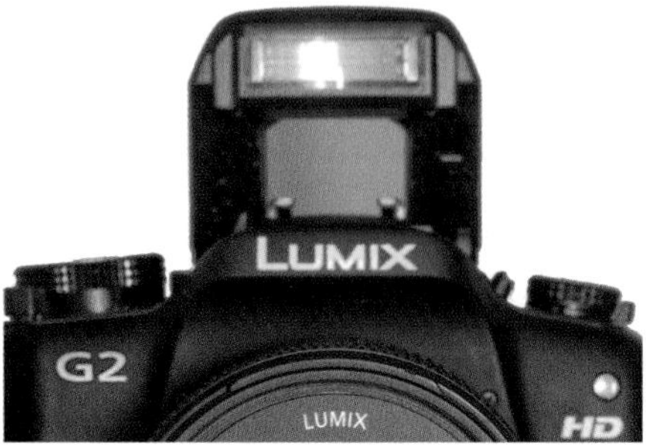

Figure 8-1a: The top of the camera showing the flash open lever;
Figure 8-1b: The flash head is raised and it is ready to be fired

The Panasonic G2 camera's built-in flash is always under your control. It can be fired only after you manually raise the flash head by sliding a small button called the flash open lever on the roof of the camera (figure 8-1a). This is a blessing in that you can be certain that the flash will not fire unintentionally. Once raised, the flash is usable in every mode except those involving video.

The Panasonic G2 camera has multiple flash settings. Table 8-1 lists the available flash options. The Panasonic G2 camera's manual (page 68) contains an extensive chart of which flash options are available for each of the camera's modes. This is a useful comprehensive list, but its very size is daunting. Fortunately, you do not need to memorize this chart. After you select your mode, the camera will automatically determine which flash options are allowable. You will find the allowable settings by going to the following command:

MENU/SET>REC>(pg 2) FLASH

Once there, the FLASH command will be displayed with the complete list of options. Deep black letters and icons indicate the options that are enabled (figure 8-2a). Light gray letters and icons indicate options that are disabled.

You might wonder how the camera controls exposure when the flash is fired. First, remember that flash exposure from the built-in flash is always controlled automatically. It is accomplished by the camera firing two flashes—a weak, preflash followed by a powerful illuminating flash. The preflash is not used for recording the image. It is a low-intensity light that serves as a reference of how much light will be needed in the second flash. Its light is reflected from the subject, collected by the camera lens, and measured by an internal meter. From this, the camera calculates how long the second, illuminating flash should last. A longer duration provides more light and a shorter duration provides less. Under all conditions, the internal flash intensity is automatically set.

When working with the internal flash, you first need to decide how the flash will fire in response to ambient light. From there, decide the time separation between preflash and illuminating flash. Your final decision is determining whether the camera's main shutter should be open for a long period (slow shutter speed).

Icon	Name	Function
	Forced Flash OFF	Flash will not fire. The built-in flash unit is not raised. To cancel command, raise the flash unit. Note that this is not a command option and is visible only on the display screen.
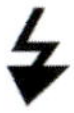	Forced Flash ON	Flash will always fire, independent of ambient lighting.
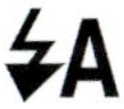	AUTO	Flash may fire depending on ambient lighting. Fires when the shutter speed slows and the "jitter" icon appears.
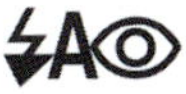	AUTO/Red-Eye Reduction	Flash may fire. Needs low light and tends to prevent red-eye.
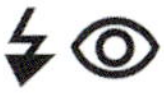	Forced Flash ON/ Red-Eye Reduction	Flash will always fire and tends to prevent red-eye.
	Forced Flash ON/ Slow Sync.	Flash always fires. Shutter speed slowed in order to lighten a dark background.
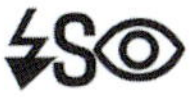	Forced Flash ON/ Slow Sync./Red-Eye Reduction	Flash always fires. Shutter speed slowed so dark background will be lightened. Red-eye reduction activated.

Table 8-1: FLASH command option's icons and descriptions

Table 8-1 lists seven icons. Six of the icons are settings available through the FLASH command to control the type of the flash. The remaining icon, Forced Flash OFF, is not under software control and is seen only on the display screen when the built-in flash is not open. As you review the available options, you will see that several options are a combination of four components: Forced Flash ON, AUTO, Red-Eye Reduction, and Slow Sync.

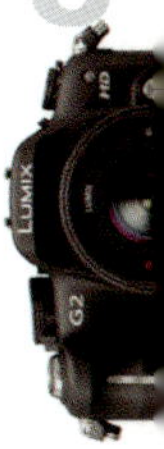

Forced Flash OFF

When the flash is closed, you will see an icon with a jagged arrow in a circle with a diagonal line on the display screen (table 8-1). This is the Forced Flash OFF icon. The mechanical switch for raising and lowering the flash head controls this icon. Once the head is raised, the icon will be replaced with the selected FLASH command's option. What FLASH command option you select depends on how and when you want the flash to operate.

AUTO

You have the option to have the flash fire automatically when needed. To do so, select the AUTO option (the icon is the letter *A*). With the AUTO option selected, the flash will fire only under dim light conditions. If the camera judges that there is enough light to take a sharp picture, the flash will not fire. In other words, the flash is treated as a supplemental light source to be used as the camera sees fit. In a sense, you lose control of whether the flash is fired or not. The camera makes the determination based on its interpretation of sufficient lighting.

The command for setting this is as follows:

MENU/SET>REC>(pg 2) FLASH>[*AUTO*], [*AUTO/Red-Eye Reduction*]

Note that AUTO can be combined with the Red-Eye Reduction function, which will be explained later. The key point is that the flash may or may not fire in AUTO.

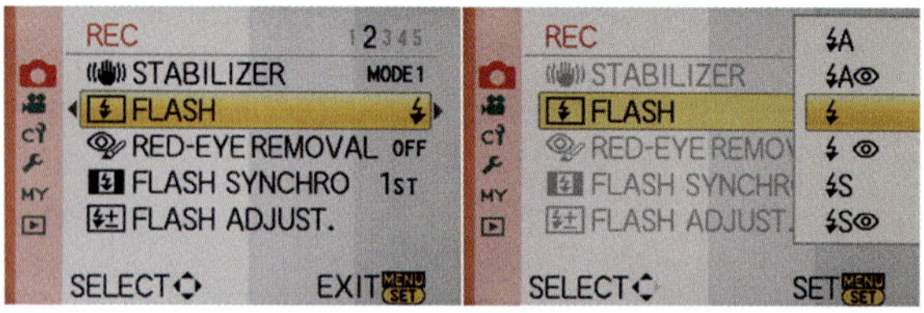

Figure 8-2a: The FLASH command within the REC menu; Figure 8-2b: Available FLASH command options with Forced Flash ON highlighted

Also remember that AUTO does not mean automatic exposure—with the internal flash unit, you always get automatic exposure. AUTO only refers to the flash firing as being under the camera's control. The camera will supplement the low light level by firing the flash, allowing the camera to speed up the shutter and capture the image clearly. Many photographers will prefer this setting.

Forced Flash ON

The Forced Flash ON option allows the flash to be used in daylight as a fill flash. That is to say, if the subject is back illuminated, it will receive additional light to ensure that it will not be hidden in its own shadow.

This option puts you in control of the lighting since you always know that the flash will fire. There is no uncertainty of whether or not it will supplement the light in the scene. It always will do so. If you feel that the flash will detract from the scene, you can cancel its operation by simply closing the flash head.

The command for setting this is as follows (figure 8-2b):

MENU/SET>REC>(pg 2) FLASH>[*Forced Flash ON*], [*Forced Flash ON/ Red-Eye Reduction*], [*Forced Flash ON/Slow Sync.*], [*Forced Flash ON/Slow Sync./Red-Eye Reduction*]

Forced Flash ON can be combined with the Red-Eye Reduction and Slow Sync components, which will be covered later in the chapter.

The Flash Icons on the Display Screen

When you open the flash head and see the selected flash icon, it does more than just show what flash controls are active. It also shows whether the flash is ready to be fired. When you press the shutter-release button halfway, the flash option's icon turns red, indicating that the flash is ready to be fired. When the flash is fired, the red icon starts blinking, indicating that the capacitor for the flash is being recharged. You cannot fire the camera while this blinking occurs. When it becomes a steady red light, you can fire the camera and flash again.

Additional Controls for Preflash and Internal Shutter

Red-eye Reduction

Another icon that may appear is a representation of an eye (table 8-1). This command is for red-eye reduction and a bit of background may be needed to clarify its function. The camera's flash unit will send out light, and if a person—or an animal—is looking into the lens, the light will enter the eye and be reflected back to the camera. Since the human eye has a rich vascular system, the reflected light will be colored red, resulting in a photograph with the person's pupil's glowing eerily. As an aside, animals (such as a cat) have a reflective layer behind their retinas (tapetum lucidum).

8

This causes a cat's eye to glow yellow rather than red when it looks toward an electronic flash. This is significant for pet photographers in that automated software removal for red-eye may fail to take the glow out of the cat's eye.

Red-eye reduction attempts to reduce this effect. According to the Panasonic G2 manual, the interval between the preflash and the firing of the illuminating flash is lengthened. We noticed that this command is not 100 percent effective in eliminating red-eye, and you may wish to use another way to reduce this condition. See the sidebar "Alternate Ways of Reducing Red-Eye," where we list additional strategies that will help in eliminating this phenomenon.

Alternate Ways of Reducing Red-Eye

Red-eye is a phenomenon caused by light reflecting out of the eye and into the camera lens. It occurs when the subject has dilated pupils and the flash is placed close to and in line with the photographic lens. This makes sense if you think about it. If the pupils are wide open and the flash is close to the lens, the chances of the flash's light being reflected back into the camera is enhanced by having a larger opening for the subject's eye and having the illuminating light traveling close to the lens optical axis.

There are three strategies for eliminating red-eye. The first is to displace the flash away from the camera's lens, reducing the chance that light entering the subject's eye will be reflected back into the camera's lens. This is one reason external flash units are popular—you position the external flash at an angle, thus reducing the chance of light from the flash reflecting back from the subject's eyes directly into the camera's lens.

The second strategy is to constrict the subject's pupil by increasing the surrounding light. So do not take portraits of people sitting in a darkened room.

The final strategy is to not have the subject look directly into the camera. Have them look at a point to the right or left of the camera, thus reducing the chance of the reflected light from their eye going back to the camera lens.

Slow Sync.

The final FLASH command option is represented by an icon consisting of the letter *S*, representing Slow Sync. Since you will be using the flash when the ambient light is low, there is a tendency for the flash to provide all the light to the subject. Because it is a low-power short-range device, it frequently fails to illuminate the background, rendering it jet-black. One way to lighten the background is to increase your exposure. This can be accomplished by slowing the shutter to allow the camera's sensor to capture more ambient light. The flash will still expose your subject, but you have lightened the darker background by using a longer shutter speed.

Recommendation

In the P, A, S, and M Modes, you have the full menu of flash options available to you. We recommend using the Forced Flash ON option. This guarantees that your flash will fire when you open up the flash unit, ensuring that the flash will always be available as a fill flash for use in daylight. With the AUTO option, you will not know if the flash will fire until you press the shutter-release button fully—and while it is desirable in the interest of conserving battery power to limit the use of the flash, this can be easily accomplished by simply lowering the flash when it is not needed.

In regard to whether you need to use Panasonic's red-eye correction, we are unconvinced that it significantly reduces this phenomenon. But it is something that you might as well leave on, simply because even a slight reduction in red-eye can't hurt.

So how do you eliminate red-eye if the built-in flash creates it? Well, the simplest way is to avoid having the subject look straight into the camera lens. It is better if they are glancing away at some object to the left or to the right of the camera. Second, the idea of constricting the subject's iris by brightening the room lighting may be another easy way to accomplish this task.

Finally, you may wish to consider getting an external accessory flash unit. This will position the flash tube further from the lens and at an angle, reducing red-eye. Also, with the most expensive units, you can use the bounce flash technique (described at the end of this chapter).

Altering Exposure

When using the flash, you may wish to either lighten or darken its effect by adjusting its output. This is easily accomplished with another command.

MENU/SET>REC>(pg 2) FLASH ADJUST>[*a scale of-2 to +2 f-stops in increments of 1/3*]

When you select this command, a scale (figure 8-3) spanning from -2 to +2 f-stops is displayed. This allows you to adjust the flash output—either increasing or decreasing it by up to 2 f-stops. Use the rear dial or the left and right directional arrow buttons to move the slider along the scale to select the flash adjustment. When using this command, take some test shots to determine if your selected adjustment is acceptable.

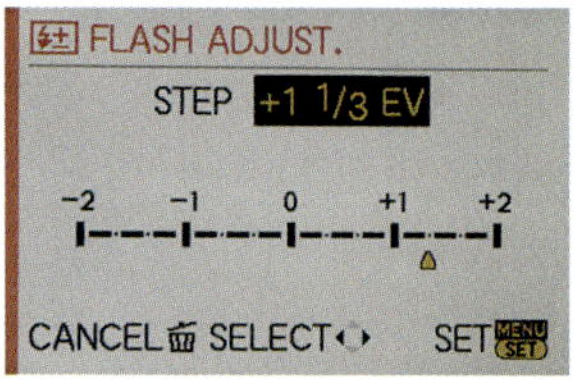

Figure 8-3: FLASH ADJUST command set for 1 1/3 f-stop overexposure

Flash and the Internal Shutter

Finally, we will discuss how to synchronize the flash to the camera's internal shutter. Although this is something we do not use, it may be of interest to those who want to create special effects.

The following command controls the synchronization of the flash with the camera's shutter:

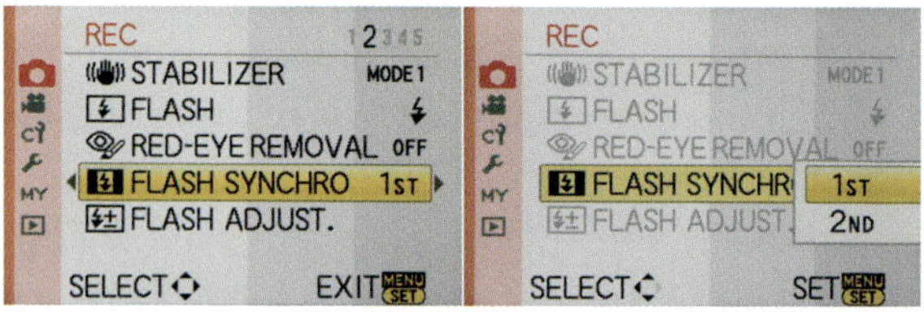

Figure 8-4a: Setting the flash to fire on the initiation of the shutter-release button; Figure 8-4b: Showing the option to fire the flash when the shutter closes

MENU/SET>REC>(pg 2) FLASH SYNCHRO>[1ST], [2ND]

The movement of the shutter is sometimes referred to as the movement of the shutter's curtain since it is essentially the movement of something opening and then closing, much like a curtain.

Normally, the flash is fired at the onset of the movement of the shutter curtain (figure 8-4a).

However, it can be triggered to fire at the point the internal shutter ends (figure 8-4b)—the close of the shutter curtain.

This is done for special effects, such as, for example, when you are "writing with light" and showing the subject after you complete your script. This is accomplished in the following manner:

1. Pose a person in a blackened room with a lighted flashlight.
2. Open the shutter for a long exposure.
3. During this interval, the person moves the lighted flashlight, using it as a pen to "write" by generating a trail of light against the black background.
4. Fire the flash just before closing the shutter. This will illuminate the subject and allow the camera to capture an image of the writer, holding the flashlight at the end of his glowing script. It will appear as if the writer has written glowing letters in mid air. This type of control is used for special effects.

If you closed the shutter without firing the flash, you will have just the glowing script against a black background.

1ST Option

This option is the default. The flash is timed to fire as the shutter curtain opens. If you photograph a moving car with its headlights on, you will "freeze" the car in position with its headlights glowing.

2ND Option

Selecting this option times the flash to fire just before the shutter curtain closes. This is not used except when you want to provide a special effect such as "writing with light" as described earlier.

Another example is purposely using a slow shutter speed when photographing a moving car with its headlights on. This blurs the car's body as it moves, and the headlights form an elongated streak. When the flash is fired, just as the shutter closes, the flash will "freeze" the car in position. In appearance, the car's body will have a blurred tail behind it and the headlights will show up as an elongated streak. Together, this will give an illusion of motion. Note that this option cannot be set when the flash is set to red-eye reduction.

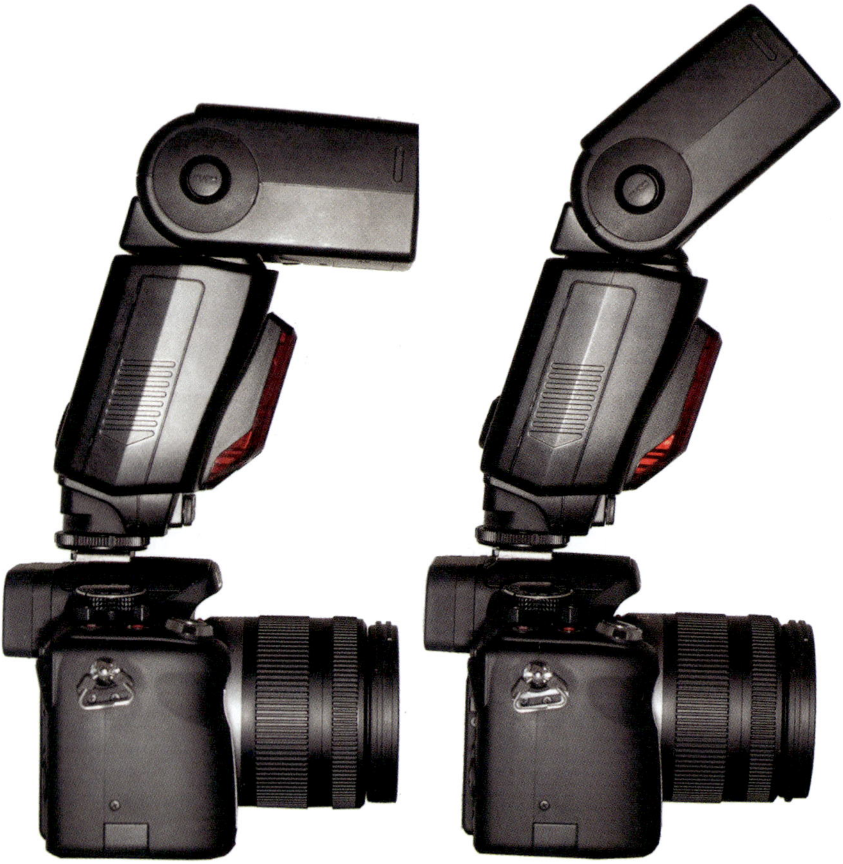

Figure 8-5a: An external Olympus FL-50 flash set for direct lighting;
Figure 8-5b: The flash head tilted to provide bounce flash

External Flash

There are basically two groups of external flashes: one group that is completely separate from the camera and another that attaches to the camera's electronic flash's hot shoe. We will be covering only the external flash units that can directly attach to your Panasonic G2 camera's electronic hot shoe (figure 8-5a).

Panasonic sells three external flash units. All share a common advantage—they generate more light than the camera's small built-in flash.

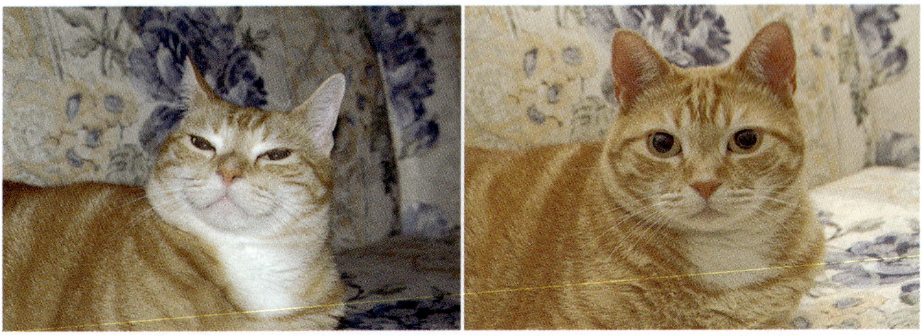

Figure 8-6a: Direct flash provides harsh lighting and causes a blink reflex ;
Figure 8-6b: Bounce flash provides a softer light. There is no squinting in this shot.

The smallest and least-expensive unit is the DMW-FL220 that takes two AA batteries and directs its flash directly onto the subject. Essentially, this is a more powerful replacement for your built-in flash unit and it helps preserve your camera's battery if you shoot a lot of flash. It is the smallest unit, weighing only 111 gm (about a quarter of a pound).

Although heavier and more expensive, the Panasonic DMW-FL 360 and the DMW-FL 500 models will give you greater control on directing their light output. Both flash units also have tilting heads (figure 8-5b) so you can position where the flash will be projected. They both attach to your camera's hot shoe. This way the flash units' internal electronics can interpret the camera's optics and settings so the flash unit can use its electrical motor to better adjust the lighting according to your subject's needs.

When you're using the camera's zoom lens, the external flash unit will adjust its flash's coverage as you zoom in and out. As you move from telephoto to wide-angle, the flash adjusts and spreads its beam to fully illuminate the field that the lens sees. Similarly, if you zoom to a telephoto setting, the flash concentrates the beam into a narrower field to match the view seen by the telephoto.

An even more useful feature is that these external flash units' tilting heads allow their beam to be directed away from the subject. This obviates the problems of direct flash (figure 8-6a). You can aim the light up at the ceiling, away from your subject. This technique is described as bounce flash, and it provides a flattering light for many subjects. When you use the ceiling as a reflector, light is diffused and redistributed, softening the shadows, helping to hide facial wrinkles, and providing softer, more evenly distributed lighting (figure 8-6b). By contrast, direct flash, where the light is cast directly onto the subject, can create harsh shadows, squinting, and emphasizes wrinkles.

Recommendation

Panasonic's built-in flash is generally adequate for typical flash work, but attaching external flash units to your camera's hot shoe is better. You are able to soften the results of a direct flash hitting your subject. Using an external flash unit allows you to create more depth and ambiance, thus strengthen your resulting picture.

Both Panasonic and Olympus sell units of this type. We have used the Olympus unit FL-50 and FL-36 interchangeably on the Panasonic G2 and the Olympus E series SLR camera. If you already own a compatible Olympus unit (FL-50, FL-50R, FL-36R, or FL-36), there is little need to buy one of the Panasonic units.

To see if your Olympus hardware is compatible with the Panasonic camera, check the following web address: **http://panasonic.jp/support/global/cs/dsc/connect/g1.html**. You will find that some Olympus flash units are not recommended (FL-40, FL-20) and that the wireless function of the FL-50R and FL-36R cannot be used.

9

Video

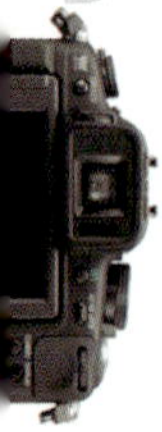

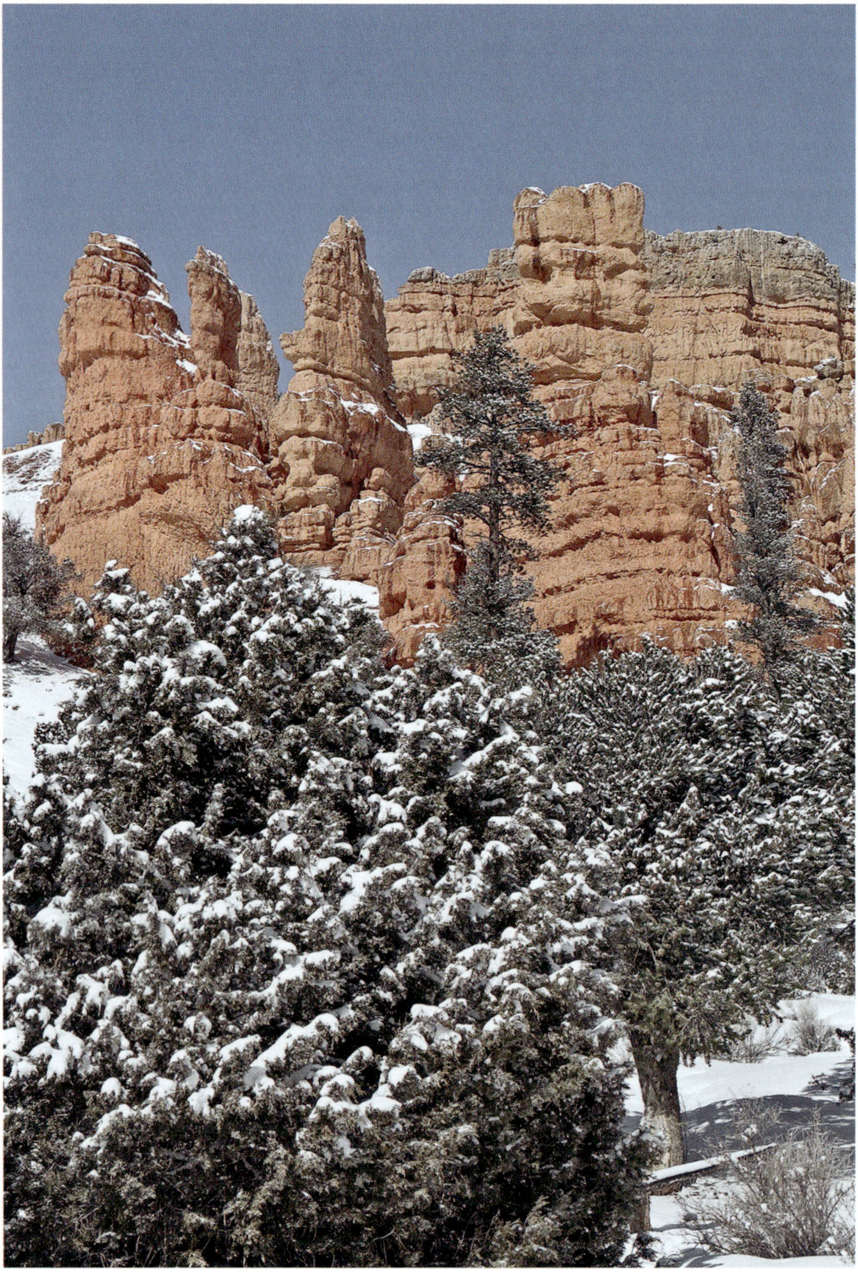

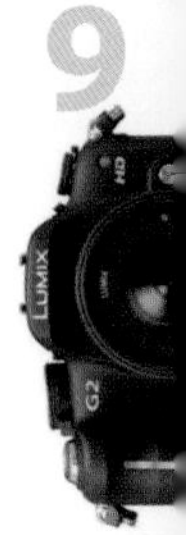

Introduction: Video

The Panasonic G2 camera is not only a capable still camera but also a high-resolution video camera, or as Panasonic refers to it, a motion picture camera. Switching from still to video photography is simple; it requires either a press of one button or the turn of the mode dial.

However, using a video camera requires the operator to compose in time as well as in three-dimensional space. Now the photographer must be concerned with the appearance of a scene lasting several seconds or more and have the skill to ensure that the viewer is not distracted by poor technique. A skill as basic as holding the camera takes on greater significance because camera stability must last for the length of the entire video clip. Unlike with still photography, where the camera records only a fraction of a second, a video clip will run in seconds and perhaps minutes, and sloppy technique can ruin the sequence. A video clip taken with an unsteady camera will annoy the audience by displaying a subject that randomly moves about within the frame.

Another concern is that with movies you don't have as extensive exposure controls as you do with a still photograph. You don't have the ability to vary the shutter speed over a broad range. Instead, for the Panasonic G2, your shutter speed will range from 1/50 to 1/125 of a second. This translates to a limited ability to work under dim lighting. Since videos are taken at about 30 frames per second, the longest shutter speed will be 1/50 of a second. To provide a brighter image in dim light, the camera has to open the lens aperture or increase the sensitivity of its sensor (gain) to ensure a proper exposure for the clip. Your camera will be controlling exposure automatically, adjusting its lens aperture or the sensitivity of its sensor to ensure proper exposure.

In this chapter, we are going to discuss how videos work and how to get the most out of your camera's video capabilities. Since many of the components were covered in earlier chapters, there may be some redundancies. But we will try to keep it to a minimum and give references to subjects covered earlier rather than discussing them again. Of course, if there is new information you need now that we are covering videos, we will cover it fully at this point.

Just as for pictures, there are MOTION PICTURE menu commands, which govern how your videos will be created and stored. Many of them mimic some of the REC menu commands, with some new ones pertaining just to video functionality. In addition, you can record videos using the Intelligent Auto Mode, the predefined scene modes, semi-automatically or completely manually. You can review the video settings before you start recording, review them after recording has completed, play them back through the PLAYBACK MODE, play them back on your TV, or download them from your camera's memory card onto your computer. You have most of the same general functionality you have with taking still pictures. One function we have covered that is specific to pictures and not available with videos is the capability of storing name, age, baby, and pet information. In addition, Face Recognition functionality is not available for videos. The good news is the Panasonic G2 camera can still detect faces in videos and use them as focusing targets.

Setup

Video Setup

The main menu includes a MOTION PICTURE menu option (figure 9-1). There are several commands controlled within this menu option. These command settings are utilized when you are recording a video. You can review the total list in Appendix C* within the MOTION PICTURE menu section.

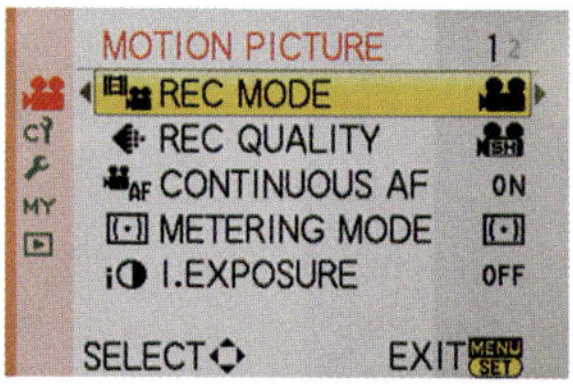

Figure 9-1: The MOTION PICTURE menu

As with RAW and JPEG formats for still pictures, the Panasonic G2 camera has two video recording types: AVCHD Lite and Motion JPEG. Use the following command to choose your video format:

MENU/SET>MOTION PICTURE>REC MODE>[*AVCHD Lite*], [*Motion JPEG*]

AVCHD Lite is a sophisticated compression algorithm, saving your videos in a compact digital file. The data compression is advanced, and its primary limitation is that it does not lend itself to editing directly. Most of us will have to transcode (translate) it to another format before it can be edited. You might note that the Panasonic manual recommends using this format for playback on high definition television (figure 9-2a) and using an alternate format (motion JPEG) if you intend to play back on your PC (figure 9-2b).

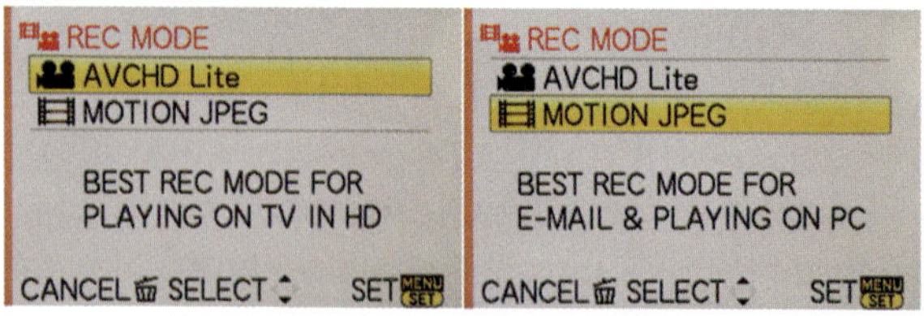

Figure 9-2a: Saving video as AVCHD Lite;
FIgure 9-2b: Saving video as Motion JPEG

* To view the Appendix, see: http://rockynook.com/PanasonicG2

We believe this advice is based on the difficulty of working directly with AVCHD Lite files on computers. In fact, you can work with AVCHD Lite files on your computer, but you need to spend more time and perhaps additional money to do so. Most of us do not own a computer fast enough or powerful enough to work directly with AVCHD Lite files. So we will have to transcode them into a less-compressed file format in order to edit them.

The Panasonic-supplied software, PHOTOfunSTUDIO 5.0 HD Edition, will perform this function for PCs using Windows 7. It does require some time to do the translation, but for most of us, this inconvenience can be tolerated.

Apple computer owners can use iMovie software to do this translation. For example, if you purchase the iLife disk, the included iMovie application translates AVCHD Lite files so you can edit them. New Apple computers come with iLife software preinstalled.

Regardless of the type of computer you have, be prepared for a wait. It will take time to transcode the AVCHD Lite files. If you prefer the immediacy of simply transferring the file to your computer's hard disk and working directly with it, save the files as Motion JPEG. This file format is easy to edit in programs like QuickTime 7 Pro. This program can be downloaded, and you can find a version to work on either a Windows or an Apple computer. It is understandable why Panasonic recommends setting your video files' REC MODE command to [*Motion JPEG*] format if you intend to work with your videos on your computer.

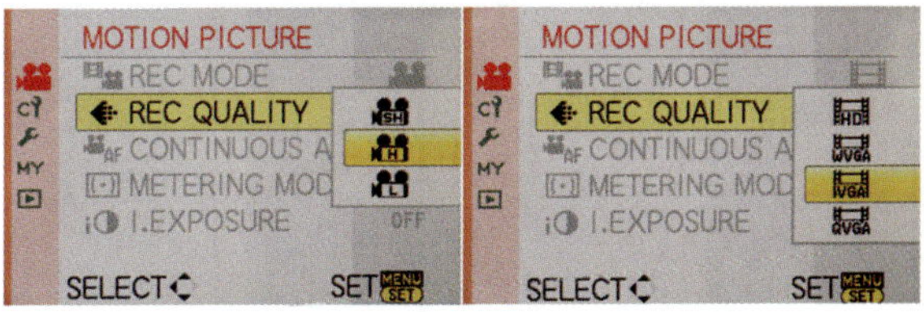

Figure 9-3a: Compression of AVCHD file set to H ;
Figure 9-3b: Compression of Motion JPEG set to VGA

Just as you did with your pictures, you will need to choose an associated level of quality to record your videos. The available MOTION PICTURE menu's REC QUALITY command values are dependant on the selected REC MODE command value. Table 9-1 contains the relationship between REC MODE and REC QUALITY command values for video settings. What you select depends on what you intend to do with the resulting video. As a rough guide, if you want to be able to play back your videos on your HDTV, choose [*AVCHD Lite*]. Use [*Motion JPEG*] if you intent to move your videos to your computer and possibly send it in an email message or upload it to the Web.

Your quality choice will in part depend on your video's subject. If you intend to record fast-moving objects for AVCHD Lite and you want to ensure that they are captured clearly, use [SH]. If you are willing to sacrifice quality for disk space, then use the [H] or [L] quality setting (figure 9-3a). We routinely use [SH] and never use [H] or [L]. Use the following command to set your video quality level:

For the MOTION PICTURE menu's REC MODE = [*AVCHD Lite*]:
MENU/SET>MOTION PICTURE>REC QUALITY>[SH], [H], [L]

For the MOTION PICTURE menu's REC MODE = [*Motion JPEG*]:
MENU/SET>MOTION PICTURE>REC QUALITY>[HD], [WVGA], [VGA], [QVGA]

REC. MODE		REC. QUALITY	
Menu Option	**Name**	**Menu Option**	**Description**
	AVCHD Lite	[SH]	Records highest quality at 17 Mbps
		[H]	Records highest quality at 13 Mbps
		[L]	Records highest quality at 9 Mbps
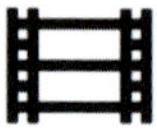	Motion JPEG	HD	Records at the highest quality level. Sets ASPECT RATIO value to [16:9].
		WVGA	Records at the second quality level. Sets ASPECT RATIO value to [16:9].
		VGA	Records at the third quality level. Sets ASPECT RATIO value to [4:3].
		QVGA	Records at the lowest quality level. Sets ASPECT RATIO value to [4:3].

Table 9-1: Relationship between the MOTION PICTURE menu's REC MODE and REC QUALITY command values

Note that when you compress the files in AVCHD Lite, they will always be displayed as 1280 x 720 pixel arrays. However, if you choose Motion JPEG, there will a reduction in the pixel array when you save the file. In HD mode, Motion JPEG will be 1280 x 720 pixels, but there will be a reduction in the pixel array to 848 x 480 pixels when you compress to WVGA. As you compress the files further to VGA (640 x 480 pixels) and QVGA (320 x 240 pixels), the array is made smaller (figure 9-3b).

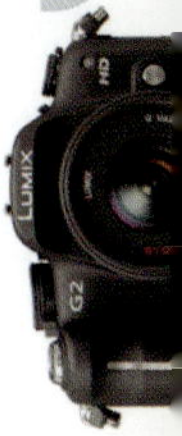

ACVHD Lite vs. Motion JPEG

AVCHD Lite (Advanced Video Coding High Definition) format is used to record high definition video for playing back on your HDTV using an HDMI (High-Definition Multimedia Interface) connection. Technically, the video is recorded storing every other frame. The playback device plays each frame twice.

Motion JPEG is used for recording standard definition video for playing back on your computer. Technically, Motion JPEG compresses each individual frame as a JPEG image allowing the user to trade off picture quality for smaller file sizes and therefore take up less space on the memory card.

Audio Setup

The Panasonic G2 camera uses a built-in mono microphone to record sound with your video. It also has the capability of accepting a stereo microphone, although the microphone is not supplied with the camera. Check with Panasonic's manual or website to determine acceptable stereo microphone accessories.

Unlike still pictures, where you need to enable the MENU/SET>REC>(pg 5) AUDIO REC. command to enable audio recording, the audio functionality for video is always enabled. At most, you can control the sound for videos two ways: VOLUME and WIND CUT. The VOLUME command controls the recorded level of sound for both still pictures and videos. The values range from [0] to [6], where [0] represents no sound and [6] represents the loudest level of sound being recorded. Although [0] is obvious, you should test the remaining audio levels to actually hear how loud each is and determine what seems right for you.

MENU/SET>SETUP>VOLUME>[0], [1], [2], [3], [4], [5], [6]

Recording outdoor scenes can often be challenging, especially if there is wind. Not only can the wind negatively affect the subjects you are recording, the wind's sound can be very disruptive when capturing the audio.

The WIND CUT command can help reduce the effects of the wind blowing during your video recording (figure 9-4a).

MENU/SET>MOTION PICTURE>(pg 2) WIND CUT>[OFF], [LOW], [STANDARD], [HIGH]

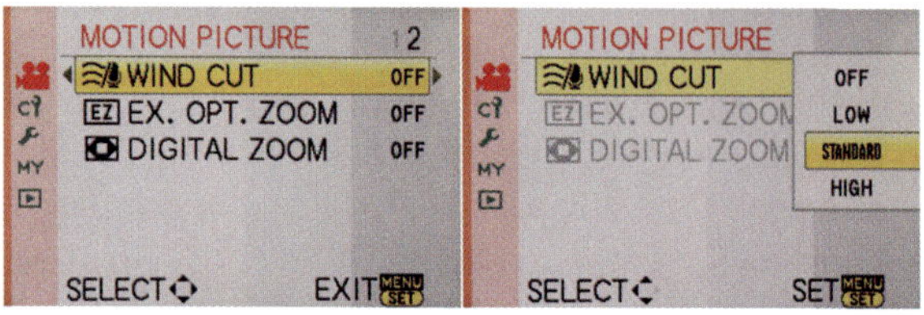

Figure 9-4a: Audio susceptible to wind noise;
Figure 9-4b: Audio set to remove standard level wind noise

Setting the WIND CUT command to [LOW] enables light wind noise reduction, and [HIGH] reduces high wind noise. Given windy enough conditions, you might have to accept some wind noise being captured even when this command is set to [HIGH]. Typically, you will start by using the [STANDARD] setting and determine its effects on your video clip (figure 9-4b).

Several other actions can cause unwanted noise to be captured on your videos. Using auto focus for your videos will cause the focusing motor to move when adjusting the focus automatically during your recording. If you are recording your grandchild running around in the backyard, the focus motor may be constantly in action. The sound of the motor running will be recorded on your video.

One solution for avoiding the lens motor noise is to replace the 14-42 mm lens supplied with the camera with the Panasonic 14-140 mm HD lens. It has a quiet focusing motor and is designed to work with video recording. In addition, this lens has an extended zoom range, and because of this, we use it as our standard lens. We feel its extra weight, size, and expense is justified by its 10x zoom capability as well as its silent auto focus.

The Panasonic G2 camera does help eliminate the sounds created when the shutter-release button or Motion Picture button is pressed. The beginning of your video recording is delayed about 0.5 seconds from when you push the button to start the recording. When you push the button again to end the recording, the camera's software cuts off the recording about 0.5 seconds before the point at which you pushed the button. This way, any of the sounds occurring from pressing the buttons to start and end your video will not be recorded. This also means the video's recording does not start or end exactly when you push the button. You need to keep that in mind so you don't end up with something very important being cut off.

The silver lining might be that you won't hear the comment "It's recording!" that frequently starts many videos, nor will you have the jarring of the camera when pushing the button.

One additional note is that the audio portion of Motion JPEG videos and still pictures is not compatible with older Panasonic LUMIX digital cameras launched before July 2008.

Recommendation

We save our files by using [*AVCHD Lite*] with [SH] selected. We have become addicted to the highest-quality movie clips. Even though we work mostly with computers for displaying our files, we find it worthwhile to invest the extra time and effort to working with the AVCHD Lite files. We use either an Apple computer with iMovie '11 or a Dell computer using PHOTOfunSTUDIO 5.0 HD Edition. Be advised, however, that when you are recording videos, you should keep an eye on how long you make the recording. A long continuous recording can be difficult to edit, and you will find it advantageous to make short recordings. Plus, you can always splice the shorter video clips together for a longer-running video clip.

If you do not want to work with PHOTOfunSTUDIO 5.0 HD Edition or iMovie '11, you may save your files as Motion JPEG and work directly with them using QuickTime 7 Pro on your computer.

LCD Screen vs. Viewfinder

You can use the LCD screen or the viewfinder to frame your subject and control the recording of your video. Each has its advantages and disadvantages.

Using the LCD screen to frame and view the video recording of relatively stationary subjects is the easiest. When doing so, you should use a tripod whenever possible. Having the camera mounted to a tripod helps prevent involuntary camera movement and, if necessary, will enable you to pan the scene smoothly on an even plane. There will be times when you need to handhold the camera to record a video. Using the viewfinder pressed against your face helps steady the camera and reduces the effects of involuntary body movements. It also helps produce a smoother panning of the scene. In addition, if you are in bright lighting, the viewfinder will allow you to view the subject more easily.

Conversely, using the LCD screen broadens your view to what is going on around you to help you record that which you want and avoid that which you don't want. You can see a stranger about to walk into your video before they get there, giving you time to prevent the disruption.

You will need to evaluate each situation to determine whether to use the LCD screen or viewfinder as your tool to keep track of your subject during video recording. Just remember that the audio is always running while you are recording.

Image Data Display Screen Formats

As discussed in chapter 3, the LCD screen and viewfinder data display formats will also apply to your videos. As with still pictures, you will be framing the beginning of your video by aiming your camera and pressing the shutter-release button halfway to have the camera apply its interpretation of the image per the selected iA button or mode dial option. You will be able to view the camera's settings through the viewfinder or on the LCD screen. How you see the data will depend on the selected data display screen formats based on the selected values for the LCD DISP. STYLE and LVF DISP. STYLE commands described in chapter 3. You will have the same four data display screen formats to choose from. Press the DISPLAY button to cycle through the four format styles, choosing the style which best suits your needs.

Video Recording

Starting/Stopping a Video

The best way to initiate a video is to use the Motion Picture button positioned just behind to the shutter-release button on the top right side of the camera. The Motion Picture button has a large red dot in its center encircled with a silver ring (figure 9-5), This button starts video recording and will incorporate settings per the selected mode dial option or Intelligent Auto Mode (iA button). To stop the video recording, push the Motion Picture button again.

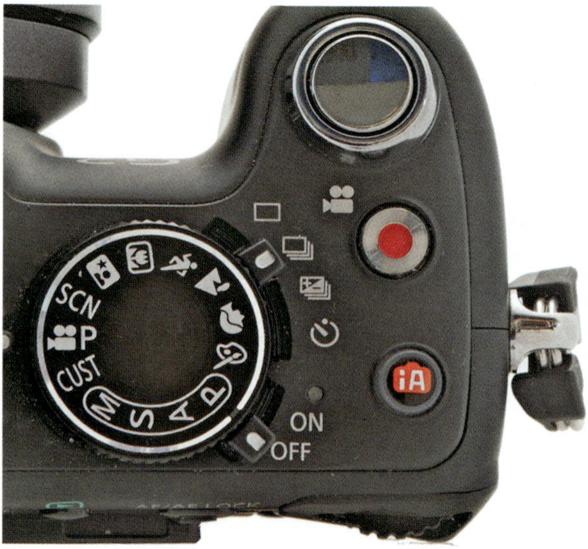

Figure 9-5: The Motion Picture button with its red center dot enclosed within a silver circle

You can use the shutter-release button to start and stop a video when the mode dial is set to the Motion Picture P Mode (figure 9-5), but we don't recommend this. The other mode dial options allow you to start and stop video recording using only the Motion Picture button. To help maintain consistency, we recommend that you always use just the Motion Picture button to control the starting and stopping of your videos regardless of the mode you are in. As you will learn later, the shutter-release button will allow you to take still pictures during videos. Using it to also start and stop videos will mean you will always need to be cognizant of what mode you are in when you are recording videos—something not always possible when you are completely absorbed with capturing the action at hand.

Enabling the Motion Picture button is controlled by the following command:

MENU/SET>CUSTOM>(pg 5) *Motion Picture P* BUTTON>[OFF], [ON]

Set this command to [ON] so you can use the Motion Picture button to start and stop videos. Without it, you will not be able to use the Intelligent Auto Mode or any of the mode dial options other than the Motion Picture P Mode, which will require you to use the shutter-release button.

Selecting Video Mode

You can record videos in all of the mode options on the mode dial plus while in Intelligent Auto Mode. Each selected mode will utilize the same general functionality as it did when you were taking still pictures, with some variations. In the case of Intelligent Auto and the predefined scene modes, the camera will set the most appropriate camera settings to match your subject, just as it would for still pictures. In the case of P, S, A and M Modes, you will have the same functionality and will be able to make the same adjustments to best record your subject.

Keep in mind, though, that you will not have the full range of shutter speeds, nor will you have control of ISO when in video. Shutter speeds will be limited and the camera will be in AUTO ISO when taking the video.

The mode dial's Motion Picture P Mode option has some advantageous features that will be described in the section on Motion Picture P Mode. But you do not take still pictures with this mode directly—although you can do so indirectly, and we will address how later in the chapter.

Assigning Categories

Videos are assigned categories just as still pictures are. If you have selected a predefined scene mode, your videos will be assigned the selected mode's category with one exception. Face Recognition functionality is not available during videos. So if you have selected one of the baby predefined scene modes, the video will be assigned a portrait category instead.

Intelligent Auto Mode's software has five iA categories it uses for videos. Just as they do for still pictures, each iA category has its own core settings and determines specific values per the environment. The Intelligent Auto Mode will take control and determine the camera's settings based on its software and the image it encounters during the recording. The camera will determine the iA category based on lighting, face detection, and distance between camera and the subject. If the camera's software cannot assign one of the specific categories to the subject, it will assign the iA General icon.

i-Portrait	i-Scenery	i-Macro	i-Low Light	General
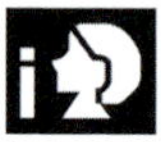	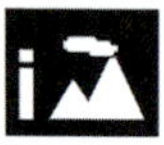			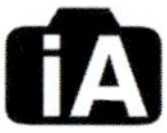

Table 9-2: Intelligent Auto Mode available video categories and displayed icons

Once the Intelligent Auto Mode has determined the video's category, the associated icon will be displayed in the lower-left corner on the display screen and the category will be saved with the video (table 9-2).

When you're recording videos in the Intelligent Auto Mode, the iA button's light will be extinguished during recording to prevent unwanted lighting from interfering with the quality of the recording. The blue light will return once the recording is completed.

Intelligent Auto Mode takes precedence over whatever the mode dial is set to except when the mode dial is set to the Motion Picture P Mode. In this case, the shutter-release button will still allow you to start and stop the video recording instead of taking a still picture.

Motion Picture P Mode

The advantage of using this mode is its control of the video image. It provides control of the video's exposure through Exposure Compensation. It also provides control of the video's depth of field, which Panasonic calls peripheral defocus. In addition, you can vary the shutter speed to reduce the flickering resulting from subjects illuminated with arc-type lighting (fluorescent tubes, mercury vapor lamps, or neon lighting).

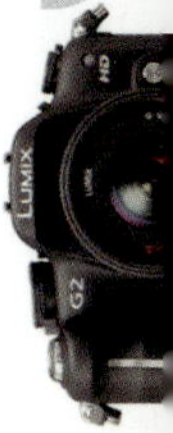

Exposure Compensation

As with pictures, you have the option to adjust the video's exposure using Exposure Compensation. It works the same way it does with pictures. Press the rear dial to activate the Exposure Compensation. If the Exposure Compensation scale is glowing yellow, turn the rear dial right or left to increase or decrease the exposure (figure 9-6).

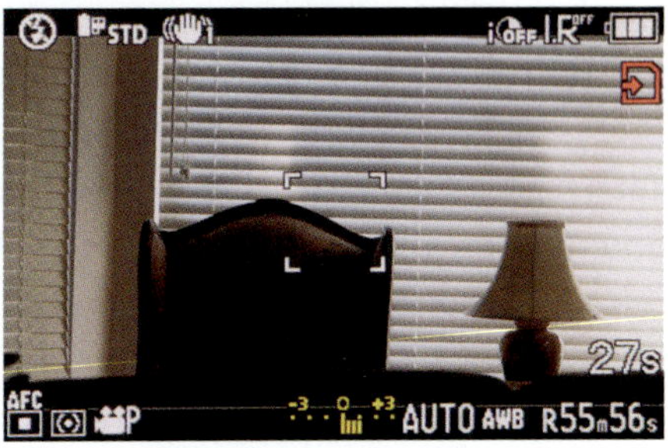

Figure 9-6: Display of Motion Picture P Mode while adjusting exposure

You can change Exposure Compensation while you are recording videos when you are using the Motion Picture P Mode. Keep in mind, any sound generated by turning the rear dial can sometimes be recorded. When you're using a mode other than the Motion Picture P Mode, Exposure Compensation must be adjusted prior to initiating a video.

Peripheral Defocus

Press in the rear dial again and you activate its second function, Peripheral Defocus. This controls the opening and closing of the aperture to vary the depth of field.

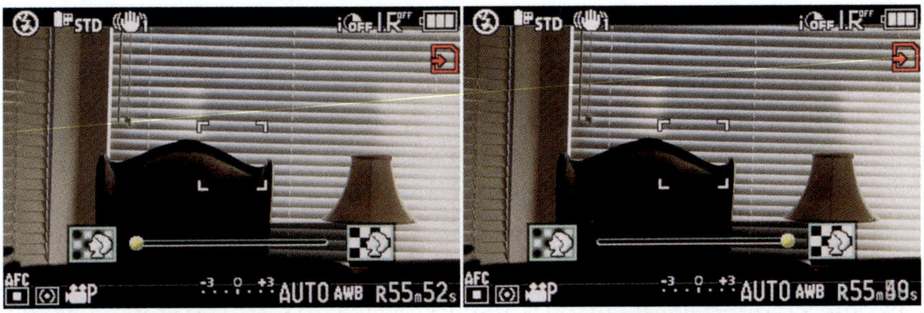

Figure 9-7 (a–b): Adjustment for minimum depth of field (a) and maximum depth of field (b)

With most consumer camcorders, the sensor and lens are optically constrained and generate an image with a great depth of field. However, the larger sensor on the Panasonic G2 camera allows you to reduce the depth of field, and you can concentrate the viewer's attention on the subject while blurring out the background. This is a unique feature and is limited, usually, to professional video equipment. If you press the rear dial, you will see a scale showing a profile at either end with a checkered background. Turning the rear dial to the left moves the scale indicator toward blurring the background (figure 9-7a). Turning the rear dial to the right brings more of the full picture into focus (figure 9-7b). You will see this effect on the display monitor.

You can change the Peripheral Defocus value while you are recording videos when using the Motion Picture P Mode. The predefined scene modes each have a Creative mode, which allows you to modify focusing related settings and thus, be able to adjust the still picture's depth of field. In the case of the scene mode, its Creative mode option is called Peripheral Defocus, and it operates the same as the Peripheral Defocus function initiated through the rear dial while you are using the Motion Picture P Mode. Again, keep in mind the sound generated from turning of the rear dial during a video can sometimes be recorded.

Flicker Reduction Function

Sometimes there is a marked flicker or striping in videos. This usually occurs working under fluorescent, mercury vapor, and neon lights. These bulbs, unlike an incandescent lamp, generate light intermittently, flickering at 50 or 60 cycles per second. This is not noted by the naked eye, but it can be recorded during a video recording.

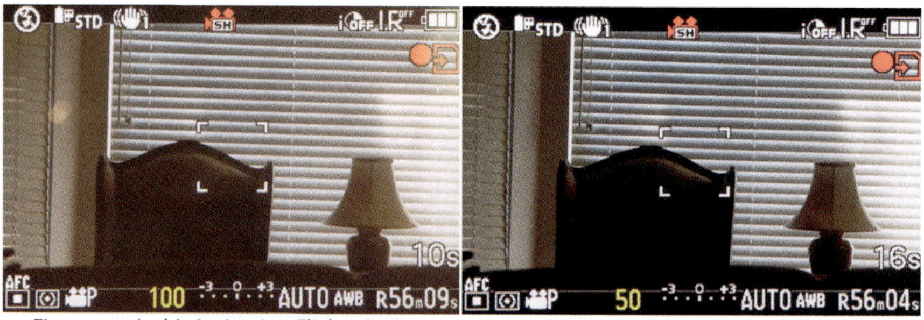

Figure 9-8 (a–b): Activating Flicker Reduction (a), Setting shutter speed to 1/50 second (b)

One way to counterbalance this effect is to vary the shutter speed to avoid this defect. The Flicker Reduction function only works within the Motion Picture P Mode. The following steps enable the Flicker Reduction function:

1. When the video is recording, press the Trash Can button. The Flicker Reduction Function is activated. The Shutter speed is changed to 1/100. Note that 100 will be displayed on the lower portion of your screen (figure 9-8a).

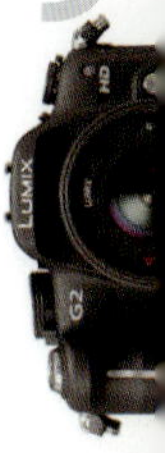

2. If flicker persists, turn the rear dial to adjust the shutter speed further. Turning the rear dial to the right once will change the shutter speed to 1/120. Turning the rear dial to the left once will change the shutter speed to 1/60. Turning it to the left one more time will change the shutter speed to 1/50 (figure 9-8b). You can rotate the rear dial left and right to go back and forth through the allowable shutter speeds. Any additional turns past the allowable shutter speeds will have no affect.
3. Finish recording your video. The following message will be displayed:

FLICKER RED. CANCEL *Trash Can icon*

Shutter Speed	1/50	1/60	1/100	1/120
Displayed Value	50	60	100	120
Rear Dial Action	Turned to the left twice	Turned to the left once	Pressed (initial setting)	Turned to the right once

Table 9-3: Flicker Reduction function's available shutter speed values

The Flicker Reduction shutter speed value (table 9-3) is retained for future videos until either you press the Trash Can button to cancel the value or the camera goes to "Sleep" (**MENU/SET>SETUP>(pg 2) ECO>SLEEP MODE**), whichever comes first.

When using the Flicker Reduction setting, you will no longer be able to do peripheral defocus.

You may not be able to get rid of flickering by using the camera controls, and there is no recourse but to change how the subject is lighted. Incandescent lights or daylight will not generate this phenomenon.

You may have to remove the affected portion by image processing using the VIDEO DIVIDE command in the PLAYBACK MODE menu. The VIDEO DIVIDE command allows you to divide a saved video into two videos. If you have a problem with the beginning or end of a video, you can divide it into two parts, separating the good part from the bad part, and then delete the bad part. You can also offload your video to a computer and use either the supplied Silkypix Developer Studio software or another third-party software package. Chapter 10 covers the PLAYBACK MODE menu, and we also discuss the VIDEO DIVIDE command and offloading your pictures and videos to your computer.

Recording Videos

It is easy to record a video. The following steps will walk you through it:

1. Select either Intelligent Auto Mode or a mode dial option.
2. Frame your subject and press the shutter-release button halfway to initiate the camera's software and focus the image.
3. Review the camera settings. If necessary, use the DISPLAY button to change the information display format for more visibility into the camera's settings. You can make adjustments using the Exposure Compensation function described in chapter 3.
4. You can also make some adjustments to the video volume and review the menu commands. Note that an appropriate category is assigned to the pending video based on the camera's interpretation of the scene and the selected mode dial option.
5. Press the Motion Picture button to start your video recording. Note that the MOTION PICTURE commands are in effect now.
6. Press the Motion Picture button to stop your video recording.
7. Use the Playback button to play back the video to see if you got what you wanted. You can again use the DISPLAY button to review the camera settings.

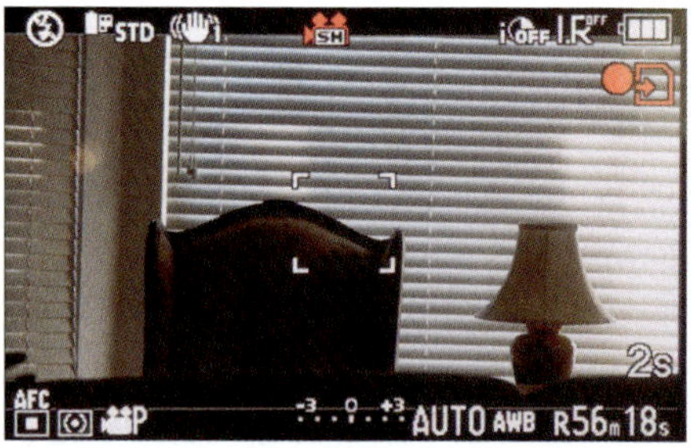

Figure 9-9: Flashing data displayed during video recording

Regardless of what method you use to kick off your video, once it has started, a couple of things will be displayed on your screen (figure 9-9). The Recording State Indicator, a large solid green dot in the upper-right corner of your display screen, will turn red and flash. The selected recording mode and quality indicator in the center top portion of the display screen will also turn red and flash in unison with the Recording State Indicator. The elapsed recording time in minutes and seconds is displayed in the lower-right corner of your display screen. At the very bottom, on the right side of your display screen, the remaining available video recording time in hours and minutes is displayed and updated periodically as the video is being recorded.

Focusing

Video focusing is controlled by a combination of the focus mode lever and the video-related CONTINUOUS AF command, which allows the camera to continuously auto-focus while taking videos (table 9-4). The CONTINUOUS AF command is as follows:

MENU/SET>MOTION PICTURE>CONTINUOUS AF>[OFF], [ON]

There is one potential drawback. The sound of the camera continuously setting its aperture and focus action can sometimes be captured on the audio portion of a still picture or video. If this is a problem, set the command to [OFF]. As mentioned earlier, you may want to replace the 14-42 mm lens supplied with the camera with the Panasonic 14-140 mm HD lens. This way, the focusing motor's sound will not be captured in your videos.

Focus Mode	CONTINUOUS AF	Focus Results	
		Shutter Pressed Halfway	Video Recording Initiated
AFS/AFC	ON	Set initial focus	Will focus continuously as video is recorded
	OFF	Set initial focus	Will use initial focus throughout the recording
MF	ON	Requires manual focusing	
	OFF		

Table 9-4: CONTINUOUS AF command's relationship with the three focus mode lever options

Focus is determined four ways. You can select Face Detection, AF Tracking, 1-area-focusing or 23-area-focusing options on the auto focus mode dial. Selecting Face Detection will cause the camera to maintain focus on the detected face throughout the video as long as it continues to be detected.

You can set tracking using the AF Tracking option in your video and have the camera continue to focus on your tracked subject. Using 1-area-focusing will allow you to establish a single point for the camera to focus on. As long as you have CONTINUOUS AF set to [ON], the camera will refocus as the subject moves. If you select the 23-area-focusing option (which for videos Panasonic calls multi-area focusing), the camera will execute an algorithm to select multiple areas to determine focus, and depending on the selected focus mode and CONTINUOUS AF commands setting, the camera will determine where and how it will focus within your video.

Commands Disabled During Videos

There are several commands that either do not function or are disabled and set to default values while in video mode. The following is a list of camera commands that are not functional during video recordings:

FACE RECOG. (note, not face detection)
Flash-related functionality
I.RESOLUTION
AUTO REVIEW
ASPECT RATIO
PICTURE SIZE
STABILIZER
BURST
AUTO BRACKET
AUTO POWER LCD
SLEEP MODE
FOCUS PRIORITY
MF ASSIST when using DIGITAL ZOOM
ISO LIMIT SET

The following is a list of commands that cannot be adjusted. They are set to these values:

ISO sensitivity is set to [AUTO].
AF Mode will be switched automatically to Multi Auto Focus Mode if:

- **AF Mode = 23-area-focusing**
- **AF Mode = Face Detection and no face has been detected**

Recording Times

One thing you do not want to have happen is to have the battery drained or the memory card become filled to capacity while recording a video. When either of these two things happens, the recording stops immediately. To minimize this inconvenience, carry a fully charged backup battery and an empty memory card. Check the battery indicator in the upper-right corner of the display screen to judge if your battery has enough charge to complete your next video.

The amount of recordable time depends on the memory card's size, the selected file format, and the recording quality selected. The more memory card capacity, the lower the recorded file quality, and the more compressed the file type, the more recording time available. Conversely, the smaller the memory card, the higher the quality, and the less-compressed the file type, the less overall video recording time available. Again it depends on your chosen memory card and command selections. Experiment with REC MODE and REC QUALITY values and see what best fits your video needs.

The camera can give you some help. The REMAINING DISP. command displays an approximate amount of remaining video recording time based on available space on your memory card, recording quality, and file type. This information is displayed prior to starting a video and will be updated afterward to help keep you informed of the approximate available remaining recording time.

MENU/SET>CUSTOM>(pg 5) REMAINING DISP.>[*# of remaining pictures*], [*remaining video time*]

The remaining video time is displayed in minutes and seconds (figure 9-9). The REMAINING DISP. command defaults to [*remaining video time*] when the Motion Picture P Mode option is selected. For all other mode dial options, the command must be set in order for the remaining video time to be displayed on the display screen.

Creating Still Pictures from a Video

There are two ways to create still pictures from a video within the Panasonic G2 camera. You can take a still picture while you are recording a video or you can create a still picture during playback, after the video has been recorded. Both have their restrictions that you need to know at the time you are taking the video. Only JPEG images can be created in both cases.

During Video Recording

This option does not work during two conditions:

- The mode dial is set to Motion Picture P Mode
- REC QUALITY is set to [VGA] or [QVGA] when REC MODE is [Motion JPEG]

Once you have started recording a video, press the shutter-release button fully to take a picture. A maximum of 20 pictures can be recorded during a video. The camera software will be using the focus and mode dial option's settings set at the time you recorded your video.

Only JPEG type pictures will be created. The resulting picture's quality will be determined by what you have set in the MENU/SET>REC>QUALITY command (table 9-5).

During Video	Resulting Picture's		
MENU/SET> REC>QUALITY	QUALITY	ASPECT RATIO	PICTURE SIZE
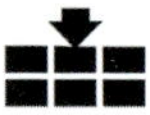	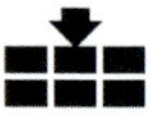	16:9	[S] (2 M)
	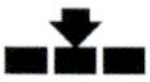	16:9	[S] (2 M)
RAW	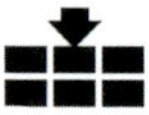	16:9	[S] (2 M)
RAW	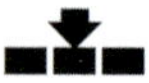	16:9	[S] (2 M)
RAW	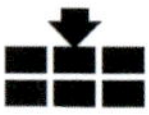	16:9	[S] (2 M)

Table 9-5: Resulting picture's file information when taken during video

After Video Recorded

There is no limit (other than the available memory on your camera's memory card) to how many still pictures you can create from a recorded video. You will not be able to created still pictures from Motion JPEG's VGA or QVGA format videos. The resulting picture's quality will always be JPEG Standard (table 9-6).

During the playback of a video:

1. Pause (press the up directional arrow) the video at the place you want to create a still picture.
2. Press the MENU/SET button.
3. You will receive the following message:

   SAVE THIS IMAGE? [YES], [NO]

   Select [YES] to save the image and then press the MENU/SET button. Select [NO] to stop the process.

4. Press the up directional arrow button to continue or the down directional arrow button to exit the video.

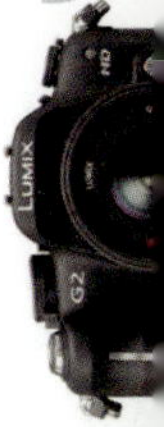

Video Settings		Resulting Picture's		
MENU/SET> MOTION PICTURE>REC. MOD	MENU/SET> MOTION PICTURE>REC. QUALITY	QUALITY	ASPECT RATIO	PICTURE SIZE
AVCHD Lite	[SH]	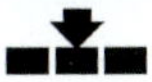	16:9	[S] (2 M)
	[H]		16:9	[S] (2 M)
	[L]	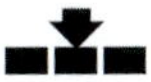	16:9	[S] (2 M)
Motion JPEG	HD	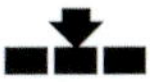	16:9	[S] (2 M)
	WVGA		16:9	[S] (2 M)
	VGA	Still picture cannot be created		
	QVGA	Still picture cannot be created		

Table 9-6: Resulting picture's file information when created after video

Recommendation

We have found taking videos to be a lot of fun. In some cases they are well planned and in other cases they become impromptu. Experiment with your camera's video capabilities. Test all of the possible color schemes and predefined scene modes. See what works for you and when.

Do not be afraid to work with AVCHD. If you take short video recordings, you can edit these files on your computer. In the case of Apple computers, you will have to buy additional software; however, the cost is nominal. The iLife series, for example, costs $50 and it provides you with three programs. Two of them you will find useful, iPhoto and iMovie. iPhoto will be useful if you wish to work with the camera's RAW files, and iMovie will allow you to work with AVCHD Lite files. If you own a PC, be sure to load Panasonic's PHOTOfunSTUDIO HD Edition program. It comes with the camera and it will enable you to work with the AVCHD Lite files. When working with these files, start working with short video clips that do not run longer than a couple of minutes. This will enable you to estimate the time it takes to work with longer video streams.

Playing Back Your Pictures and Videos

10

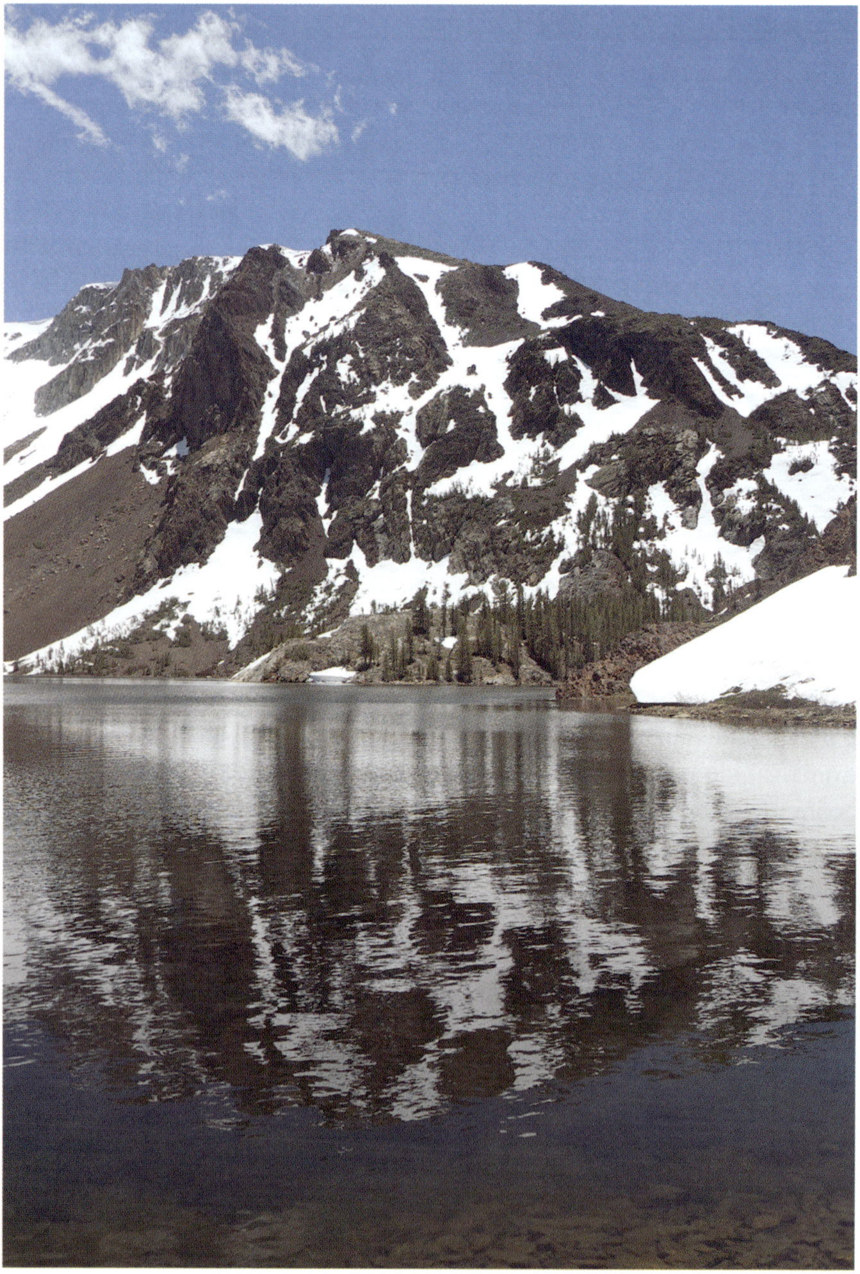

Introduction: Playing Back Your Pictures and Videos

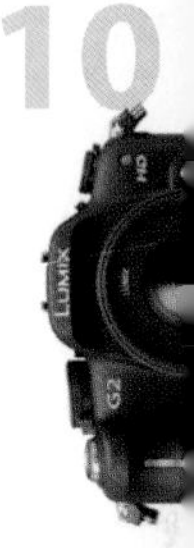

The previous chapters concentrated on describing how to take and record pictures and videos. This chapter is about how the Panasonic G2 camera can be used to play back those images stored on your memory card.

Before you start reading this chapter, you should ask yourself how you intend to review and work with your images. If you intend to do work with them on a computer, then much of the information in this chapter is not essential for using the camera. In fact, downloading your picture and video files to a computer and using third party software to organize and display them is more convenient than using your camera for this purpose.

In this respect, PC owners are lucky. They can do this immediately and with no extra cost by using the Panasonic-supplied program PHOTOfunSTUDIO 5.0 HD Edition. Users of Apple computers will probably use the programs supplied in the iLife series. Frequently these programs are preloaded on a new Apple computer, but if it is not, you can purchase it for a nominal fee ($50). If you intend to work primarily with a computer, then you should go to the end of this chapter and read the section on downloading pictures and videos to the computer.

However, there may be times when a computer is unavailable and you want to prepare an impromptu slide show for a small audience. For example, suppose you are traveling and wish to organize your day's pictures and videos and share them with your traveling companions on your camera. Other times you may wish to play back a group of stored pictures and videos on a television monitor. To undertake these tasks, the Panasonic G2 camera is equipped with a comprehensive and large menu command sequence. Included with these commands are some simple image processing commands.

Chapter Organization

This chapter covers the PLAYBACK Mode menu and managing your pictures and videos outside of the camera. The PLAYBACK Mode menu has three distinct groups of commands:

- SLIDE SHOW for showing images to an audience
- PLAYBACK MODE for viewing a group of images
- Image processing commands to assign print information or improve your images

The PLAYBACK Mode menu's SLIDE SHOW commands allow you to build and play back a slide show presentation of selected groups of pictures and/or videos from your camera's memory card.

The PLAYBACK MODE command enables you to select a group of pictures and/or videos and view them one at a time. This can help you to view what you have in a specific subject and determine how best to manage your pictures and videos before they become unmanageable.

Finally, since you want to present your images and videos in the best manner, there are image processing commands for assigning print information, adjusting orientation, cropping to the most effective area of the picture, and shortening the video clips.

The last section of this chapter will cover your option to download your files from the camera's memory card onto your computer. This way, you can free up space on your memory card for more pictures and videos and still have the existing ones for future enjoyment. Panasonic includes two software applications with your camera at purchase time: Silkypix Developer Studio and PHOTOfunSTUDIO 5.0 HD Edition. We will briefly cover both applications at the end of this chapter.

A note of caution before you read further: Although the PLAYBACK Mode menu is straightforward, we have found it can have a steep learning curve, especially for users who are not very experienced in menu structures or image processing. There are multiple menu levels that need to be navigated and managed. The image processing function has limitations and, in some cases, the results are not as exacting as they would be if you conducted the image processing via your computer.

We have utilized the PLAYBACK Mode menu features extensively to learn the process, and although we can clearly see its value and have enjoyed the results, we do not use it. We prefer to download our pictures and videos regularly to our computers to free up space on our camera's memory card. We use our computers to process our pictures and videos and write to DVDs for keepsake viewing. So you may not wish to read this chapter in its entirety, especially, if you are comfortable with working with images and videos on your computer.

PLAYBACK Mode Menu

Overview

The PLAYBACK Mode menu is a system of its own with a vast menu structure. It consists of commands that center on image processing and grouping your pictures and videos for printing or viewing them through the camera or on a computer or TV. Although you may find the PLAYBACK Mode menu functions will work very nicely,, in many cases it's better to download your pictures and videos to your computer and use specialized software.

The PLAYBACK Mode menu has three distinct sections: the SLIDE SHOW command with its supporting menu structure that allows you to construct and initiate a picture and video presentation, a quick PLAYBACK MODE command that lets you play back a group of pictures and videos one at a time, and a set of PLAYBACK image processing commands.

Preparation Criteria

If you intend to make a slide show presentation, familiarize yourself with the different available presentation formats. Listen to the types of music, watch the transition styles and test the different playback speeds before you make a decision on how to build a slide show presentation. The slide show presentation settings are retained in the camera so you can play them again and again.

PLAYBACK Mode Menu and Playback Button

The PLAYBACK Mode menu is distinct from the Playback button on the back of the camera.

The Playback button, discussed in chapter 3, allows you to view your pictures one at a time through the viewfinder or LCD screen. You will be able to scroll through all of the pictures and videos saved on the memory card in order of their recording. In addition, you can review the camera settings used to record the picture or video.

The PLAYBACK Mode menu is the last menu command within the camera's main menu. It has a series of commands for organizing, building, and playing back selected pictures and videos as a presentation or viewing them one at a time. In addition, the PLAYBACK Mode menu has a set of image processing commands to help you improve upon your saved pictures and videos.

10

CATEGORY SELECTION - Categories

The PLAYBACK Mode menu takes advantage of the categories to which your stored pictures have been assigned, as described in chapter 4. The category information is stored with the recorded picture or video, and is utilized in two places within the PLAYBACK Mode menu: SLIDE SHOW and PLAYBACK MODE (figure 10-1a, figure 10-1b).

When selecting the specific playback category, use table 10-1 to determine which recording category will fall into which SLIDE SHOW and PLAYBACK MODE category. Note that for FACE RECOG, you will be asked to select a specific registered face from which the camera will group together all of the associated pictures for playback purposes.

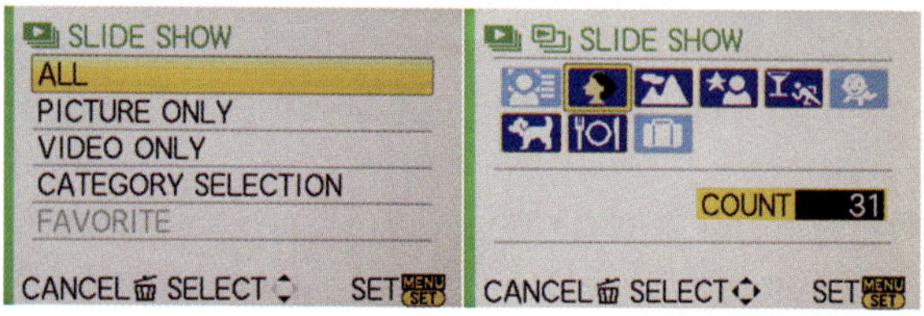

Figure 10-1a: The SLIDE SHOW command's available options; Figure 10-1b: List of available categories when building a slide show presentation

Playback Category	Recorded Categories
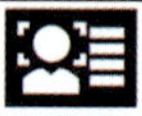	FACE RECOG.
	PORTRAIT, i-PORTRAIT, NIGHT PORTRAIT i-NIGHT PORTRAIT, BABY1/BABY2, i-BABY
	SCENERY, i-SCENERY, SUNSET, i-SUNSET
	NIGHT PORTRAIT, i-NIGHT PORTRAIT, i-NIGHT SCENERY
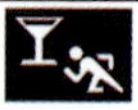	SPORTS, PARTY
	BABY1/BABY2, i-BABY
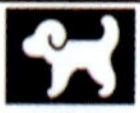	PET
	FOOD
	TRAVEL DATE
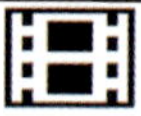	AVCHD Lite, Motion JPEG

Table 10-1: Recorded categories mapped into the available SLIDE SHOW and PLAYBACK categories

SLIDE SHOW

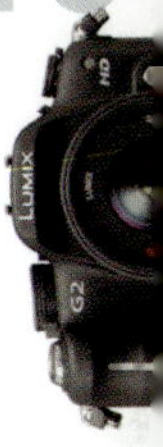

Determine Presentation Content

The PLAYBACK Mode menu's SLIDE SHOW command has a complex multi-level menu structure. You have several options for how to play your saved pictures and videos residing on the memory card within the camera. For example, you can create a slide show consisting of either just still pictures or just videos, or you can select a specific category, which includes pictures and videos. Finally, you can limit the show to only your favorite images.

In addition, there are multiple slide show presentation styles. You can vary the time interval between each picture/video, the presentation style, whether you will use the preset music, and have only recorded audio or no sound at all. Once you have determined your slide show content and style, you can start the slide show presentation and watch it on your camera's display screen or on your TV.

The first decision you make is the type of pictures and/or videos the slide show presentation will consist of. Select the value from the following command:

MENU/SET>PLAYBACK>SLIDE SHOW>[ALL], [PICTURE ONLY], [VIDEO ONLY], [CATEGORY SELECTION], [FAVORITE]

Table 10-2 describes the different SLIDE SHOW command options you have to choose from. Once you select what will be in your slide show presentation, you will need to select the playback style consisting of the transition from one picture or video to the next, the picture display style, and music.

SLIDE SHOW Options	Slide Show consists of
ALL	All pictures and videos.
PICTURE ONLY	All pictures only.
VIDEO ONLY	All videos only.
CATEGORY SELECTION	Only pictures and videos in a specific category.
FAVORITE	Only pictures and videos that are identified as Favorites. Option is enabled only if MENU/SET>PLAYBACK>(pg 3) FAVORITE>[ON] is selected.

Table 10-2: SLIDE SHOW command options

Presentation Commands

How you build your presentation is really a personal preference. We recommend that you try each of the different styles and listen to the preset music to determine what you like. Once you have selected a SLIDE SHOW command option, you will be presented with a standard presentation submenu (except for CATEGORY SELECTION) asking you to specify how you want the selected pictures and videos presented (figure 10-2). In the case of the CATEGORY SELECTION command option, you will first be presented with a list of categories to select from. Once you have selected a category, you will be presented with the standard presentation submenu.

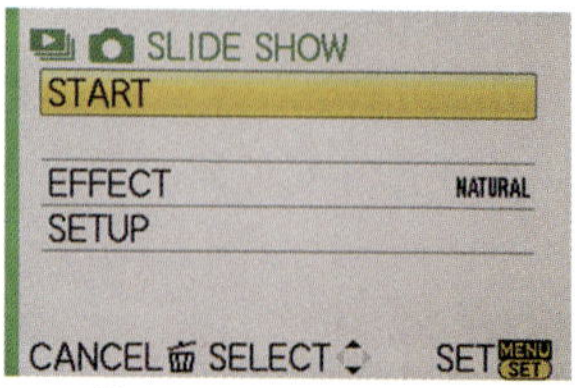

Figure 10-2: Repetitive SLIDE SHOW submenu

Because of the uniqueness of the SLIDE SHOW command's menu structure we will vary our menu path nomenclature to include "[*selected option*]" as a placeholder for the selected SLIDE SHOW command option and selected category when [CATEGORY SELECTION] had been selected.

There are a few places within the SLIDE SHOW menu structure where the available presentation styles have minor differences. For example, the camera has you select a transition style for when the slide show transitions from one picture to the next. But you do not have any transition styles to chose from when you have specified that your slide show will contain [VIDEO ONLY]. Rather than cover all of the exceptions here and potentially complicate the flow, we recommend you look for the specific option in the SLIDE SHOW portion in Appendix D*.

EFFECT Command

This command allows you to set the transition style for switching from one picture to the next picture along with the type of music. The EFFECT command is disabled when [VIDEO ONLY] is selected for SLIDE SHOW command. The slide show's style is set with the following command:

MENU/SET>PLAYBACK>SLIDE SHOW>[*selected option*]>EFFECT> [AUTO], [NATURAL], [SLOW], [SWING], [URBAN], [OFF]

Each EFFECT command option has its own transition style and music. Test them and see which works best for the selected pictures and videos. When [OFF] is selected, only the recorded audio is played. You will see that selecting [URBAN] will cause some of the pictures to be played in black and white and

* To view the Appendix, see: http://rockynook.com/PanasonicG2

that [AUTO] is only available when you have selected a CATEGORY SELECTION option. If you wish to override the recorded audio, make sure you have selected a value for the EFFECT command other than [OFF] and set MENU/SET>PLAYBACK>SLIDE SHOW>[*selected option*]>SETUP>SOUND>[MUSIC].

SETUP Command

This command has three submenu commands allowing you to set how the slide show presentation will occur. Assign the slide show's setup values using the following command:

MENU/SET>PLAYBACK>SLIDE SHOW>[*selected option*]>
SETUP>[DURATION], [REPEAT], [SOUND]

- DURATION Command
  The DURATION command is as follows:

  MENU/SET>PLAYBACK>SLIDE SHOW>[*selected option*]>SETUP>
  DURATION>[1 SEC], [2 SEC], [3 SEC], [5 SEC]

  This command controls the transition time between each image. It is automatically set to 2 seconds ([2 SEC]) when you have selected a specific EFFECT value. You can select your own duration from the allowable options if you set EFFECT to [OFF].

- REPEAT Command
  Use the following command to set whether there will be a continuous loop through the selected images or they play through once:

  MENU/SET>PLAYBACK>SLIDE SHOW>[*selected option*]>SETUP>
  REPEAT>[OFF], [ON]

- SOUND Command
  You may have been recording sound with your videos and pictures and want it to be played during the slide show presentation. The SOUND command will enable you to set how you want to handle the slide show's accompanied sound:

  MENU/SET>PLAYBACK>SLIDE SHOW>[*selected option*]>SETUP>
  SOUND>[OFF], [AUTO], [MUSIC], [AUDIO]

These options are as follows:

- OFF - No sound will play, including any saved audio.
- AUTO - Music will play when there is no recorded audio.
- MUSIC - Music will play instead of recorded audio.
- AUDIO - Only recorded audio will play.

START Command

Execute the START command as follows:

MENU/SET>PLAYBACK>SLIDE SHOW>[*selected option*]>START

There are no options within the START command. Selecting START initiates your slide show presentation. Whatever you selected in the other commands will dictate what the slide show presentation will consist of and how it will be presented. The slide show presentation style will be based upon the entered values in the other commands: EFFECT and SETUP's DURATION, REPEAT, and SOUND. The presentation will play the selected pictures and/or videos in order of recorded date and time.

Recommendations

Playing a slide show is a great way to view your pictures and videos on the fly or if you are unable to download your saved files to a computer for processing. It can be fun to view your saved memories quickly and with minimal effort. There are some drawbacks. To get the best results, you must make sure you have your pictures and videos categorized correctly and saved on your camera's memory card in order to play them back. You must also continue to store them on your memory card in order for them to be available to your camera. We recommend you use this feature as a novelty. When wishing to store your pictures and videos permanently, download them to your computer and use third-party software to organize them into a permanent slide show.

PLAYBACK MODE

Overview

The PLAYBACK MODE command (figure 10-3a) allows you to select a group of pictures and videos from the memory card and manually play through them one at a time. Use the following command to select which pictures and videos you want to view:

MENU/SET>PLAYBACK>PLAYBACK MODE>[NORMAL PLAY], [PICTURE PLAY], [AVCHD Lite PLAY], [MOTION JPEG PLAY], [CATEGORY PLAY], [FAVORITE PLAY]

Table 10-3 contains the PLAYBACK MODE command options displayed in figure 10-3a along with a description of what group of pictures and videos will be selected for each option. Select an option and press the MENU/SET button. For all but the [CATEGORY PLAY] option, the camera will group all of your pictures and videos per the selected option and present the first one on the display screen for your viewing.

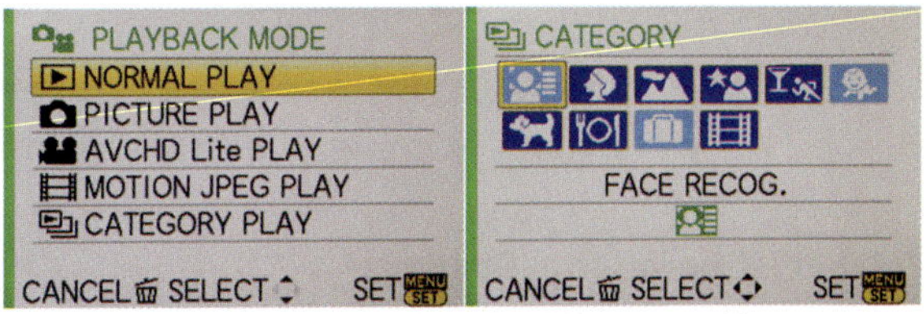

Figure 10-3a: The PLAYBACK MODE command's menu;
Figure 10-3b: The PLAYBACK MODE's CATEGORY PLAY menu

The [CATEGORY PLAY] option has an additional step to select the category you wish to have played back (figure 10-3b). Select a category and press the MENU/SET button to group all of the selected category's pictures and videos. The camera will present the first one on the display screen for your viewing. Use the right and left directional arrow buttons to move through each image one at a time. Press the MENU/SET button again to end the playback and return to live view mode.

PLAYBACK MODE Options	Description
NORMAL PLAY	Play back all pictures and videos.
PICTURE PLAY	Play back pictures only.
AVCHD LITE PLAY	Play back all videos recorded using AVCHD Lite.
MOTION JPEG PLAY	Play back all videos recorded using Motion JPEG.
CATEGORY PLAY	Play back all pictures and videos in the specific category.
FAVORITE PLAY	Play back both pictures and videos that are identified as favorites. Option is displayed only if MENU/SET> PLAYBACK>FAVORITE>[ON] is selected.

Table 10-3: PLAYBACK MODE command options

Recommendations

We recommend using the PLAYBACK MODE command as a quick and easy way to view a group of pictures and videos that would otherwise be dispersed throughout your memory card. Keep in mind, the PLAYBACK MODE command is using only images stored on your memory card, and if you are continuing to record pictures and videos on the same memory card, each playback may contain new pictures and/or videos.

If you wish to view your pictures and videos on a permanent basis, we recommend you download them to your computer and save them for future viewing via either your computer or some other medium.

Playback Operational Controls

Once you start a slide show presentation or start playing back pictures and videos via the PLAYBACK MODE command, you may want to pause the show, jump ahead, or replay an image. Table 10-4 lists operation controls to help you navigate during the playback.

Playback Operations	Description
Play/pause	Press the up directional arrow button.
Stop	Press the down directional arrow button.
Back to previous picture or video	Press the up directional arrow button (pause), then the left directional arrow button.
Skip ahead to the next picture or video	Press the up directional arrow button (pause), then the right directional arrow button.
Reduce volume	Turn the rear dial to the left.
Increase volume level	Turn the rear dial to the right.

Table 10-4: Playback operational controls

Image Processing Commands

Overview

Table 10-5 contains a list of the 12 PLAYBACK Mode menu image processing commands available to help you document and modify both your pictures and videos and print your pictures. Additional quick reference information containing each of the commands plus their subcommands, values, and high-level descriptions can be found in the PLAYBACK section within Appendix C*.

* To view the Appendix, see: http://rockynook.com/PanasonicG2

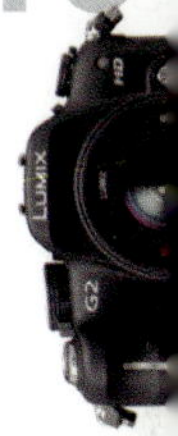

We recommend you review table 10-5 before proceeding with this section. You may already be using image processing software and therefore most likely will not be using these commands. If that is the case, feel free to skip to the section "Working outside of the Camera" near the end of this chapter. You can always come back to this section if you change your mind.

We have structured this section to allow you to zero in on a specific command and learn how to use it along with any concerns and limitations you will need to know.

Playback Command	Description
TITLE EDIT	Add a title to a picture or video to be displayed during PLAYBACK Mode.
TEXT STAMP	Collect a set of data to be printed on the picture.
VIDEO DIVIDE	Divide a video into two separate videos.
RESIZE	Reduce a picture's size so it can be emailed or posted to a website easier.
CROPPING	Identify a portion of a picture and saves it as a new picture.
ASPECT CONV.	Convert a picture with an aspect ratio setting of [16:9] to one of the following three settings: [4:3], [3:2], or [1:1].
ROTATE	Rotate a picture in 90 degrees increments clockwise or counterclockwise.
ROTATE DISP.	Display vertical pictures rotated horizontally.
FAVORITE	Identify pictures and videos as favorites so they can be played back as a group.
PRINT SET	Identify pictures to print along with print criteria.
PROTECT	Set a protection key to prevent a picture or video from being deleted by mistake.
FACE REC EDIT	Delete and replace Face Recognition information in selected pictures.

Table 10-5: PLAYBACK Mode Menu image processing commands

You can also use the supplied Silkypix Developer Studio and PHOTOfunSTUDIO 5.0 HD Edition software, which we will cover later in this chapter. Although both of these software packages have limitations, they will enable you to process your pictures and videos for a more finished and enjoyable result.

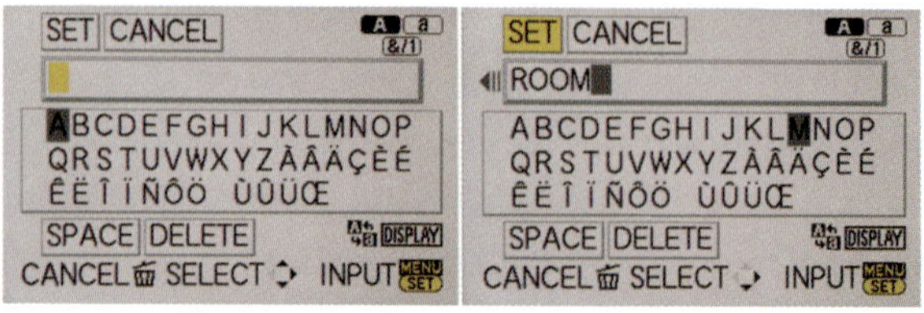

Figure 10-4a: Empty text entry screen;
Figure 10-4b: Entered text with SET icon highlighted

In many cases, the third-party software will do a better job of modifying the files, building slide show presentations, and protecting your pictures and videos. The down side is that you need to have the software, a computer to execute it, and the expertise to know how to use both to get the results you desire. This is not for everyone, and since Panasonic has supplied the camera with many desirable image processing capabilities, you can easily use these commands to improve the quality of your pictures and video.

Before we go through each of the commands, there are two common steps that are used by several of the commands.

1. Several of the commands will have you scroll through the saved images to select 1 [SINGLE] or up to 50 [MULTI] pictures/videos. When [SINGLE] is selected, you will scroll through each picture or video one at a time using the right and left directional arrow buttons. To select one, press the MENU/SET button. When [MULTI] is selected, you are presented with up to six pictures on the display screen at one time. To select one, press the DISPLAY button. We will refer to these actions as "scroll through" and "select."
2. Several of the commands have the option to associate text with a picture or video. You will be presented with a text entry screen. This is the same text entry screen used to enter in name information for BABY1, BABY2, PET, LOCATION (in TRAVEL DATE), and FACE RECOG. The screen is simple and straightforward. Pressing the DISPLAY button will cycle through capitalized alphabet, lowercase alphabet, and number/symbol keyboard pads. Use the directional arrow buttons to navigate through the keyboard and the MENU/SET button to enter the highlighted letter. Once you have entered the text, return to the SET icon on the top-left portion of the screen and press the MENU/SET button to accept your entered information (figure 10-4a, figure 10-4b). When applicable, we will refer to what you need to enter via the text entry screen.

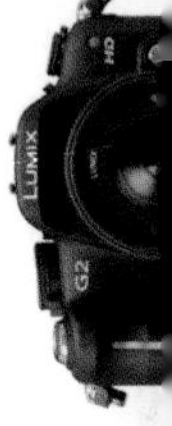

TITLE EDIT

This command gives you the option to assign title information (maximum of 30 characters) to one or more pictures at one time. The title information will be carried over and available for printing with the picture when using PHOTOfunSTUDIO 5.0 HD Edition software.

What you should know:

- Command not available for the following types of pictures:
  - Videos
  - Protected pictures
  - RAW only and RAW/JPEG format pictures
  - Pictures recorded with other equipment

To use the TITLE EDIT command:

1. Select MENU/SET>PLAYBACK>TITLE EDIT>[SINGLE], [MULTI]. Press the MENU/SET button.
2. Scroll through the saved pictures. Select the picture(s) to which you wish to add a title. Press the MENU/SET button to select.
3. The text entry screen appears. Enter in the title, position the cursor on the SET icon, and press the MENU/SET button to accept your entered title.
4. Press the Trash Can button to exit the command.

TEXT STAMP

Use the TEXT STAMP command to stamp the recording date/time, name, travel location, travel day, and/or title (entered from TITLE EDIT command) onto a new copy of a recorded picture for printing purposes.

What you should know:

- Pictures must be printed using compatible software and on a compatible printer. Some software cannot read the pictures' associated text. Some printers will cut off characters. The supplied PHOTOfunSTUDIO 5.0 HD Edition software can read this information from the downloaded pictures.
- There is no guarantee the text will be printed or positioned correctly. If you specify to have the picture's recorded date printed, it will overlay

the stamped text. Check with your print shop before having your pictures printed to determine if they will be able to print your pictures' associated text.

- Adding text may cause the picture's printed quality to deteriorate.
- Pictures made from original pictures with a picture size of [L] or [M] will be resized to [S].
- TEXT STAMP command will not work for the following type of pictures:
  - Pictures recorded with RAW only or RAW/JPEG format
  - Pictures recorded with audio
  - Videos or pictures recorded without setting the clock first

To set the text stamp information for your picture(s):

1. Select MENU/SET>PLAYBACK>TEXT STAMP>[SINGLE], [MULTI]. Press the MENU/SET button.
2. Scroll through the saved pictures. Select the picture(s) you wish to copy with a text stamp. Press the MENU/SET button and the TEXT STAMP command options appear on the display screen (figure 10-5a).
3. Select values for each option. Table 10-6 contains a list of options and their possible values.
4. Press the MENU/SET button when completed.
5. If you have selected either the [*Face Recognition*] or [*Baby/Pet*] options for the NAME command, you will receive the following question:

   DO YOU NEED AGE STAMP? [YES] [NO]

   Select [YES] to include the age with the text stamp information; [NO] to exclude the age information.
6. You will be asked if you want to save the new picture with the text stamp information. The message you receive depends on the size of the original picture(s).

   If picture size = [L] or [M], the following message will display:

   IT WILL BE STAMPED ON THE PICTURE RESIZED TO S. SAVE NEW PICTURES? [YES] [NO]

10

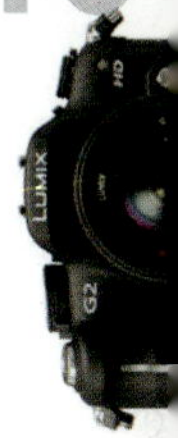

If picture size = [S], the following message will display:

SAVE NEW PICTURES? [YES] [NO]

Select [YES] to save the new picture(s) (figure 10-5b). Select [NO] to not save the new picture(s) and return step 3.

7. Press the Trash Can button to exit the command.

Commands	Options	Value Description
SHOOTING DATE	OFF	Don't include recorded date and time.
	W/O TIME	Include recorded year, month, and day.
	WITH TIME	Include recorded year, month, day, hour, and minute.
NAME	OFF	Do not include saved registered name information.
	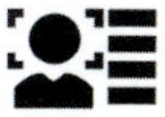	Include Face Recognition name. When asked to include age, if you select [YES], age information will be added.
	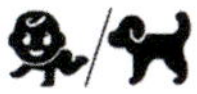	Include registered name settings of BABY1, BABY2, or PET. When asked to include age, if you select [YES], age information will be added.
LOCATION	OFF	Don't include MENU/SET>SETUP>TRAVEL DESTINATION>[LOCATION] information.
	ON	Include MENU/SET>SETUP>TRAVEL DESTINATION>[LOCATION] information.
TRAVEL DATE	OFF	Do not include calculated number of days elapsed since travel departure date.
	ON	Include calculated number of days elapsed since travel departure date (ex. "5" for Day 5).
TITLE	OFF	Do not include saved title for picture(s) from MENU/SETUP>PLAYBACK>TITLE EDIT.
	ON	Include saved title for picture(s) from MENU/SETUP>PLAYBACK>TITLE EDIT.

Table 10-6: TEXT STAMP command options with descriptions

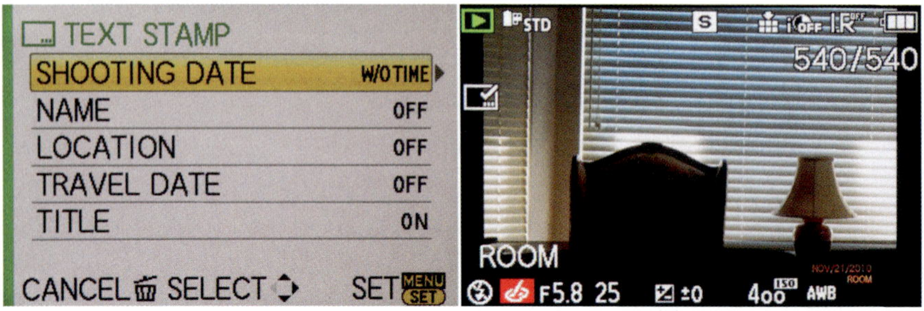

Figure 10-5a: TEXT STAMP command menu options;
Figure 10-5b: TEXT STAMP command information displayed in red in the lower-right corner

Each new picture will have a Text Stamp icon in the upper-left side of the display screen and the saved text stamp information displayed in red in the lower-right corner of the display screen (figure 10-6b). The text information is small and easy to miss. Once you realize what you are looking for, you should have no trouble finding it.

VIDEO DIVIDE

This option allows you to divide a saved video into two parts and save both parts. Keep in mind that the original video will be shortened to the point where you divide it and the portion of the video after the division point will be saved in a new video file. For example, if you have a 50-second video and you decide to divide it into two parts at the 40-second mark, you will end up with two video files, one with a length of 40 seconds and a new file with a length of 10 seconds. The audio portion will also be divided accordingly and kept with each portion of the divided file. Once you have divided a video, you cannot put them back together with the camera software. You will need to download them from your camera's memory card and use third-party software to put them back together.

We have noticed that you cannot divide a video at an exact frame and therefore if you want to divide a video at a precise point, you would be better served to download the video onto your computer and use third-party software to control the point of the division to an exact frame.

What you should know:

- You cannot divide the following kinds of videos:
  - Videos set as a favorite
  - Protected videos
  - Videos with a total recording time of about 2 seconds or less

- You cannot divide a video if one of the resulting videos will be about 1 second or less.
- PRINT SET is cancelled for divided videos.
- Dividing [Motion JPEG] videos reorders the file numbers. For example, suppose there are 105 files on your memory card. You divide video file #100. Resulting videos will be file #105 and #106, with #105 being the original video up to the point of division and #106 the new video containing the portion after the division.
- Dividing [AVCHD Lite] videos does not reorder the file numbers. For example, suppose there are 200 files on your memory card. You divide video file #160. Resulting videos will be file #160 and #201, with #160 being the original video up to the point of division and #201 the new video containing the portion after the division.

To execute a VIDEO DIVIDE:

1. Select MENU/SET>PLAYBACK>VIDEO DIVIDE.
2. Select the video you wish to divide.
3. Press the MENU/SET button to play the video.
4. Press the up directional arrow button at the location in the video you wish to make the divide. The video will pause.
5. Press the down directional arrow button to execute the divide.
6. You will receive the following message:

   DIVIDE THIS MOVIE FILE? [YES] [NO]
   DO NOT REMOVE THE BATTERY/MEMORY CARD WHILE PROCEEDING.

   Using the left or right directional arrow buttons, select [YES] to complete the divide or select [NO] to stop the divide.
7. Press the Trash Can button to exit command.

It might be easier to find the video first before starting the VIDEO DIVIDE command. Use the Playback button to locate and play back the video to determine where you want to divide it. Once you have found the video and decided where to divide it, initiate the VIDEO DIVIDE command.

RESIZE

The RESIZE command will create a copy of a picture with a reduced picture size (number of pixels). This makes the new picture easier to post to web pages or attach to emails. For example, if you have 100 files saved on your memory card and you execute the RESIZE command for picture file numbers 80 and 81, the results will be 102 files on your memory card with file number 101 being a resized version of file number 80 and file number 102 a resized version of file number 81.

What you should know:

- You can only resize pictures from a larger size to a smaller size:
  - Original picture size of [L] can be resized to [M] or [S}
  - Original picture size of [M] can be resized to [S] only.
- You cannot resize the following types of pictures:
  - Video files
  - Pictures with audio
  - Pictures taken with picture size of [S],
  - Pictures taken with RAW only and RAW/JPEG formats
  - Pictures stamped with text stamp information.

To resize your picture(s):

1. Select MENU/SET>PLAYBACK>(pg 2) RESIZE>[SINGLE], [MULTI]. Press the MENU/SET button.
2. If [SINGLE] selected:
   a) Scroll through the saved pictures. Find the picture you wish to resize. Press the MENU/SET button.
   b) If you have selected a picture that is already sized [S], you will receive the following error message:

      THIS PICTURE CANNOT BE RESIZED

      Select another picture or stop the process.
   c) If the picture you selected is currently [L] or [M], a screen is displayed with the selected picture's current size and an arrow pointing down to the possible resize choices:
      - Picture size of [M] can be copied to [S] size.
      - Picture size of [L] can be copied to [M] or [S] size (figure 10-6a, figure 10-6b).

Use left or right directional arrow buttons to select a resize value and press the MENU/SET button.

3. If [MULTI] is selected:
   a) A screen appears listing both the [M] and [S] picture sizes with all of the possible aspect ratio values and related sizes. Use the up and down directional arrow buttons to select [M] or [S] and press the MENU/SET button.

   b) Scroll through and select the pictures you wish to resize using the DISPLAY button. If you have selected a picture that cannot be resized to the selected new size, (step 3a), the following message appears at the bottom of the selection screen:

      THIS PICTURE CANNOT BE RESIZED

      Select another picture or stop the process.

   c) When you have found all of the pictures for resizing, press the MENU/SET button.

   Note that the Resize icon is displayed on each successfully selected picture.
4. You will be asked if you want to save the new picture(s) with the new picture size:

   SAVE NEW PICTURES? [YES] [NO]

   Select [YES] to save the new picture(s). Select [NO] to stop the process and return to scroll though the pictures.
5. Press the Trash Can button to exit the command.

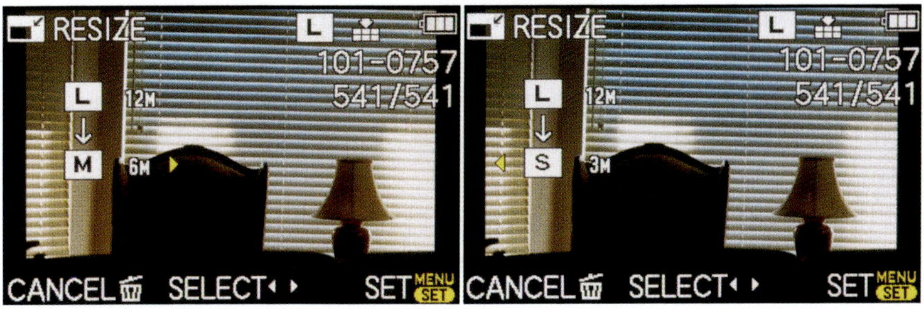

Figure 10-6a: Original [SINGLE] picture with picture size of [L] can be resized to [M]
Figure 10-6b: Original [SINGLE] picture with picture size of [L] can be resized to [S]

CROPPING

Cropping is a technique used to create a new picture containing only a portion of the original picture. The CROPPING command allows you to enlarge a picture, move the center of the picture, and then create a new picture containing what you see in the display screen. This is not an exact science. You can enlarge the picture only by set increments, plus the resulting picture size will have to fit within the set of available picture sizes.

What you should know:

- The picture quality of cropped pictures will deteriorate due to excessive enlargement.
- You cannot crop the following:
  - Videos
  - Pictures with audio
  - Pictures stamped with Text Stamp icon
  - Pictures recorded with RAW only or RAW/JPEG formats
- Face Recognition information will not be copied from the original picture to the new cropped image.

To crop your picture:

1. Select MENU/SET>PLAYBACK>(pg 2) CROPPING.
2. Locate the picture you want cropped and press the MENU/SET button.
3. Turn the rear dial to the right to enlarge the picture. Note the four yellow arrows displayed on the screen. Use the directional arrow buttons to position the picture (figure 10-7a).
4. Press the MENU/SET button.
5. The following message displays:

   SAVE NEW PICTURES? [YES] [NO]

   Select [YES] to complete the cropping; [NO] to stop the process.
6. Press the Trash Can button to exit the command.

The original picture will be unaffected and a new picture will be saved on the memory card containing the cropped image (figure 10-7b).

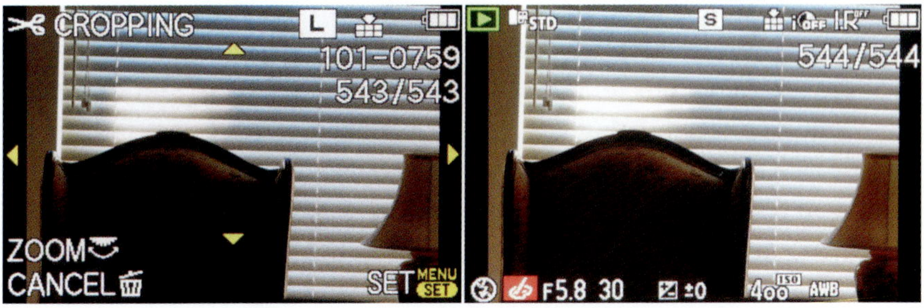

Figure 10-7a: The cropped picture prior to being saved;
Figure 10-7b: The cropped picture with a new file number

ASPECT CONV.

This command allows you to create a new picture with an aspect ratio of [3:2], [4:3], or [1:1] from a picture with a current aspect ratio of [16:9]. An aspect ratio of [16:9] does not completely fit on a computer monitor or a non-widescreen TV. If you plan to create a presentation for your TV or computer and you have pictures with an aspect ratio of [16:9], you most likely will want to convert them to a better aspect ratio for your intended purposes. This command creates new pictures, so you will not be losing the original pictures.

What you should know:

- This command does not work on the following:
  - Videos
  - Pictures with audio
  - Pictures stamped with Text Stamp icon
  - Pictures recorded with RAW only or RAW/JPEG formats
- Face Recognition information will not be copied from the original picture to the new picture.

To convert your picture's aspect ratio:

1. Select MENU/SET>PLAYBACK>(pg 2) ASPECT CONV.>[3:2], [4:3], [1:1] (figure 10-8a).
2. Locate the picture you want to create a new picture of with a different aspect ratio and press the MENU/SET button (figure 10-8b). If the selected picture is not eligible, the following error message displays:

   CANNOT BE SET ON THIS PICTURE

   Select another picture or stop the process.

3. If the selected picture's aspect ratio is 16:9, the picture will show a yellow target box representing the selected new aspect ratio size with arrows indicating that you can move the target box using the directional arrow buttons (figure 10-8c). Position the target box where you want it and press the MENU/SET button. The new picture will be cropped to the new aspect ratio size.
4. The following message displays:

   SAVE NEW PICTURE(S)? [YES] [NO]

5. Select [YES] to complete the aspect conversion. Select [NO] to stop the process.
6. Press the Trash Can button to exit the command.

A new picture with the selected aspect ratio will be saved (figure 10-8d).

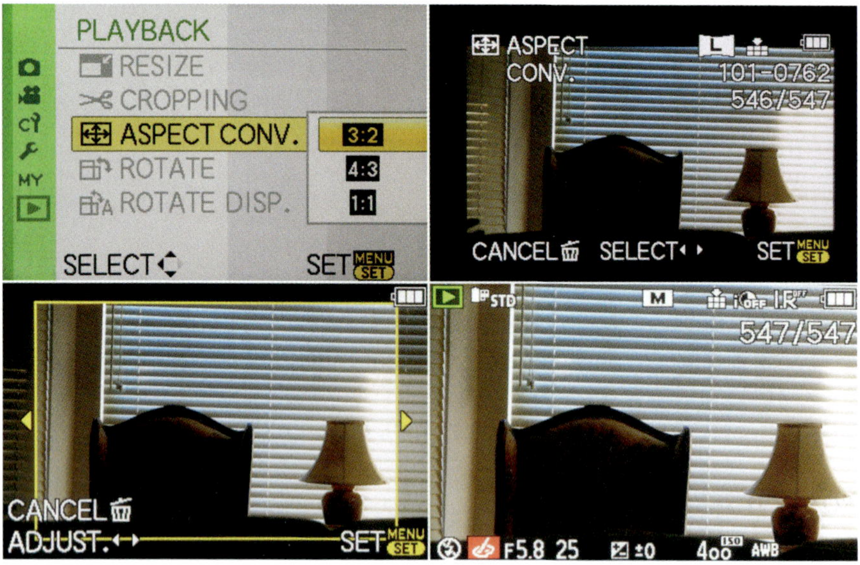

Figure 10-8a: Select new aspect ratio value;
Figure 10-8b: Original picture with an aspect ratio of [16:9];
Figure 10-8c: New aspect ratio superimposed on picture;
Figure 10-8d: New picture with aspect ratio of [3:2]

ROTATE

Although most pictures are taken holding the camera horizontally, there will be times when you will want to hold the camera vertically to snap that perfect picture. Vertical pictures can be displayed on the display screen horizontally using the ROTATE DISP. command, but when you print vertical pictures, you will find there will be two black lines, or borders, one on each side of the picture. This might not be to your liking. Rotating the vertical pictures for print purposes will eliminate the black borders on the printed version of the picture. The ROTATE command is enabled only when the ROTATE DISP. command is set to [ON].

What you should know:

- Cannot rotate the following:
  - Videos
  - Protected pictures

To use the ROTATE command:

1. Select MENU/SET>PLAYBACK>(pg 2) ROTATE.
2. Select the picture you want rotated 90 degrees and press the MENU/SET button. If the selected picture is not eligible for the command, the following error message displays:

   CANNOT BE SET ON THIS PICTURE

   Select another picture or stop the process.
3. Using the up and down directional arrow buttons, select the direction you want the picture rotated and press the MENU/SET button.
4. Press the Trash Can button to exit the command.

ROTATE DISP.

This command controls how you will view vertical pictures and videos during playback.

1. Select MENU/SET>PLAYBACK>(pg 2) ROTATE DISP>[OFF], [ON].
2. Select [ON] to have vertical pictures and videos displayed horizontally automatically; select [OFF] to retain the vertical orientation during playback. Press the MENU/SET button to accept the highlighted value.

FAVORITE

Setting a picture or video to Favorite status gives you some additional control. You can group all identified Favorite files for playback purposes through the SLIDE SHOW or PLAYBACK MODE commands. In addition, when deleting pictures and videos, the [DELETE ALL] option will exclude deleting any files identified as a Favorite.

This command has three values: [ON], [OFF] and [CANCEL] (figure 10-9a). When FAVORITE command is set to [OFF], no new pictures and videos can be marked with a Favorite status. Previously marked pictures and videos will retain their Favorite status behind the scenes, but it is not recognized by the camera's software until the FAVORITE command is set to [ON]. Once it's set to [ON], pictures and videos set with a Favorite status will have a Favorite icon in the shape of a star displayed in white in the upper-left corner. There will also be another white star along with a yellow down arrow in the lower-right corner, indicating that pressing the down directional arrow button will unset Favorite status for the displayed image (figure 10-9b). You can remove all of the favorite statuses by setting the FAVORITE command value to [CANCEL].

What you should know:

- You can set a total of 999 pictures and videos as favorites.
- Pictures with QUALITY = RAW cannot be set as favorites.
- The [CANCEL] option will be disabled if there are no pictures or videos currently identified as a Favorite.

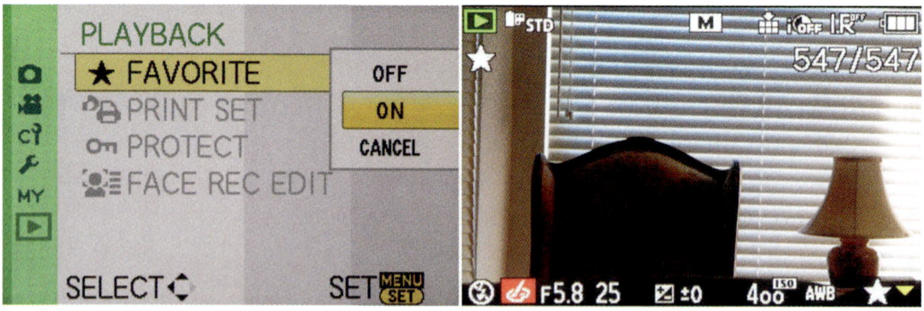

Figure 10-9a: FAVORITE command's options;
Figure 10-9b: Both Favorite icons displayed

To initiate FAVORITE functionality:

1. Select MENU/SET>PLAYBACK>(pg 3) FAVORITE>[OFF], [ON], [CANCEL].
   a) To enable pictures and videos to be marked as favorites, set MENU/SET>PLAYBACK>FAVORITE>[ON].
   b) To prevent pictures and videos to be marked as favorites, set MENU/SET>PLAYBACK>FAVORITE>[OFF].
   c) To cancel the favorite statuses for all pictures, set MENU/SET>PLAYBACK>FAVORITE>[CANCEL].
   You will receive the following message:

   CANCEL ALL FAVORITE SETTINGS? [YES] [NO]

   Select [YES] to cancel the favorite status for all pictures and press the MENU/SET button. Select [NO] to stop the process.
2. Press the Trash Can button to exit the command.

PRINT SET

This command allows you to set information to ultimately print your pictures using the DPOF (Digital Print Order Format) system that is utilized by many photo printers and photo printing services. You can select the pictures, how many copies of each to print, and whether to include recorded date/time stamp information.

What you should know:

- The print indicator and information do not automatically delete when you have printed the pictures. You will have to go back and execute the PRINT SET command's [CANCEL] option to erase the information when you are done printing the chosen pictures.

To initiate the PRINT SET command:

1. Select MENU/SET>PLAYBACK>(pg 3) PRINT SET>[SINGLE], [MULTI], [CANCEL].

   [SINGLE]

   a) Find the picture you wish to print and press the MENU/SET button. The Print Set icon displays in the top-left corner.

b) The COUNT field appears. Enter the number of prints you want (figure 10-10a). As soon as you enter, the Print Set icon with the entered count value is displayed on the left side of the display screen. The DATE indicator appears in the lower-right corner of the display screen.

c) Press the DISPLAY button to include date/time stamp information. The Print Set information consisting of the Print Set icon, number of prints and, if selected, the Date icon will display on the screen.

d) Press the MENU/SET button to store the entered print information with the selected picture (figure 10-10b).

[MULTI]

a) Scroll through the pictures. Find the picture you wish to print and press the MENU/SET button. The Print Set icon displays in the top-left corner.

b) The COUNT field appears. Enter in the number of prints you want. As soon as you enter a number, the DATE indicator appears.

c) Press the DISPLAY button to include date/time stamp information. The Print Set information consisting of the Print Set icon, number of prints and, if selected, the Date icon will display on the screen.

d) Press the MENU/SET button to set print information.

e) Repeat steps a through d until you have found and set the print information for each picture.

[CANCEL]

a) The following message is displayed:

CANCEL ALL PRINT SETTINGS? [YES] [NO]

b) Select [YES] to cancel all print settings and press the MENU/SET button. Select [NO] to stop the process.

2. Press the Trash Can button to exit the command.

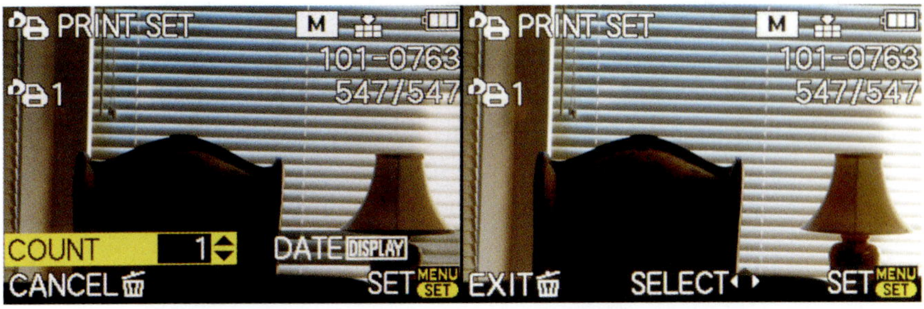

Figure 10-10a: Enter the number of prints you want printed for the selected picture;
Figure 10-10b: Print Set information displayed from Playback button

The information along with the Print Set icon will display on the screen when the picture is displayed via the Playback button or the PLAYBACK MODE command (figure 10-10b).

PROTECT

Did you ever intend to save something and you inadvertently deleted it by mistake. Pretty upsetting when that happens. The PROTECT command allows you to set an indicator on a picture or video that will prevent you from deleting it accidentally. Select [ON] to enable protection, [OFF] to disable protection, and [CANCEL] to remove existing protected status on all pictures and videos. The Protect icon is in the shape of a key displayed on the left side of the display screen (figure 10-11a). The Protect icon will also display in the top line of data when the picture is displayed via the Playback button or the PLAYBACK MODE command (figure 10-11b).

What you should know:

- [CANCEL] will be enabled only if at least one picture or video is already protected.
- You can also protect your pictures and video by setting the memory card's Write-Protect switch to LOCK.
- Protecting pictures and videos does not prevent them from being deleted when formatting the card using the FORMAT command.

To initiate PROTECT functionality:

1. Select MENU/SET>PLAYBACK>(pg 3) PROTECT>[SINGLE], [MULTI], [CANCEL] and press the MENU/SET button.

[SINGLE]

a) Find the picture or video you wish to protect.

b) Press the MENU/SET button to set the protection indicator. The Protect icon will appear on the picture or video.

To unprotect a picture or video, press the MENU/SET button again. The protection indicator acts as a toggle.

[MULTI]

a) Find the picture or video you wish to protect.

b) Press the MENU/SET button to set the protection indicator. The Protect icon will appear on the picture or video.

c) Repeat steps a and b for each picture or video you want to protect.

To unprotect a picture or video, press the MENU/SET button again. The protection indicator acts as a toggle.

[CANCEL]

a) The following message will display:

CANCEL ALL PROTECT? [YES] [NO]

b) Select [YES] to remove all protection status currently existing on pictures and videos and press the MENU/SET button. Select [NO] to stop the process.

If you wish to protect one or all of them again, you will have to execute the PROTECT command again for each one you wish to reprotect.

2. Press the Trash Can button to exit the command.

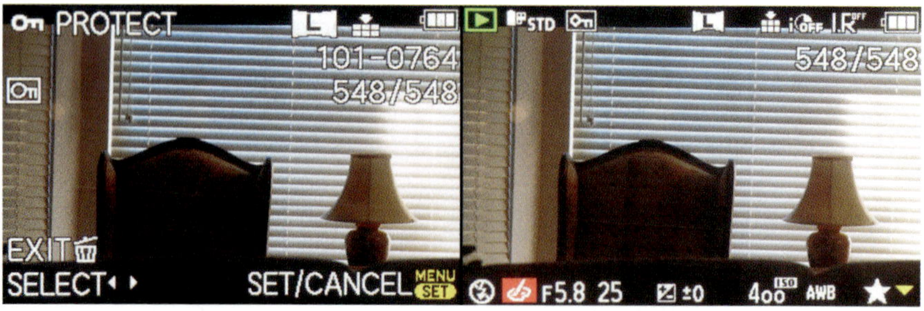

Figure 10-11a: Protect icon displayed on protected picture;
Figure 10-11b: Playback of same picture with Protect icon

FACE REC EDIT

This command allows you to replace or delete existing face recognition information associated with a selected picture.

What you should know:

- You can replace a picture's existing face recognition information only with existing information from the face recognition registry.

To initiate FACE REC EDIT command:

1. Select MENU/SET>PLAYBACK>(pg 3) FACE REC EDIT>[REPLACE], [DELETE].

   [REPLACE]

   a) Locate the picture for which you wish to change the face recognition information and press the MENU/SET button. If selected picture does not contain face recognition information, you will be presented with the following error message:

      NO FACE RECOG. INFORMATION FEATURED

      Select another picture and press the MENU/SET button.

   b) If selected picture has face recognition information, the following message will display:

      WHO TO REPLACE?

      Press the MENU/SET button and the Face Recognition screen appears containing the six registered people.

   c) Select the registered face with the face recognition information you want to have in place of the selected picture's current information. Press the MENU/SET button.

   d) The following message will display:

      REPLACE FACE RECOG. DATA [YES] [NO]

      Select [YES] to replace and press the MENU/SET button. The picture's face recognition information will be changed to the selected face registered information. Select [NO] to end the process and return to the Face Recognition screen containing the six registered people.

[DELETE]

e) Locate the picture from which you wish to delete the face recognition information and press the MENU/SET button.

f) The following message will display:

WHO TO DELETE?

Press the MENU/SET button.

g) The following message will display:

DELETE FACE RECOG. DATA? [YES] [NO]

Select [YES] and press the MENU/SET button. The picture's face recognition information will be deleted. Select [NO] to stop the process.

2. Press the Trash Can button to exit the command.

Working outside of the Camera

Overview

There is a lot of variety in how you can view and manage your pictures and videos outside of your camera. You can play them on your computer or TV, print the pictures, email them, and add them to your personal website. As technology evolves and new inventions are developed, most likely you will want to move your pictures and videos into those new arenas.

You have some current options that we will briefly discuss. What you use will depend on your available equipment and software and your level of knowledge to use both. Rather than go into details on how to use different technology, we recommend that you consult both the camera's and the connecting equipment's manuals along with their corresponding websites for specific information on how to accomplish your goals.

Playing Pictures/Videos on Your Computer/Downloading

The Panasonic G2 camera can be connected to your computer directly using the USB connection cable supplied. There are some limitations. You will not be able to play back any of the slide shows you created on the camera.

Our suggestion is to download your pictures and videos to your computer and build slide shows on your computer using either the PHOTOfunSTUDIO 5.0 HD Edition software or other third-party software you might own, such as iLife '11.

There are two ways to download your picture and video files to your computer. The first is to use a supplied cable that inserts into the USB port of the camera and connects to the USB port of your computer. Typically, if you are running PHOTOfunSTUDIO 5.0 HD you will receive a prompt for copying your files to your computer. This is a straightforward process, but you may wish to invest in a card reader rather than use your camera. Transferring files via a USB cable uses the camera's battery to access files on the memory card and send them on the USB cable. If you deplete your battery while downloading your files, you may corrupt and lose them. If you decide to use your camera and its USB cable, make sure you have a fully charged battery.

The second method is to download directly from the memory card. You can remove the card from your camera. Then by using a card reader, you can download to your computer's USB port. Card readers are inexpensive adapters that have a slot for your memory card and attach to your computer's USB port. This adapter may not even be necessary. Many laptop computers have a SD card reader built into their chassis. You simply insert the card into your computer and then start your download. Again, if you have a PC with PHOTOfunSTUDIO 5.0 HD Edition software, you will receive prompts on saving your files onto your computer. It is a straightforward process, and once the files are downloaded, you can organize them, edit them, and display them. If you wish to edit your RAW files, be sure to load Silkypix. This will provide you with the capability to alter contrast, sharpness, and color balance.

Those of you who wish to try image processing your files and want more advance controls than that provided by the software Panasonic supplies can download free software for this work. Picasa can be downloaded from Google for free (**www.picasa.google.com**). Another available software for either Windows or Apple computers is GIMP (**www.gimp.org**).

Playing Pictures/Videos on Your TV Screen

Directly linking your camera with your TV will yield more viewing options than linking your camera with your computer. The Panasonic G2 camera can be connected to your TV directly using either the AV cable (supplied with your camera) for non-HDTVs or an HDMI cable (not supplied) for HDTVs. In addition, how you link the camera to the TV is dependant on the age, brand, and type of TV you have, so we recommend that you consult both the camera's and the TV's manuals and their websites to get up-to-date information.

Once the camera is connected, you can play your slide shows on your TV. One advantage is if you have a wide-screen HDTV, you will be able to appreciate the definition, color, and contrast of both your pictures and your videos. The HDTV serves as the "screen" for your slide shows and provides an ideal venue for displaying pictures to a small audience.

Printing Your Pictures

As we have discussed with the PLAYBACK Mode menu commands, the Panasonic G2 camera has the capability of allowing you to set up commands to print your pictures. You can add text to your pictures using the TEXT STAMP and TITLE EDIT commands. You can specify which pictures you want printed and then use the DPOF print system to have them printed. There are some limitations to this because the print information is always through your camera and only deals with what is saved on your memory card. You also have the option of downloading your pictures to your computer, determining what you want printed, and then either printing them on your personal printer or sending them to an outside printing services on the Web or in local stores.

Recommendation

We recommend that you download your pictures and videos onto your computer, build the slide shows you want using either the PHOTOfunSTUDIO 5.0 HD Edition software or other-third party software you own, and then store the results on a DVD so you can play back your saved memories over and over again on your computer or TV. An added benefit is that you can also copy your DVDs and send them off to friends and family to share your memories with them. We also recommend that you consider doing your post-processing on your computer.

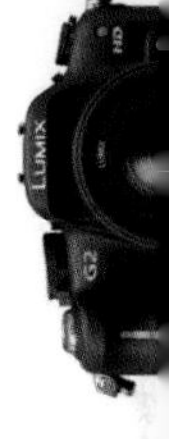

Appendix A – Setting Up The Camera

Setting Up Your New Panasonic G2 Camera

When you take you camera out of the box, you will have the following components:

- Camera – 12.1 effective megapixel Lumix DMC-G2
- Lens – F3.4-5.6, 14–42 mm Lumix G lens with MEGA OIS (Optical Image Stabilization)
- Lens cap
- Lens hood
- Lens bag
- Battery – DMW-BLB13 lithium-ion
- Battery charger/AC adapter
- Shoulder/neck strap
- USB cable
- Body cap
- A/V cable
- CD-ROM featuring PHOTOfunSTUDIO 5.0 HD Edition and Silkypix Developer Studio 3.1 SE
- Camera manuals in English, French, Spanish, and Portuguese (219 pages)

Take an inventory to ensure that you have a complete kit before starting to assemble your new camera.

Some Assembly Required

Memory Card Basics

Fortunately not much assembly is required—screwdrivers and hammers will not be needed. You will need a memory card to store your pictures and videos. This does not come with your camera, and what you get will depend on what you want to do with your camera. If you plan to take a lot of videos, you will need a large amount of memory, at least 8 gigabytes (GB). If you are going to take mainly still photos, 4 GB should suffice. See the sidebar "Memory Card Criteria" for more information. If you are upgrading from an existing digital camera, its memory card may serve for your new Panasonic camera.

Several considerations should be made when determining how much memory is right for you. First, how are you going to use the camera? Videos use more memory than still photos. RAW files use more memory than JPEG. The amount of memory you need also depends on your photo-taking style. If you tend to keep a lot of photos on your memory card, you will need more memory. If instead you continuously delete pictures you don't want and keep only a small number of pictures on the memory card, you can get by with less memory.

Regardless of your style, the amount of memory needed also depends on how often you download the stored pictures to your computer, thereby freeing up the memory to take more pictures. Many people keep an additional memory card for those occasions when they are taking a large number of pictures or have not been able to download the memory card contents to a computer.

Memory Card Criteria

SD memory card (8 MB to 2 GB)

- SDHC memory card (4 GB to 32 GB)
- SDXC memory card (48 GB to 64 GB)

Additional Information

- SDHC memory card can be used with equipment that's compatible with the SDHC memory card or SDXC memory card.
- SDXC memory card can be used only with equipment that's compatible with the SDXC memory card.
- Check the Panasonic website to see if your PC and other equipment are compatible when using the SDXC memory cards.

Panasonic website:

http://panasonic.net/avc/sdcard/information/SDXC.html

Battery Basics

The supplied lithium battery should be charged to full capacity before using. After your initial charge, you should never let the camera's battery fully drain. Doing so may damage the battery. Use Panasonic certified batteries only. Noncertified batteries are not approved for your camera. If you are unsure if your battery is certified, check with the Panasonic website or contact Panasonic technical support. Although some may tell you your camera can take a lesser-quality battery, don't succumb to temptation. You can ruin your camera and jeopardize its warranty.

The camera's battery is delivered partially charged. If you have upgraded from a Panasonic G1 or G1H camera, the batteries can be used in your new G2 camera. Assuming it has a charge, you can use the battery from your old camera while charging up your new G2 battery.

Using the supplied AC cable, assemble the cable and the charger and plug it into an electrical socket. Insert the battery with the printed side up and pointed away from the plug. The charge indicator light will glow when charging, and extinguish when fully charged. If the charger's light starts flashing, there was a charging problem, such as a defective battery incapable of holding a charge. Panasonic estimates it would take 155 minutes to fully charge a depleted battery. Future charges will take less time depending on how much residual charge remains in the battery when the recharge process is started.

Side Bar – Can I Use a Non-Panasonic-Authorized Battery?

Simple answer – No. Counterfeit batteries are not made under the same guidelines and regulations as the real Panasonic-certified batteries. In fact, the camera is designed to detect unauthorized batteries and may refuse to start up if you attempt to use it with an unauthorized battery. Using a counterfeit battery can cause degradation or, worse, damage to your electronic devices. In most cases, using nonauthorized equipment will nullify your camera's warranty should any damage occur. Therefore, Panasonic included code in the camera's software to prevent noncertified batteries from working within the camera.

Inserting the Battery and Memory Card

Once you have made sure you have everything, insert the battery and memory card. On the right side of the bottom of the camera, you will see a switch with LOCK and OPEN. Slide the switch toward OPEN and the door will pop open. Insert the battery into the bottom portion of the compartment and the memory card into the top portion. The battery has a printed arrow indicating the side that slides into the compartment first. You will hear a solid click when you insert the battery. The battery can only be inserted one way—if you do not hear a click, then the battery's contacts have not connected to the camera and you should turn it around and reinsert it. To remove the battery, push the small lever at the base of the opening on the far right side and the battery will pop up for easy removal.

The memory card slides in with the metallic reading bars going in first. You can remove the memory card using a simple push and release mechanism. Push the memory card in a bit and it will pop up for you to easily remove it. If the memory card is not properly inserted in the camera, an error message will appear on the rear LCD screen. If this occurs, simply remove the memory card and reinsert it and the message should go away. If it does not, the card may be defective and it will have to be replaced. Check Appendix B*, "Common Error Messages and Resolutions."

Attaching a Lens

Next, connect the lens to the camera body. Remove both the rear lens cap and the camera's body cap. Each is easily removed by turning the cap counter clockwise. Store both in a safe place for future retrieval—most likely in the camera's lens bag since it will not be in use when the caps are off and the lens is attached to the camera body. There is a red bump at the base of the lens and a red dot on the camera body where the lens is attached. Insert the lens into the camera body so the two red marks match up. Turn the lens clockwise to seat it properly. Make sure you do not have the lens at an angle. It will not seat properly in that case. There will be a distinctive click when the lens is properly mounted. If the lens is not seated properly, an error message will appear on the rear LCD screen when you turn the camera on informing you that there is a problem detecting the lens. The easiest fix is to check to see that the lens has been rotated fully clockwise. If the problem persists, check Appendix B*.

Neck Strap Basics

Last but not least, install the camera shoulder/neck strap. The strap should always be secured to the camera and either around your neck or over your shoulder when you're carrying the camera around or taking pictures.

Turning the Camera On and Off

You are ready to turn on your camera. The ON/OFF switch is on the top right side. Switch the small lever to ON. A small green light displays next to the ON option.

* To view the Appendix, see: http://rockynook.com/PanasonicG2

Additional Downloadable Resources Website

As a final reminder, there is a downloadable resources webpage for this book. It contains additional Appendix sections that provide added information on camera operation. The webpage is located at the following website address:

http://rockynook.com/PanasonicG2

All references in this book to Appendices B–D refer to information that is available from the downloadable resources webpage.

INDEX

Numbers & Symbols

A

B